CHINA'S GREEN RELIGION

CHINA'S GREEN

RELIGION

Daoism and the Quest for a Sustainable Future

James Miller

Columbia University Press   New York

Columbia University Press

Publishers Since 1893

New York   Chichester, West Sussex

cup.columbia.edu

Library of Congress Cataloging-in-Publication Data

Names: Miller, James, 1968– author.
Title: China's green religion : Daoism and the quest for a
sustainable future / James Miller.
Description: New York : Columbia University Press, 2017. |
Includes bibliographical references and index.
Identifiers: LCCN 2016039619 (print) | LCCN 2017017828 (ebook) |
ISBN 9780231544535 (electronic) | ISBN 9780231175869 (cloth) |
ISBN 9780231175876 (pbk.)
Subjects: LCSH: Taoism—China. | China—Religion. | Human
ecology—Religious aspects—Taoism. | Sustainability—China.
Classification: LCC BL1923 (ebook) | LCC BL1923 .M55 2017 (print)
| DDC 299.5/14—dc23
LC record available at https://lccn.loc.gov/2016039619

Cover photos: James Miller

For Eric Tang

天地相合以降甘露
民莫之令而自均

Heaven and earth unite to drop down sweet dew.
No one commands the people, yet they naturally achieve equality.

Daode jing, chap. 32

Contents

Acknowledgments

I gratefully acknowledge permission from the State University of New York Press to incorporate into the current book material from my essay "Aesthetics and Daoist Body Cultivation," first published in James McRae and J. Baird Callicott, eds., *Nature in Asian Philosophical Traditions* (2014). Likewise, thanks are due to the Council for Research in Values and Philosophy for permission to use material from my essay "Manifesto for a Daoist Theology of Messianic Wisdom," published in Vincent Shen and Willard Oxtoby, eds., *Wisdom in China and the West*, Chinese Philosophical Studies 22 (Washington, DC: Council for Research in Values and Philosophy, 2004). I draw on the Ph.D. thesis of Ian Alexander Cuthbertson (Queen's University, 2016) for some of the ideas and sources cited in chapter 1. Ideas from my previous publications also appear throughout the text, but in new formulations and with new perspectives. Notably, for discussions of Highest Clarity Daoism, I draw on my book *The Way of Highest Clarity: Nature, Vision, and Revelation in Medieval China* (Magdalena, NM: Three Pines Press, 2008), and for discussions on the Daoist body, I draw on chapters from *Daoism: A Beginner's Guide* (Oxford: Oneworld Publications, 2006).

Thanks go to Andrew Hood, Jennifer Lemche, Ke Junyu, Ryan Pino, Matt Riley, and Xiang Zairong for reading, commenting on, or assisting with various drafts of the manuscript. Louis Komjathy read an early draft of the manuscript and gave detailed and helpful comments and criticisms. Heartfelt thanks go to Jason Kelly, who spent two weeks with me in China reading, discussing, and commenting on the manuscript. He provided invaluable insights and helped me considerably to refine my arguments. This draft was then rewritten following the detailed comments and criticisms of Natalie Gummer and two anonymous reviewers. I owe them thanks for helping me to clarify my arguments and express myself more precisely. The editorial team members at Columbia have been outstanding in their professionalism and commitment. Their hard work has ensured that the manuscript improved at every stage, and for this they have my utmost thanks.

I would also like to express my gratitude to the School of Social Development and Public Policy at Fudan University, Shanghai, and in particular to Vice-Dean Cheng Yuan, who gave me the use of an apartment in Shanghai in the fall of 2015; this provided me with the ideal space in which to think and write. While in China I presented some of the book's material at Nanjing University of the Arts, South East China University, and Nanjing University of Information Technology. Many thanks to my hosts for providing me with these opportunities and to the audiences for giving me valuable feedback.

Finally I must express my unending thanks to Mary Evelyn Tucker and John Grim. They have graciously encouraged my research in this area, brought me into conversation with a wealth of colleagues and friends, and been a constant source of inspiration and wisdom.

Introduction

The question of China's sustainability, whether economic, demographic, ecological, political, or financial, is one that rightly concerns people across the world. China is the world's largest economy in purchasing power parity terms, the second largest in real gross domestic product terms, and has witnessed staggering economic and social development over the past generation. Its massive investments in resource development in Africa and Latin America, as well as its extensive financial and trade relationships with developed economies in North America and Europe, mean that to an increasingly large extent China's future is also the world's future. The decisions taken in Beijing over the next generation will have a profound effect not only on the 1.3 billion people who live in China, but also on countless others across the world whose lives are, in some small way at least, dependent on China.

Given the complexity of the social, economic, political, and environmental problems that China faces, it is almost absurd to imagine that an obscure, misunderstood religious tradition that very nearly died in the twentieth century can have anything substantial to do with the most important question facing the world in the twenty-first century: how to create a sustainable way of living for the human species. As the world reaches a population of nearly 10 billion people in 2050, as climate change provokes unexpected transformations in weather patterns, as sea levels rise, and as water and food security become paramount concerns for nations, how China manages these challenges will have serious implications across the world. No one wants China's vast economic, political, and environmental experiment to fail. At the same time, it is evident that the way that contemporary Western and Chinese societies are structured together in a system of global finance, trade, and economic exploitation is ultimately unsustainable and will lead to the drastic reordering of the fundamental relationships between the planetary biosphere and the species that inhabit it.

The source of this economic and ecological unsustainability is the inability of modern neoliberal ideology and its attendant cultural forms to conceptualize and operationalize a way of being in the world that inscribes human prosperity within the prosperity of planetary life. Rather, we have come to conceptualize human prosperity in a way that is alienated from the ecological systems that make such prosperity possible. As a result, the modes by which we pursue human prosperity serve only to diminish its long-term viability by destroying the ultimate foundation for prosperity: the capacity of the natural order to produce of its own accord the creative vitality that can support the flourishing and well-being of all species. Such a capacity I term the subjectivity of nature. Modern human culture, by denying nature's subjectivity and arrogating subjectivity and agency to itself alone, has sowed the seeds of its own destruction.

This book develops a normative critique of this aspect of modernity from an ecocritical analysis of ideas and values found within Daoism, China's indigenous religious tradition. It also aims to produce an alternative vision for a culture of sustainability that is of relevance to China and the world in the mid-twenty-first century. This vision draws in part on my attempt to produce the first thematic introduction to the Daoist religion, more than ten years ago. At that time, existing accounts of Daoism presented the historical contours of the tradition without directly engaging what the tradition itself might consider to be normative cultural paradigms for framing Daoist practitioners' own views of their own experience. This was because most of the leading interpreters of Daoism were historians, keen to construct a historical narrative of how Daoist ideas were transmitted from generation to generation and how each historical period produced its own ways of relating Daoism to broader social, cultural, and political forces. My own interest, however, as one trained in comparative theology, was to understand the ways in which Daoism itself sought to form a normative culture that would not simply adapt or adhere to the hegemonic ideology of the dominant political discourse (though that, of course, is in some ways inevitable) but also sought to distinguish itself from (and also shape) dominant sociocultural paradigms by articulating the Daoist experience of reality through a distinctive vocabulary.[1]

This way to think about the impact of religion is perhaps somewhat different from the mainstream approach to thinking about the relevance of religion for sustainability. Indeed, when many people consider the value, positive or negative, of religion in contemporary society, they often make reference to the social power of religion as identified by the number of its adherents. In this way, Catholicism and Islam may be regarded as powerful social forces because they command a billion or more adherents across the globe (though of course they are organized in radically different ways). An example of this argument is made by Gary Gardner in his paper *Invoking the Spirit: Religion and Spirituality in the Quest for a Sustainable World*. He writes:

[Religions] know how to inspire people and how to wield moral authority. Many have the political clout associated with a huge base of adherents. Some have considerable real estate holdings, buildings, and financial resources. And most produce strong community ties by generating social resources such as trust and cooperation, which can be a powerful boost to community development. Many political movements would welcome any of these five assets. To be endowed with most or all of them, as many religions are, is to wield considerable political power.[2]

In an earlier discussion of this paper I commented:

All of this is designed to point out why religions are significant in the world's societies: in a sense they resemble transnational corporations, straddling the world's ethnic and national boundaries, wielding political power and influence, and, in fact, constituting a significant sector of the economy. These arguments seem to say that religions exist, they are present, they have power, and therefore they should be taken seriously.[3]

What motivates Gardner's argument is clear: many modern people believe that religions are irrelevant as social forces, and that to suggest that religions may play an important role in contributing toward a sustainable future is hard to comprehend. Gardner's argument tries to reassert the importance of religions in a secular society by simply pointing to the fact of their existence, their size, and their potential for social influence.

This argument, however, overlooks the key question of whether religions actually shape their adherents' lives differently from the dominant economic, political, and technological ordering of modern societies. Perhaps it does not matter how many religious people there are in the world if in their daily lives they do no more than acquiesce to the social forces that drive the continuing ecological crisis. In fact, it may well be that the power of secularization is not to make religions disappear from the world but rather to domesticate them so that their continuing functioning is relatively irrelevant. If there are a billion Christians who all want to buy bigger houses, drive bigger cars, and consume more natural resources, then the value of Christianity as regards the sustainability of the planet is nil.

From this perspective, the more important aspect of religions is not the numbers of adherents they can command, but whether or not they assert a worldview and value system that pushes against the operative social order of the times in a way that is relevant to sustainability. Religions are not interesting principally as collective social organizations, but rather as collective traditions of culture and practice that react to, engage with, and transform the broader collective identities in which they operate. It is their capacity for collective social dissonance that is of singular relevance to the question of ecological sustainability precisely because our dominant social order is socially dysfunctional, economically unviable, and ecologically unsustainable. The topic this book explores, therefore, is the value of Daoism not as a Chinese religious organization, but as a cultural system that may be relevant for providing a critical edge over the dominant social-political orderings of the times and enacting in their place a culture of sustainability.

My research into this area is not based on interviews or data acquired from contemporary fieldwork in China, although I have done that kind of work in the past. Rather, my aim is to read through key themes and concepts that arise within the tradition itself in the context of our current ecological crisis. The reader will readily note that those categories and concepts, though produced from within the worldview of Daoism itself, are not deployed to serve the interests of "Daoists" or "Daoism" in the way that an insider might likely deploy them. This does not, on the face of it, render such a deployment suspect. The fact is that self-identified "Daoists" would likely disagree among themselves on how to deploy those categories to serve the interests of their tradition, and in so doing would likely conflate their own locations and interests with those of the "tradition" as a whole. Religious adherents are not simply passive recipients of religious doctrines, but rather actively shape and reimagine those doctrines in ways to serve their own interests and motivations.[4] Moreover, the claim that "Daoism" is somehow the intellectual preserve of "Chinese people" is also on the face of it untenable when it is accepted that the production of racial and ethnic categories that underpin such a claim themselves originate in the hegemonic deployment of cultural power (whether Orientalist or nativist).

The reader should also note that this interpretation of Daoism should not be read as a romantic Orientalist attempt to resurrect something "beautiful" or "traditional" that has been "lost in modernity." I am reasonably cognizant of the challenges and pressures that China faces today, and I have no desire to turn the clock back and resuscitate tradition at the expense of social justice, or of the improved health, security, freedom, and economic power of China's people. The achievement of China's people over the past century has been one of the most important contributions to world peace, social justice, and gender equality. But the method for doing so has been, as Tu Weiming notes, an explicit strategy of Westernization,[5] and one that has had devastating consequences for the natural environment. As Bruno Latour notes,

> The various manifestations of socialism destroyed both their peoples and their ecosystems, whereas the power of the North and the West have been able to save their peoples and some of their countrysides by destroying the rest of the world and reducing its peoples to abject poverty. Hence a double tragedy: the former socialist societies think they can solve both their problems by imitating the West; the West thinks it has escaped both problems and believes it has lessons for the others even as it leaves the Earth and its peoples to die.[6]

Between the failed strategy of Western industrial modernization on the one hand, and the reactionary, Orientalist exaltation of something like "Confucian values" on the other hand, lies an alternative space. By eschewing the failed hegemonies of both Western modernity and Confucian tradition, a space opens up in which Daoism, the more marginal tradition of China's past, can be brought into dialogue with emerging alternatives to contemporary neoliberal capitalism. To bridge the margins of Chinese tradition and the margins of contemporary ecopolitics is to begin the process of opening up a third space, a decolonial space that resists the ways Daoism has conventionally been framed. Indeed, as this book argues, the way modernity conventionally frames religion and nature is a problem to be overcome.

This step toward a decolonial reading of Daoism and ecology together must begin by recognizing the power of the margins to bear witness to alternative framings of society. It is a reading that emphasizes Daoism's capacity for subverting and resisting China's dominant collective ordering by perpetuating a lineage of ethical values, cultural frameworks, and social habits that is deliberately off center. This is not to say that Daoism never became subservient to the state or that its elites never framed Daoism in ways that reinforced hegemonic patterns of social order, but to say that Daoism has, from its inceptions, functioned as a powerful dissonant note in China's complex civilizational history, and as an alternative to Confucianism's dominance in state politics. To see Daoism's dissonant side, therefore, is to see is decolonial side. It is to resist the framing of Daoism in terms of the categories drawn from contemporary Chinese and Western political orderings and to consider the quality of its insights and their relevance for planetary sustainability.

This approach draws upon a strategy for interpreting Daoist texts described by Michael LaFargue as "confrontational hermeneutics." He writes:

> Confrontational hermeneutics entails two different elements. The first element should aim at understanding the text precisely in its otherness from our own views and values, focusing on the ways the basic thought patterns of the text's original authors and audience were fundamentally different from our own. Doing this requires temporarily setting aside our own most cherished assumptions so as to produce for ourselves a strong opponent to wrestle with, so to speak. The second element should be the wrestling itself, considering the pro's and con's of this reconstructed view of the world vis-à-vis our own views or other views we might be attracted to.[7]

LaFargue's perception of the value of reading Daoist texts draws on his own work in understanding the meaning structure of the major early

Daoist text, the *Daode jing* 道德經 (ca. fourth century B.C.E.). This text is known for its aphoristic nature, its use of paradox, and the way it seems to resist obvious meaning. LaFargue's insight into this text was to delineate a common meaning structure that frequently recurs in the text, which he described as the "polemical aphorism." He gives as an example the English saying "slow and steady wins the race."[8] This aphorism is contrary to the received wisdom that to win a race one must be quick. It offers a general image rather than a universal law, inspiring the listener to imagine a situation in which conventional wisdom is unlikely to prove correct. Finally, it represents the values and attitudes of the speaker regarding the particular context in which it is offered. In this case, the speaker is saying, "maybe in this particular situation you shouldn't rush to complete the task but take care to make sure that it is done correctly." LaFargue believes that the polemical aphorisms of the *Daode jing* reflected the values and orientations of a midlevel political class in Warring States China who sought not to completely overthrow society but to reform it from the inside. They did so by holding onto wisdom that was antithetical to the dominant traditions of the time, but which they thought would ultimately be more effective. Take, for example, chapter 29:

> If one wants to take hold of the world,
> and act on it—
> I see that he will not succeed.
> Well,
> the world is a sacred vessel,
> and not something that can be acted on.
> Those who act on things will be defeated by them. Those who take things
>   in their hands will lose them.[9]

As this passage makes clear, although the conventional way to act in the world is to grasp things directly and shape them, there may be some situations where handling things (like a sacred vessel) with delicacy, skill, and respect is more important than directly manipulating a situation to one's immediate advantage. This early Daoist text, therefore, offers the suggestion that conventional wisdom about how to do things may not be universally successful, and that the astute Daoist should be alert to situations in which the exception may prove to be more useful than the rule. In our current time of unprecedented ecological crisis, never has this kind of thinking been more necessary.

At the same time, the strategy of "confrontational hermeneutics" invites the contemporary reader to consider not simply the meaning of this text in its original historical circumstances (as if that were possible), but also to challenge the conventional frameworks and assumptions that guide the reader's own cultural situation. The Daoist tradition is not simply data to be mined and processed by the scholarly gaze, but is also itself a tradition of inquiry and reflection that has the power to respond to scholarship with questions of its own. In this way, one can begin to make advances toward a decolonial reading of Daoism as a religious tradition and to perceive where Daoism has embodied a tradition of dissonance within itself.

In this regard, it is helpful to imagine Daoism not simply as a tradition hermetically sealed within its own walls, but rather as a tradition that has operated within a dominant social framework with which it has not always agreed. That is to say, Daoism, rather than being a tradition of social harmony and quietism (which is perhaps the quintessential conventional Confucian and modern Western interpretation), has largely functioned as an argumentative, polemical, and countercultural tradition. This tradition functioned in two dominant modes: the first was to encourage eremitism, a withdrawal from conventional society; the second was to engage in debate and conflict. Both should be interpreted through the ways they relate to the dominant social ordering of the time.

As a brief example of Daoist eremitism, consider the hagiography of the Daoist saint known as Perfected Purple Yang. His *Esoteric Biography* (*Ziyang zhenren neizhuan* 紫陽真人內傳; DZ303),[10] preserved within the Highest Clarity tradition of Daoism, records how the protagonist, Zhou Yishan 周義山 (80 B.C.E.–?), left a conventional life and roamed through the mountains in search of spiritual transformation. Julius Tsai, in his reading of the text, notes that Zhou's rejection of conventional society should not be read as a rejection of earthly power in exchange for spiritual enlightenment, but rather as a quest for alternate, religiously constituted, forms of power and authority.[11] Traditions of monasticism or eremitism should not automatically be construed as quietistic rejections of normative social orderings, but rather as quests to articulate socially significant alternatives. They involve alternative ethics of relation to nature and society, and alternative forms of economy and patterns of consumption. The fact that a biography such as Zhou Yishan's was written, circulated, and preserved within the Daoist tradition suggests that the view of Daoism as a dissenting or exceptional tradition of social power was deemed significant within the tradition. His story was written down, circulated, and emulated, and it became part of a socially significant tradition alternative to the dominant culture. In the same way, alternatives to dominant social orderings founded upon the recognition of a true ecological crisis can be found throughout Western society today, though they are rarely remarked upon in the mainstream media.[12]

An example of Daoism's more direct engagement with society can be seen in the consistent efforts of the Celestial Masters (Tianshi 天使) tradition to oppose popular religious practices in which priests received money from the people to perform blood sacrifices to the gods. According to historical evidence, such practices were common in southern China in the Six Dynasties period (220–589 C.E.), when the Celestial Masters were attempting to establish themselves as a religious organization. In so doing, the Daoists of the time were clearly repudiating the religious framework of conventional society, in which communication between humans and spirits took place by means of the blood drawn during animal sacrifices. In contrast, Daoists were to be bound by a "pure covenant" (qingyue 清約) that rejected animal sacrifices and also the financial system that underpinned conventional religious activity. In this way, the Daoist tradition functioned not simply as a "spiritual" tradition but also as a way of undermining the social and economic power of rival, mainstream traditions.[13] The contemporary world similarly demands alternatives to neoliberal ideology that are not simply utopian fantasies but are materially embedded in cultural forms, thereby providing alternate financial and economic processes.

The aim of a decolonial reading of Daoism, then, is to provide an alternative framework for understanding the Daoist tradition. It is based not on the conventional understanding of religion as a collective social organization, which, in Daoism's case, only began in the middle of the second century C.E. Nor is it to regard Daoism as a quietistic tradition that sought peaceful coexistence with prevailing social norms and institutional power. Rather, from its inception Daoism can be defined as a tradition of praxis that functioned in critical tension with dominant social orderings. Finally, to read Daoism in a decolonial way is to read it from the perspective of LaFargue's "confrontational hermeneutics" in which the reader allows the text to disturb and resist his or her own cultural framework.

This decolonial approach is carried out in this book through reading Daoist texts and concepts from the perspective of how they can resist and reframe contemporary Western ideas of nature and environment. The core of the book, chapters 2 to 6, examines key Daoist concepts such as Dao (Way), *wuwei* (nonaction), *qi* (vital power), and the like that are generally well understood from existing studies of Daoist philosophy and religion, but which are interpreted here from an ecocritical perspective. This discussion is then redirected toward key Western ideas such as "the environment" or "ecological ethics" in order to present a Daoist theoretical approach to Western thought. This is a reversal of the normal Orientalist procedure of interpreting Asian traditions from Western theory.

The book begins, however, with an overview that examines how religion and ecology have come to be related in modernity and how scholars have approached this topic in the past. The goal here is to suggest, as many have, that the logic of modernity is in fact a contingent logic, a network of concepts and relations that is not exceptional in and of itself. This modern network of concepts is then supplanted with a Daoist ordering of religion and nature, one that can stand as an alternative to the network of modernity, and one that refuses to be tamed by it. The chapter argues that this Daoist logic, though no more or less contingent than the logic of Western modernity, has a greater pragmatic value in terms of producing the optimal flourishing of life as the world approaches a population of ten billion. This Daoist approach is then examined in further detail in chapters 2 to 6.

Chapter 2, "The Subjectivity of Nature," uses Daoist cosmological ideas to reverse the normative Western understanding of nature as "environment." Instead, it suggests how nature can be reframed as the infusion or insistence of the cosmos within the body of the individual.

Chapter 3, "Liquid Ecology," examines concepts of *qi* 氣 flowing in the body and in the landscape to suggest that the fundamental stuff of nature is not material substance, but liquid process. The chapter then divides this liquid process into two modes, genealogical and ecological, and suggests that these are two key dimensions of Chinese cosmology.

Chapter 4, "The Porosity of the Body," analyzes Daoist visualization meditations to dissolve the fundamental modern dichotomy of body and world, inside and outside. In its place, I suggest a vision of the body as fundamentally porous to the world that surrounds it and consider the implications of this for a queer sexual ecology.

Chapter 5, "The Locative Imagination," uncovers the Daoist imagination of space not in terms of the abstract geometry of modernity but as hierarchies of power and places of transformation and redirects this imagination toward theories of environmental ethics.

The focus on ethics continues in chapter 6, "The Political Ecology of the Daoist Body," which takes as its starting point the Daoist notion of the body as radically porous to the world. This notion then influences the way human relations and relations between humans and the nonhuman world are to be construed, and gives examples from contemporary China.

The final two chapters of the book bring together some concluding arguments on how this process of allowing Daoism to resist and disturb normative modern Western claims about religion and nature affects the study of religion and contemporary thinking about sustainability. Chapter 7, "From Modernity to Sustainability," analyzes how the modern concept of religion has produced the basic set of questions that has driven modern Sinological scholarship on Daoism up to the present day. Rather than continuing in this mode of scholarship, guided by questions that were key for the production of modern societies, the chapter suggests that a new ordering framework is required for scholarship, namely, that of sustainability. The chapter offers an outline of what such a scholarship could look like and how it might interrogate Daoism not as a "tradition" that engages "modernity" but as an interlocutor in the realization of a sustainable future.

The second of the concluding chapters, "From Sustainability to Flourishing," takes a step toward articulating a Daoist vision of sustainability not simply as the maintenance or preservation of a status quo, as though nature were no more than a resource to be conserved for future generations. Rather, it considers what global environmentalism might look like if we consider that it is not the responsibility of humans to "save nature" but rather to enable the natural world to continue its work of bringing forth the flourishing of things. This vision of a flourishing, rather than a sustainable, future is examined in four key modes: aesthetic, ethical, political, and spiritual. Each of these is related to important environmental issues in China in order to show how a Daoist vision might concretely intersect with contemporary issues.

CHINA'S GREEN RELIGION

1   Religion, Modernity, and Ecology

My aim in this book is to think through China's indigenous religious tradition, Daoism, from the perspective of sustainability, and to think through sustainability from the perspective of Daoism. The reason for this is to provide a new way of thinking about Daoism as a religious and cultural tradition, and also to provide a new way of thinking about sustainability. My hope is that these new considerations will be relevant not only to China's contemporary quest to construct an "ecological civilization," but also more broadly to global movements to transition human society toward ecologically responsible forms of culture, economics, and politics. But what do these two things, Daoism and sustainability, have to do with each other? Are they even things that can or ought to be related?

Religion and Ecology

In a conventional modern Western understanding, religious traditions are primarily concerned with beliefs about the transcendent, supernatural world: Is there a God? What happens to us after we die? They are secondarily concerned with universal questions of social ethics: Is abortion ever justifiable? What crimes warrant the death penalty? Thirdly, they are concerned with group identity: How should men and women dress? What foods are permissible to eat? None of these three areas is, on the face of it, substantively connected to the question of sustainable ways of living. Surely the West is, or ought to be, a largely secular world, at least as regards ethics, public policy, science, and nature?

Academic scholarship on religion has come to analyze and explain the way that the modern idea of "religion" has been produced. Religion, we now know, is not simply a category that exists of its own accord as a kind of cultural or anthropological "given." It is not self-evident that human beings have been religious everywhere and at every time in a similar way to one another. Rather, each culture in each historical period has invented its own understanding of the kinds of things that we have lately come to consider to be "religion." As one simple example demonstrates, Chinese language did not have its own word for the Western concept of "religion" until the nineteenth century. The demands of translation caused a neologism, *zongjiao* 宗教, to be invented. This does not mean that there was no religion in China before then, but rather that Chinese people conceptualized the kinds of traditions and cultural complexes that we call religion differently enough to warrant the invention of a new term.

Equally important is the way that this modern idea of "religion" has also produced our modern understandings of "secularity." That is to say, secularity is not the absence of religion as a general category, but rather a particular cultural and social form that emerged from the historical transformations and responses to religion in the modern West. Two academic works are particularly important here. Bruno Latour undertook what he termed the anthropology of science in *We Have Never Been Modern* and demonstrated that the forms in which scientific research took place in early modern Europe were deeply connected to emerging ideas about politics and society. So also Talal Asad undertook the anthropology of the secular, revealing how secularity is not simply the absence of "religion" but rather is shaped and constituted by it in particular ways.[1] In short, what we think about "religion," "nature," or even "science" is influenced by particular historical, social, and political trajectories of thought.

This interaction among religion, secularity, and nature in the worldview of modernity has left those of us who inhabit modernity in a quandary when it comes to thinking about the relevance of "religion" for the ecological crisis, in that the key ways in which "religion" has been framed seem to leave it silent in the face of the world of geophysics, climate change, or geoengineering. The key question facing the human species at present might seem to be, first and foremost, about the material world rather than the immaterial world of gods, ghosts, and ancestors. It is a question that invites answers in terms of food supplies, species populations, climate change, and renewable energy, in short, questions to be answered by the natural sciences rather than theology. For this reason, bringing religion into play seems to muddy the waters at best. At worst, truly theological questions of gods and the afterlife may seem to be wicked distractions from the serious material questions that face the human species. Surely, one might argue, the amount of effort and ingenuity put into impossible and unsolvable theological questions might more profitably be directed at dealing with the pressing issues of climate change or renewable energy sources.

The arena of social ethics, however, seems a slightly more promising venue to bring religion and sustainability together. The question of sustainable forms of living can be understood as an ethical question. Do we have the right, for instance, to live in such a way that makes the lives of our grandchildren unviable? Do we have the right, as Harvard climate scientist Michael McElroy asked, to change the chemical composition of our atmosphere?[2] Surely our religious traditions have something to say about these key questions regarding the long-term sustainability of the human species? The answer, frequently, is that they do not. Religious traditions are surprisingly useless when it comes to thinking about the questions that truly matter for the sustainability of life on earth. This is largely because the dominant religions of the present world are formed around the dominant ethical questions of the Axial Age, some 2,500 years ago. Although principles derived from these ethical systems can be applied to present-day issues, none of these traditions ever had to deal with the question of sustainability as faced by the human species today, and none of these traditions lived with the scientific knowledge to even formulate a question such as that of McElroy. As a result, although religious traditions can help us to think about ethical issues, when it comes to the question of sustainability, they are not as helpful as one might think.

Moreover, as Durkheim explained, religious traditions are particularly important for the formation of group identities at a larger scale than that of the clan.[3] Religions forge the shared values that help human beings transcend their genetic ties and form into larger social networks such as those that enabled people to cooperate in the development of large-scale civilizations.[4] Some religions, such as Buddhism or Islam, have been so successful in this regard that they have spread across the world, helping to forge multinational collective identities that assist in the development of global trade networks, and, alongside nation-states and their armies, play important roles in geopolitics to this day. From this perspective it might also be argued that religions have something positive to contribute to the formulation of an ecologically sustainable way of living for the human species. The religious forces that help to shape collective identities at levels larger than the clan, however, are the same forces that create religious rivalries. Group identities are always asserted over and against another group's identity. Identity, whether religious identity, national identity, or gender identity, is always created in relation to the Other. For this reason, while global religions may have played an important role in helping to forge the major civilizations that shape the world today,[5] they might be seen to be of relatively little use, or even positively unhelpful, when it comes to dealing with the issue of the long-term sustainability of the human species.

For these reasons—and doubtless more can be adduced—it would seem absurd to imagine that a religion, such as Daoism, can play an important role in helping to bring about a transition to a sustainable way of living for the human species in the twenty-first century: religions deal with the immaterial world, not the material world; they are rooted in the problems of the past, not the problems of the present; and their rivalries inhibit us from acting for the collective good of the species.

Despite such arguments against the relevance of religion for sustainability, there has been a considerable body of scholarship on the ways in which "religions" have historically understood "the environment" and the ways in which they can play useful roles in addressing today's environmental challenges. A major approach to the study of religion and ecology has been undertaken in a series of books published by the Harvard Center for the Study of World Religions based on conferences organized at Harvard by the Forum on Religion and Ecology. This series of conferences in the late 1990s was instrumental in establishing the academic field of religion and ecology today and in spurring both religious practitioners and academics to explore the ways in which religious traditions could fruitfully address the question of the environment.[6]

This approach to considering religious environmentalism can be characterized as having two phases. The first is that of examining religious texts and other foundational documents and statements to see the ways in which each religious tradition might understand the natural environment. Such approaches could examine myths of creation, view of nonhuman animals, or ethical texts that detail how human beings ought ideally to act in the world, and whether the natural environment might deserve some special protection for religious reasons. The second phase would be that of engaging with religious traditions to promote green policies and practices within the parameters of each tradition's beliefs and values and engaging in constructive theological or philosophical reflection on how each tradition might perceive and positively contribute toward solving environmental issues. Such work involves both scholars and religious professionals.

On the religious front, the Chinese Daoist Association has been positively engaged on these issues, producing a series of policy statements and action plans on environmental issues from the late 1990s onward.[7] In partnership with the Alliance of Religions and Conservation, they have established an "Ecology Temple" in the Heihe National Forest Park near Mt. Taibai, Shaanxi Province, where they have enshrined Laozi as the God of Ecology.

At the same time, academic scholarship has made considerable headway toward understanding how Daoists have historically engaged with the natural environment, what values might drive those engagements, and what principles lie behind such values.[8] Such work has at least given credence to the notion that elements of the Daoist tradition bear a strong affinity with ideas of an ecological sense of self, in which the individual's self-understanding cannot ultimately be divorced from his or her environmental context.[9] It has also helped promote understanding of the ethical principles that have driven Daoists and others to take care of the local environments around Daoist sacred sites.[10]

Given this recent scholarship, we may more clearly understand the role that Daoism might play in dealing with environmental issues. Moreover, even if the numbers of Daoist priests and monks in China is very small, Daoism nonetheless plays an important role in the basic shape of Chinese culture. It is China's indigenous religious tradition and also a repository of deep cultural capital and philosophical orientations that resonate widely across Chinese culture even if Chinese people are not themselves "Daoists." As Yang Der-Ruey explains, there are "many new types of agents becoming involved in Daoism as a social sphere," ranging from business leaders and unofficial lay groups, to charismatic masters without formal training and online networks and bulletin boards.[11] As the reform and opening of China continue, Yang concludes, the patterns of relationship among those who might be identified with Daoism go well beyond the official orthodoxy of the Chinese Daoist Association and may function more like business networks in a market economy. The potential for Daoist ideas, values, and culture to engage with a wide range of people in China beyond a narrow class of religious professionals is quite profound.

Similar work has been undertaken by scholars in regards to many of the world's traditions, and as a result a whole new field of scholarship has been born. These kinds of arguments do make valid points about the way Daoists have traditionally imagined, valued, and acted in the natural world, but this book hopes to make a different kind of argument. My goal is to move beyond the relatively narrow goal of ecocritical analysis and to consider Daoist studies from the broader perspective of sustainability. To do so is not simply to see which kind of values and motifs are "useful" for the modern world, but rather to use those core values and motifs as diagnostic tools for interpreting and assessing the categories of imagination that have produced "religion," "nature," and "the environment" as fundamental themes of modernity. This expanded approach to the study of religion and nature also seeks to draw inspiration from some of those historical ideas and values to articulate a new, constructive approach to thinking about environmental problems and the relation of culture (including religion) to environmental issues.

Green Religion

A second approach to the field of religion and ecology is captured by the term "green religion," which denotes modes of religious or quasi-religious activity explicitly focused on nature or the natural world. Bron Taylor distinguishes here between "green religion" (which posits that environmentally friendly behavior is a religious obligation) and "dark green religion" (in which nature is sacred, has intrinsic value, and is therefore due reverent care).[12] Taylor's goal here is to distinguish the way that some religions can develop environmentally friendly aspects to them, or promote environmental ethics as part of their general religious orientation, from modes of religious activity that have at their core the reverent attention to nature. Such activity may not be regarded as religious in a standard modern sense, but may also refer to a whole class of cultural activities that fall under the broad heading of religious naturalism, in which devotion to the natural world or specific aspects of it motivates the values and behavior of the devotee. This may include surfing spirituality or radical environmentalism, both of which in various ways are motivated by a sense of the natural world as an ultimate sacred value.

In positing Daoism as a "green religion" it is possible to examine the ways in which various Daoist traditions fit into Taylor's framework of green versus dark green religion. Certainly there are Daoist ethical codes that include what we would, in retrospect, regard as environmental ethics.[13] A careful analysis of such codes in their historical context might yield clues as to whether the desire to protect aspects of the natural environment was motivated by the perception of the natural world as "sacred" or whether these "green values" were the by-product of some other ordering principle of religion. Through such an analysis, one would be able to say whether a particular Daoist activity or text was "green" or "dark green" according to Taylor's scheme.

As in the previous discussion of how religion and ecology have traditionally been related in scholarship, I would like to reframe the question and move scholarship in a new direction. Instead of articulating whether such and such a religion is "green" or "dark green" according to various criteria articulated by the academic community, I would like to point out the ways that Daoism as a tradition has articulated concepts of "religion" and "nature" that differ from how we might articulate them in contemporary discourse. Next, I would like to demonstrate how taking those Daoist conceptions seriously might prove useful in contributing to academic scholarship on how to think about the categories of religion and nature functioning together. To put it another way, I do not take Daoism simply as data to be analyzed according to a conceptual scheme devised by the academic world. Rather, I take Daoism as containing a wide range of texts, values, and practices that are shaped by common ways of articulating fundamental categories of experience of the world, categories that may be relevant for rethinking the place of human beings in the world, and the world in human beings. Such categories and ways of ordering the social imagination toward the construction of an ecologically sustainable society are interesting in their own right.

This larger conceptual project, aimed at the modern Western social imagination of nature, the perception of environmental degradation, and the present sense of ecological crisis, requires moving beyond traditional ways of conceptualizing the engagement of religions and ecology. Such traditional ways derive from a particularly modern Western view of religion, and from a particularly modern Western view of what constitutes the "environment" and why it might need to be "saved." By turning to religions beyond the modern West, it is possible to discover that, not only do they have different views about theological questions, but they also have different views about what "religion" actually is. Equally importantly, their views of what "religion" actually is relate, in turn, to how they conceive of "the world" and its relation to "the human." To put it another way, religions do not simply have different "answers" to the same set of questions about the world, such as "is there a God?": they even ask different fundamental questions, and call in to question the very categories of "religion," "god," or "nature" by which moderns organize their basic perception and experience of the world. Religion and nature are not terms that are given to us ex nihilo. They are contingent logics of ordering and categorizing reality that are shaped by centuries of historical and cultural processes.[14] As a result, to suggest that we have an "ecological crisis" is not only to say something about the physical degradation of the natural environment and the ecosystems that support human health. It is also at the same time to suggest that we have a crisis in how we have come to frame "the world" and the place of human beings in it. To address the question of the "environment" is therefore to address the question of how the "environment" has been produced in the human cultural imagination in the way that it has and how it could be produced differently. This is essentially a question of the values inculcated in humans by the modern social imagination.

The Modern Imaginary

Charles Taylor has characterized the modern social imaginary as one in which the self is "buffered" from the world, rather than being "porous" to it.[15] By this he means that a dominant tone of the collective way that moderns imagine themselves is that they are buffered or isolated from the effects of an imagined outside world, whether characterized by invisible spirits and forces or other supernatural phenomena. Concomitant with this concept of modernity, Taylor takes a "porous" social imaginary as being a chief characteristic of premodern societies, when the dominant social imagination of the body was that it was susceptible to penetration by all manner of supernatural or other forces.

For Taylor, the shift toward the social imagination of a buffered self is not simply a matter of modernity's favoring rational explanations over religious or magical explanations for events, but rather that in the modern social imagination it is largely inconceivable to sense what it would be like to live in a world conditioned by the porosity of the self to the world. He writes, "disenchantment to me is not a matter of changing theory but rather of a transformation of sensibility."[16] This sensibility, furthermore, operates at a cultural level, with the consequence that although some modern people may believe in supernatural forces that pervade their bodies, their beliefs are not consistent with the dominant feeling of the culture. Such feelings and beliefs are problematized and become associated with the "premodern" social imaginary. The question that arises from this is how they can exist within a modern, rational secular society. Conversely, those whose beliefs and feelings cohere with that of secular rationality feel no burden to "explain themselves" to the dominant cultural group.

Taylor is concerned chiefly with the cultural affect, the dominant feeling about the world, that such a buffering produces. In particular, he is concerned with this feeling as regards our sensibility toward supernatural agents such as ghosts, spirits, and gods, and is largely concerned with the process of secularization as the loss of a sense of a religious world interacting with the human world. But it would also be true to say, following Weber's concept of disenchantment, that this feeling about the self in relation to the world can be attributed to our experience of the natural world. That is to say, the modern sense of the disenchantment of the world is not simply about making belief in supernatural beings implausible, or at least demanding explanation, but also changing our feeling about nature itself. Ernest Gellner summarizes this feeling as follows:

> It is not only the procedures of organizations which are in this sense 'bureaucratised'; the same also happens to our vision of nature, of the external world. Its comprehensibility and manipulability are purchased by means of subsuming its events under orderly, symmetrical, precisely articulated generalisations and explanatory models. This is Disenchantment: the Faustian purchase of cognitive, technological and administrative power, by the surrender of our previous meaningful, humanly suffused, humanly responsive, if often also menacing or capricious world. That is abandoned

in favour of a more predictable, more amenable, but coldly indifferent and uncosy world.[17]

Note how Gellner concludes by stating that disenchantment produces a different feeling about the world, that it renders the world "coldly indifferent and uncosy," rather than "menacing or capricious." The process of disenchantment and secularization is not simply about a new point of view that emerges in modernity, but also a new affect, a new culture of feeling about the world.

This cultural affect has been studied by geographers particularly in relation to urbanization. For example, Steve Pile writes:

What makes a city a city is not only skyscrapers or the shops or the communication networks, but also that the people in such places are forced to *behave in urban ways*. For some, this involves an ever-increasing pace of life, the necessity of blocking out most of what goes on in cities, and a mental attitude based on calculation, rationality, and abstract thought. In many ways this implies that city dwellers are "locked down" emotionally: reserved, detached, distant, calculating.[18]

In this way, modernity produces a certain view of the world, and with that view produces the spaces that modern people inhabit and then the affective states of urban residents. Inasmuch as disenchantment produces a world that is "indifferent and uncosy," it also produces people who are similarly detached and indifferent. The political consequences of this are clear to Jane Bennett, for whom disenchantment becomes a kind of social force that "ignores and then discourages affective attachment."[19] As a result, she argues, we may lack the energy to contest injustice and simply conform to the blandness of the world that modernity produces.

This feeling of disenchantment is also evident in the fundamental categories that become culturally dominant in modern conceptions of the self and the world. Indeed, a key aspect of how moderns view themselves as modern concerns the way they break down experience into three fundamental categories: the world of inner, mental subjectivity; the world of nature and the environment; and the world of theology and the supernatural. These three categories are also instituted socially in the academic disciplines that modern universities have produced to study them: philosophy, science, and religion. These three disciplines are, to the modern

Skyscrapers of Hong Kong. (Author)

way of imagining the world, foundational. That is to say, the modern social imaginary regards these three categories as self-evidently distinct from one another, even though it is certainly possible to see the places where they overlap. The fundamental divisions between these three realms concern their relationship to the modern concept of nature. Science treats nature as an objective, empirical reality whose laws can be discerned through scientific methods of observation and experimentation. Religion ostensibly concerns itself with the nonobjective, nonempirical world of gods, heavens, and spirits. Philosophy derives neither from nature nor from the supernatural world, but from the inner, mental activity of human beings.

From this we can see that the modern conception of nature breaks down our sense of the world, and our means of approaching it, into three realms: the interior world of the mind; the external world of nature; and the transcendent world of the gods. Philosophy, science, and religion, in the modern social imagination, are seen as engaging distinctively with these three realms. The places where these distinctions are not so clear, the places where the human, the natural, and the supernatural overlap, constitute the basic ethical fault lines of modern Western culture. Do humans have the right to create, alter, and destroy life absolutely? Can there be a legitimate place for religion in the public sphere? Is believing in gods silly at best and immoral at worst? Are humans created by God or did they emerge from a process of evolution?

These are serious questions for contemporary culture precisely because of the way the modern social imagination conceptualizes nature. In this modern imagination, the realms of the supernatural, the natural, and the human are fundamentally distinct from one another, and the three disciplines of religion, science, and philosophy focus on each of these three realms respectively. The cultural disputes arise in the places where our knowledge of the world breaks down or blurs the preconceived distinctions of our cultural imagination. Evolutionary science, for instance, blurs the boundaries between the human and the natural worlds and causes us to ask whether humans are truly distinct from other animals, and whether other animals possess language, consciousness, and feelings, that is to say, the cognitive processes of individual subjectivity that modern people have traditionally reserved for human beings. Since the science of evolution questions the distinctive boundaries between humans and the natural world that are assumed in the modern concept of nature, the science of evolution thus becomes culturally divisive. By this I mean that evolution becomes a topic for cultural argument, because the boundaries it questions are cultural boundaries, which constitute the culturally shared framework by which modernity fundamentally organizes our experience of the world.

While it is fairly easy to see that evolutionary science causes problems for the modern humanist distinction between humans and nature, it is perhaps harder for us to imagine a way of experiencing the world that questions the distinction between the natural and supernatural worlds. But perhaps this is not so hard to imagine as it may first seem. For example, four centuries after the origin of humanism, when Darwin's views became well known, it is still extremely hard to abandon the notion that humans are ultimately distinct from nonhuman animals, or the larger processes of nature. But given the overwhelming evidence from science, we have been compelled to rethink what constitutes our uniqueness as a species, and we are now fascinated by stories of how animals communicate with each other, have emotions, or conduct mourning rituals.[20] Perhaps the distinction between the inner world of human mentality and the outer world of natural processes has begun to dissolve somewhat. We can see here a process of cultural change, of redefining our categories of human and natural so that now it has become common to refer to animals as "nunhuman animals," reinforcing the point that the category "animal" includes us humans too. And just as it has become possible for us to rethink the human/animal distinction, we can begin to see how it could be possible, in theory at least, for us to rethink the human/god distinction, for this distinction is just as much a cultural construct as the human/animal distinction, or the consciousness/nature distinction.

The reason this distinction is hard to overcome, however, concerns the history of Western theology, which has largely been premised on an absolute distinction between gods and humans. This theological view has carried over into modern concepts of secularity, in which an equally sharp distinction is posited between the supernatural world and the natural world. Within this theological worldview, gods and humans are distinct from each other by virtue of the theology of creation: God alone creates, and everything else is his creature. In Islamic theology, to assert divinity of something that is creaturely is considered *shirk*, the highest form of heresy. Nothing is allowed to breach this divide. Judaism similarly imposes a prohibition on uttering the name of God, since names are the attribute of creatures, not of the Creator. This is also why no likeness of God is permitted in Jewish and Islamic culture.

The case of Christianity, however, is slightly different. Christians hold the view that there was, miraculously, one instance of one person in which the boundary between creature and creator was absolutely dissolved, namely, Jesus. But Christians assert that Jesus is a special, indeed a unique case, and that it is impossible that there could be other instances of the divinity so absolutely and perfectly manifested within a human person. While some generous Christians allow that other religious traditions might approximate the full revelation of God that is present in Christ, most hold fast to the uniqueness of the Christ figure.[21]

But the Daoist tradition that is revealed in this book proposes a cultural world that conceptualizes nature and religion differently. It does not draw a fundamental distinction between the "supernatural" and the "human" worlds and indeed posits a major organizing category that blurs the boundaries between what we moderns call "natural," "supernatural," and "human," namely Dao, translated as "Way" or "Path." This idea of Dao, which blossomed into the rich and complex cultural web of Daoism, is in essence a radically different way of conceptualizing the world in its most fundamental nature. Rather than conceiving of the world as consisting of three distinct realms, human, natural, and supernatural, the Daoist cultural imagination regards the production of these three realms as a recursive process in which each is folded into and constitutes the other. In the Daoist imagination there is no absolute distinction between "humans" and "nature," and there is even no absolute distinction between "humans" and "gods." As a result, the whole tenor of the Daoist approach to what we categorize as "nature" and "religion," or "science" and "theology," is fundamentally different.

To think about Daoism and ecology, then, is to think about how human beings imagine, experience, and act within the natural world. This is in part a theoretical task, in the sense that it seeks to understand how humans theorize or gaze upon the world in which they live. Its fundamental assumption is that this theorization of nature is a cultural activity, meaning that different cultures in different parts of the world imagine, experience, and act upon nature differently. Along with this goes the notion that the human theorization of nature is also a historical activity, in that the way that humans have imagined, experienced, and acted upon nature has changed in some fundamental ways over time. Of course, the basic parameters for how human beings have engaged nature are set by our general constitution as physical beings: our senses provide us with visual and other data that we use to build up an image or other experience of nature. Senses allow us to experience certain aspects of nature, and we have also developed technologies that allow us to observe aspects of the world that lie beyond our normal sensory range. Indeed, through the development of technologies for sensing distant stars, and therefore ancient times, scientists have recently begun to produce an entirely new vision of nature as the history of cosmic evolution stretching back some 13.7 billion years to the big bang.[22]

The fundamental existential question that faces human beings is how we make sense out of this experience. This is partially a pragmatic question: are there better, more coherent, and functional ways to make sense out of these experiences? It is also a moral question: given what we know of the world in which we live, how ought we imagine, experience, and act within that world? Put this way, it becomes clear that experiencing the natural world and asking questions about it are related. Our changing sense of our environment, and in particular the scale with which we are able to sense our environment, shapes the parameters of our sense of morality and ultimate purpose. Our values are shaped, for instance, by whether we understand ourselves primarily as members of a local community, or as planetary citizens, or as the inheritors of a massive history of cosmic evolution. Through the development of technologies that have expanded our sense of our context, we begin to feel the need to respond with values and judgments that are appropriate to these expanded horizons.

From this basic observation, we can glimpse how cultural views of nature are entwined with views of ethics and, ultimately, religion. The human imagination, experience, and engagement with nature are part and parcel of the human imagination, experience, and engagement with religion. In the modern West, however, it is sometimes hard to acknowledge this basic relationship among our views of religion, ethics, and nature, for the reason that the main achievement of modernity as a worldview has been to separate the world of nature from the world of religion in order to organize our fundamental understanding and experience of things. Latour refers to this process as "purification."[23] Moderns strive for a conceptual purity in which these worlds do not interact and institute social practices that aim toward it. Nature, in the worldview of modernity, deals with objective reality, the world "out there," to be theorized by science, transformed by technology, and made productive by economic activity. As a consequence, religion is pushed inward toward spirituality or upward toward theology. Szerszynski argues, for instance, that because of what he calls the "long arc of monotheism," the modern sense of the sacred becomes oriented toward the world of "spirituality" or the "inner life" on the one hand, or, on the other hand, toward the world of the "supernatural" or transcendent gods, whose basic characteristic is to be immaterial, invisible, and unavailable to objective science.[24] As a consequence, the "real world" and the "religious world" came to be conceived as two separate realms that, in this theory, ought not to engage with each other, a construct that is strongly defended by Stephen Jay Gould.[25] In modern culture, we can see this in the notion that religion ought properly to be a private affair or an activity of the conscience, and not the subject of public discourse.

The basic point here is that the modern ways of theorizing religion and theorizing nature are cocreated. Following the Weberian theory of disenchantment, the worlds of nature and religion are created as separate and ideally nonoverlapping realms. But this does not tell us anything essential about either nature or religion. It simply tells us that the way we imagine one of these terms is related to the way we imagine the other of these terms. The most important consequence of this argument for the purposes of this book is that one cannot truly understand how we think about nature without understanding how we think about religion, and conversely one cannot truly understand religion without understanding nature. The problem is that because the modern Western conception of these terms appears to be basically a dichotomy—either one, or the other, but not both together—modern approaches to religion have focused on religion at the expense of nature, and modern approaches to nature have focused on nature at the expense of religion.

Of course, all of these supposed distinctions of modernity, the emphasis on the buffered sense of the body, the disenchantment of the world, and the separation of nature and religion, are not "true" in the sense of accurate descriptions of modern reality or social experience. Rather, they are to be understood as theoretical ideals and social practices posited by the framework of modernity. They demonstrate what modernity values and, at the same time, what it conceals. As Latour demonstrated over thirty years ago, just as much as modernity aims toward a kind of conceptual "purification," the main effect of this is to obscure the ways in which all of these aspects of culture are deeply entwined with one another in modern society. This does not amount to a "debunking" of modernity, but rather a recognition of the irreducibly hybrid, complex nature of modernity.[26]

There have, for instance, been several influential attempts to integrate nature and religion in the West, beginning with Spinoza's concept of God as/and Nature (*Deus sive natura*), and continuing with such modern nature mystics as Walt Whitman and Richard Jeffries. However, such approaches have never captured the mainstream of Western philosophical or theological thinking, precisely because their teachings undermine the theoretical ideals of the modernist project.

The social and political impacts of these theoretical ideals are well known through the discourse of "Othering." The worldview of modernity holds as axiomatic that this modern view of the separation of religion and nature is modern in the sense of later than and superior to that which has gone before. Modernity in this sense automatically implies the representation of itself as a step forward from previous ways of imagining the world. It thus contains an inbuilt value judgment that is fundamental to the modern condition: that the way moderns see the world today must by definition be "better" than what has gone before or what takes place elsewhere. This assumption has empowered and justified a thoroughly colonial discourse toward non-Western "others." Since those others are "others" not simply to the West, but also to "modernity," they must by definition be regressive, deficient, or inferior to the modern, Western way of seeing the world. This worldview is truly the bane of cultural politics across the globe: it inspires people across the world to look, do, and be "Western,"[27] and it imperils the development of a genuine critical consciousness toward what modernity entails.

Such a cultural discourse can be undermined in a significant way by bringing nature and religion back together, to look at religion as though nature matters, and to look at nature as though religion matters. It is thereby possible to construct a view of both nature and religion from outside the framework of modernity. In so doing, such a view dislocates the discourse of modernity and constructs a transgressive discourse of religion and nature, transgressive at least from the perspective of modernity. But why is this necessary? Why go to the trouble of seeing religion and nature differently? What difference does it make to construct a nonmodern view of the cofunctioning of these two terms?

There are three fundamental answers to this question, all of which are articulated in various ways in this book but which deserve to be summarized together at the outset. The first answer is that the modern disconnection of religion and nature makes it difficult to theorize, or see aright, religious cultures that do not emerge from a modern Western framework. I make this argument by drawing examples from Daoism, habitually referred to by scholars as the "least understood" of the world's major religious traditions. Most scholars, myself included, have repeated this formula for too long without asking the basic question: why is Daoism so misunderstood? What is it that prevents modern people from truly grasping what Daoism is all about? Why have there been so many misconceptions, mistheorizations, and misappropriations of this profound and meaningful tradition within Chinese culture? The answer lies in the fact that the modern Western categories of religion-separate-from-nature and nature-separate-from-religion make it particularly difficult for people seasoned in the cultural imagination of the modern West to understand Daoism.

To articulate a Daoist framework for seeing religion and nature together is, secondly, to make the argument that the Daoist tradition indeed has an important contribution to make to discourse in the environmental humanities. Daoism proposes a radically different view of the natural world, and consequently religion, than that of modernity. This view is anchored in the subjectivity of nature, a term that derives from the concept of "Dao follows its own nature" (*Dao fa ziran* 道法自然). This then leads to an understanding of Daoism as a mode of praxis or action in the world, based on a second foundational concept, conventionally translated as "nonaction" or "effortless action" (*wuwei* 無為). This Daoist approach, which I frame as transactions within an ecology of cosmic power, explains certain important features of Daoist religious activity and also functions as the basis for an environmental ethics that is relevant to contemporary ecological questions. This theorization of Daoist action leads to a way of analyzing Daoist activity in relation to the places where it occurs. This geographic or "locative" approach to religion seeks to understand human activity from the contexts in which it takes place. From this perspective, actions may be understood to have meaning not in and of themselves, but chiefly in relation to their environments or locations.

The third and final reason for constructing this theoretical framework for understanding Daoism in its own terms rather than from the perspective of the modern imagination of religion and nature is to make a Daoist-inspired argument about how human beings should properly understand their place in the world. Constructing a Daoist framework for seeing "religion" and "nature" does not simply explain why Daoism has been so misunderstood, nor does it necessarily mean that such a framework does a better job of explaining Daoism than conventional approaches drawn from the modern academic study of religion. Rather, my attempt to understand Daoism eventually led me to formulate a normative argument that this Daoist approach to religion and nature is a pragmatically better one than the one that has become familiar in the modern social imaginary.

The Daoist approach is better in three respects: first, as a basic paradigm for apprehending the world we live in, it fits better with the findings of evolutionary science, ecological science, and environmental science. Second, as a basic paradigm for orienting human life toward the world we live in, it provides a spirituality and a worldview that is creative and life-sustaining. Third, as a mode of practical engagement with our world, it is profoundly relevant for the global quest to create an ethical framework that produces a flourishing world for the betterment of human life and the sustainability of the planet humans depend on for their survival.

To understand the potential usefulness of this approach, consider the way in which the modern social imaginary articulated by social theorists such as Taylor is already breaking down and, indeed, to paraphrase Latour, may never have been true. In a world characterized by the uncertainty of human abilities to buffer the self from the world, or to transform the world in a straightforwardly positive way through technology, it is becoming increasingly apparent that modernity's fundamental theoretical framework can no longer hold true.

Already, the human drive to subdue and organize the natural world has produced a new modernity characterized by the requirement for self-reflection, as Ulrich Beck notes. He writes: "We are therefore no longer concerned exclusively with making nature useful, or releasing mankind from traditional constraints, but also and essentially with problems resulting from techno-economic development itself."[28] Beck characterizes this new modernity as a "risk society" concerned with the reasonable distribution of "tolerable side effects" of economic development, whether ecological, psychological, or social. More than thirty years after Beck's diagnosis of the new paradigm of modernity, it is increasingly clear that modern society has not solved the problem of how to distribute risk in a reasonable, ethical, or tolerable way, and that the very paradigm of modernity, premised on the "buffered" self that ideally operates autonomously from the world, is at risk of being largely undermined.

As early as 2007, for instance, China's State Oceanic Administration warned of a rapid rise in sea levels that could "threaten China's densely populated east coast." Given that sea levels are already rising at the rate of 2.5 mm per year, the report of the UN International Panel on Climate Change predicted that year that sea levels would rise up to 59 cm by the end of the century.[29] As such climate change events become more widely recognized as threats to modern urban civilization, it will become increasingly likely that the modern social imaginary of the "buffered self" as articulated by Taylor may fall apart.

A second example can be drawn from the rise of bacteria that are resistant to common antibiotic drugs, most notably Methicillin-resistant Staphylococcus aureus (MRSA). The Mayo Clinic notes:

MRSA is the result of decades of often unnecessary antibiotic use. For years, antibiotics have been prescribed for colds, flu and other viral infections that don't respond to these drugs. Even when antibiotics are used appropriately, they contribute to the rise of drug-resistant bacteria because they don't destroy every germ they target. Bacteria live on an evolutionary fast track, so germs that survive treatment with one antibiotic soon learn to resist others.[30]

One explanation why doctors have been misprescribing antibiotics for viral infections is that when the modern social imaginary fails to hold true, and the body is revealed to be a porous body rather than a wholly buffered one, a high level of anxiety ensues in which patients demand drugs that aim to seal the body's porous nature, even if such drugs have no effect. A small study in Australia revealed that doctors feel a strong pressure to prescribe drugs for the patient in front of them, rather than consider the long-term effects of misprescribing drugs, even if they knew such drugs to be largely ineffective.[31] Treating patients at the individual level, without considering the broader or longer term effects of such treatment, even when it is not necessarily in the patient's best interest, shows a flaw in the ethical thinking that the culture of the modern social imaginary tends to produce. Treating patients for diseases solely at the level of the individual body, without extending the parameters of moral decision-making to include the broader community, in fact produces outcomes that are neither in the best interest of the individual patient nor the community at large.

Whether at the macro level of climate instability and rising sea levels, or the micro level of the rise of drug-resistant bacteria in hospitals, two problems are evident. The first is that there is a failure to make good ethical decisions that are in the long-term interests of the community. Individual agents are prioritized with no forward thinking about the consequences of such a prioritization, or no wider systematic thinking about the implications for broader communities. The second is that the modern social imaginary of individuals buffered against the effects of nature (whether germs or rising sea levels) is shown to be inconsistent with scientific reality. Despite the best efforts of modern technological society to insulate itself from the effects of nature, the reverse may in fact be true, and the massive explosion of technological projects that characterize modernity, from the petroleum economy to cloud servers that power our phones and computers, serve only to produce the long-term instability of the natural world vis-à-vis human society.

As such instabilities with the natural world continue to increase, as seems will be the case, so also the conceptual purity of the modern social imaginary will break down and a paradigm shift will occur. In this case, a new social imaginary will be created, or perhaps an old one will be resuscitated, one based on the overall feeling of nature pervading human bodies, human societies, and the human sense of being an autonomous self. With the advent of such a new paradigm and an accompanying new social affect, posthumanist culture will be organized around a sense of nature as a powerful force permeating human bodies, human politics, and human cities, taking advantage of the genuinely porous flesh of human beings, the porous borders between nations, and the flimsy barriers between land and sea.

I wish :/

2   The Subjectivity of Nature

The Vitality of the Landscape

Hangzhou, the capital of Zhejiang Province, is a dynamic modern city of some 21 million inhabitants close to China's east coast. In many ways it epitomizes the best of modern China. It has a high per capita GDP of over US$12,000. It is home to the Alibaba Group, whose initial public offering on the New York Stock Exchange raised US$25 billion, the largest in history. It hosts a number of top universities, including Zhejiang University (a C9 University, China's equivalent to the U.S. Ivy League). It is also one of China's most famous tourist destinations, most notably due to the well-preserved West Lake tourism area, a UNESCO world heritage site. As a city prized for its natural beauty, cultural heritage, economic development, and advanced technology, it perfectly embodies the changing question of nature in the modern Chinese social imagination. Can nature be responsibly exploited as a resource for tourism development? Can the world's Internet economy be powered in an ecologically sustainable way? How is the human experience of nature's beauty inexorably entwined with China's cultural history? What is the significance of this natural beauty and cultural history for China's national ambitions? Lying behind these questions is the sense of China as a country in the process of modernization, a country whose sense of cultural identity is caught between the weight of history and the demands of a future waiting to be realized. In a city like Hangzhou, this uncertainty and tension is etched onto the landscape, literally and figuratively, as the demands of culture, history, ecology, and economy change the face of the earth, create new forms of engagement with nature, and write themselves into the cultural imagination in new and perhaps unpredictable ways.

One of the lesser known tourist attractions on the north side of West Lake is the Daoist temple known as Baopu daoyuan 抱朴道院. It is a temple devoted to Ge Hong 葛洪 (283–343), a scholar from an influential family that, over subsequent generations, had a profound impact on the history of Daoism. Ge Hong's scholarly ambition was to collect the tales and legends of immortals, men and women who had changed their bodies through an alchemical process and transcended the world. He was convinced that such stories contained more than a grain of truth, and that the riches of the natural world could be unlocked for the benefit of human beings in a way that few could imagine. Far from advocating the exploitation of nature for social and economic development, the tales that he collected held forth a vision of nature more rich and life enhancing than anything that could be obtained through a narrow rational calculus. They described the extraordinary powers of minerals, metals, flora, and fauna that could be concocted into an elixir of immortality, a prize sought by earlier emperors who had bankrupted the state in their megalomaniac desire to rule forever. For Ge Hong, however, such a quest was not driven by a desire to serve the ambitions of the powerful. His was a profoundly religious ambition bound up with the requirements of faith, devotion, and proper moral orientation.[1]

Today, the temple is a complex of buildings improbably stacked together on the side of a steep mountain overlooking the lake. It contains several shrines, a teahouse, and living quarters for a small community of Daoist nuns. Although impoverished by the ravages of China's century of revolutions, the temple thrives to this day and preserves the memory of Ge Hong, the Master Who Embraced Simplicity, welcoming both pilgrims and tourists who have perhaps tired of the flashy Buddhist temples and historical monuments that surround the lake below. Above a small shrine on the right side is inscribed the following couplet: "Obtain the aligned vitality of the landscape" (De shanshui zhengqi 得山水正氣), and, on the left,

West Lake Pavilion and Water Lilies, Hangzhou. (Daniel Vorndran / DXR [CC BY-SA 3.0 (http://creativecommons.org/licenses/by-sa/3.0)], via Wikimedia Commons)

"Gather the grand sights of heaven and earth" (Ji tiandi daguan 極天地大觀). They point to Ge Hong's desire to deeply observe all that the natural world had to offer, and also to obtain something from it, its vitality or essence. The questions that faced him were how to see what nature could truly offer and how properly to obtain such "aligned vitality."

A clue to the answers can be found in the unusual Chinese character that is used for the word "obtain." Normally written with the radical 彳 (meaning "to walk"), it is instead written with the radical 氵 (meaning "water"). This hints that obtaining the true vitality of the landscape is in some sense a fluid process. It does not involve grasping or extracting nature's power, but rather taking advantage of that power, allowing it to flow into the body and transform it. In this way, the vitality of the landscape is properly aligned with that of the individual and thus able to exert a properly transformative effect upon it.

The second half of the couplet points to another basic relationship between human beings and the natural world, that heaven and earth afford humans "great sights." Indeed, the Chinese character used here for a "sight" or an "observation" (guan 觀) is also used for a Daoist monastery. This term serves to indicate that a key element of Daoism involves observation as both a natural and a religious act. Many Daoist temples or observatories are located in sites of outstanding natural beauty that afford practitioners the ability to "observe" the landscape that surrounds them. Although Daoist temples can be located in cities and other community spaces, the monastic tradition that continues to this day has generally favored high mountains and beautiful landscapes far from the busy life of the town. By observing the scenery, Daoists are perhaps better able to take advantage of the vitality that flows through the landscape, known in Chinese as the "Dao" or the "Way," aligning themselves with it and being transformed by it. To observe the Dao, therefore, is not simply to be a passive recipient of sensory data. It is to engage in an act of transformation, known in Chinese as "cultivating the Dao" (*xiudao*). Such an act of cultivation thus connects the outer landscape of mountains and streams (the Chinese term is *shanshui*) with an inner world of bones, viscera, blood, and breath, a landscape of the inner body nourished by the same vital energy, or *qi*, that flows through the earth.

This Daoist vision for human engagement with the natural world, at least as articulated by Ge Hong, is not directly concerned with "saving it" for its own sake. Indeed, for him, the notion that humans could possibly "save nature" would seem hubristic in the extreme. His idea was more accurately the reverse: that nature could save human beings from their own bodies. This pharmacological view of nature lies at the interface between the Daoist tradition and Chinese medicine. Indeed, Tu Youyou 屠呦呦 (b. 1930), who won the Nobel Prize for Medicine in 2015, cited Ge Hong's pharmacological work as a direct inspiration for her work in developing Artemisinin, a drug therapy for malaria.[2] To pursue such an approach to the environment thus means to pursue a view in which humans paradoxically recognize their dependence on the natural environment in order to transcend it. This relationship is one in which humans "cultivate Dao" through what I call an "ecology of cosmic power." This ecology recognizes the complexity of relations between human beings and their natural environment and cannot simply be reduced to the notion of "protecting" nature according to some preordained vision of its "authenticity."[3] To allow the natural world to save human beings, however, requires an understanding of how the vitality of the human body is constituted by the vitality of the landscape. It also requires an openness to the notion that the natural world possesses to a certain degree its own subjectivity and its own agency. Indeed, to understand the Daoist approach to ethics and to the natural environment requires a deep investigation into the notion of nature's own subjectivity.

The Place of Nature

Daoism proposes a radical reversal of the way that modern human beings think about the natural world. Rather than understanding human beings as "subjects" who observe the "objective" world of nature, Daoism proposes that subjectivity is grounded in the Dao itself, the wellspring of cosmic creativity for a world of constant transformation. This does not mean that humans principally are "objects" upon which "nature" acts. This would be to suggest that they possess no genuine subjectivity, freedom, or agency, and this is certainly not what the Daoist tradition implies. But, this grounding of subjectivity in the Dao does pose a challenge to modern ideas about humans as individual, subjective agents. Since Descartes, the modern humanist imagination of the self has located subjectivity within the cognitive functioning of human beings. From this point of view, self-consciousness and the capacity to think freely and creatively take place in human minds. These rational abilities are not a function of our being "creatures of flesh," a quality that we share with other animals and "nature," but rather uniquely endowed in human beings by virtue of our mentality.

But if we now imagine that human subjectivity derives from or is in some way inherited or "modeled" from "nature," then this causes a profound shift in what we understand this nature to be. The capacity to think, imagine, and act freely in the world is not what sets humans apart from nature: it is what nature enables humans to do. To explain this shift more fully, I would like to propose that we examine the way we think about the "place" of nature. The basic argument here is that when modern humans imagine nature as object, they at the same time imagine nature as external to the body. By contrast, when Daoists imagine nature as subjective, they at the same time imagine nature as internal to the body. Positing nature as subjectivity means that nature can be apprehended and experienced internally.

Nature as Environment

The very term "environment" suggests something that is around or about human subjects. In scientific literature, environmental factors are ones that are external to the operation of an organism or organization and that may exert some influence over it. In this sense, one may define environmental elements as things that lie beyond the domain of subjectivity of the individual or organism. While humans can control their own bodies, for instance, through their subjective decision-making capacities, human bodies are still subject to the influence of external, environmental factors over which individuals have no control. Examples of this are the influence of the weather on emotions and being infected by viruses that contact the body. In these cases, the mind loses some subjective control over its body, a state that modernity normally pathologizes as "illness." The ultimate loss of subjectivity is, of course, death.

The perception of an environment or a world that surrounds us is thus key to the modern human sense of self. Subjectivity, or the sense of self, can be defined quite precisely as whatever is not "the environment." In Cartesian thinking, which has dominated the humanistic tradition of the modern West, this distinction between subjectivity and environment is also understood as a distinction between thought and matter. Human subjectivity is bound up with the ability to think, and from this perspective the Cartesian formula of "cogito ergo sum" (I think, therefore I am) can be understood with an emphasis on the first person singular of the two verbs: *I* think, therefore *I* am. My existence as a person depends upon my sense of myself as a subject who thinks about things. This sense of oneself located chiefly in the mental processes of cognition implies a contrast with the realm of things that is not "myself" and that does not "think." This unstated contrast is in fact the objective, material world that is cognized by the rational human mind. This "world" thus functions as the backdrop in front of which human subjectivity takes place, the neutral space from which the human mind stands out as intelligence that coalesces in one's sense of self. In modern terms, this world surrounds and delimits human subjectivity, and in fact constitutes our environment. To have a sense of self as thinking, rational ego, therefore, is always and already to imply the sense of a surrounding world, one from which the mind distinguishes itself by its capacity to think.

The Chinese philosophical tradition developed a comparable understanding of "the environment," in the term *ming* 命, which is commonly translated as "fate." In classical China, this term appears paired with the word for heaven (*tian* 天) in the binome *tianming* 天命, which is usually translated as "the mandate of heaven." The idea here is that certain aspects of the human social order are governed by factors that are external to human control, in effect environmental factors. This term was most commonly used to explain the fall of a dynasty. In this case, it was said that "heaven" had "changed its mandate" and given the authority to rule to a new dynastic house. In classical Chinese philosophy, the term *tian* can be translated either as "heaven" or "nature" depending on the context. Its basic meaning, however, is the realm beyond the human that is seen as acting toward the human world in some way. When this is chiefly understood as the operations of the natural world, then it is more common to translate this term as nature; and when it is chiefly understood as the operations of a supernatural or divine power, then it is more common to translate the term as heaven.[4] Crucially, however, the concept of heaven/nature implies that it has some kind of force or agential power. It is not simply a neutral background upon which humans project their own subjectivity, but rather a force to be reckoned and engaged with.

The overlapping of "nature" and "heaven" in the concept of *tian* is useful for understanding the relationship of nature and religion in Chinese thought. Inasmuch as this force or power beyond human control is envisaged as natural, in the modern sense of belonging to the empirically observable world of material objects, then the problem of the human condition is conceived as basically a technological one. It is the task of human beings to extend their subjectivity over this external world through technological innovation and engineering prowess so as to bring as much as possible of this "external world" into the domain of human subjective control. The closest analogy to this in the Western tradition is that of Francis Bacon (1561–1626), who argued that the moral duty for human beings is "the enlargement of the bounds of Human Empire, to the effecting of all things possible."[5] His approach suggests that the environment should ideally possess no subjectivity itself, but rather be rendered thoroughly objective by the ordering power and discipline of human technological prowess. Here, the function of technology is precisely to de-subjectivize nature and to bring all of the natural world into the single order of "the environment."

Within the Chinese context, this approach to the natural world is summed up most clearly in the Maoist ideology of "defeating" nature/heaven through the collective deployment of the human will. Here, it is not so much technological prowess that marks the unique capability of human beings, but rather the collective will of humanity to reshape the world to its own advantage.[6]

The concept of *tian* as heaven/nature also opens the possibility for what in modern terms would be understood as a religious response to the question of the subjectivity of the environment. This possibility arises when the dominant form of nonhuman agency is envisaged as chiefly supernatural in the modern sense of belonging to an immaterial world of invisible, culturally postulated superhuman agents. From this perspective, the task of human beings is either to submit absolutely to this external power or force or to negotiate with or otherwise attempt to change the "will of God." The former position, that of submission, is essentially the main theological insight of Islam. In Islamic theology, God alone is great, and the task for human beings is submission, or compliance with his laws. This is the basic meaning of the term "Islam," which in Islamic theology thus leads to the related condition of peace or harmony (*salaam*; cf. Hebrew *shalom*). The chief task for human beings is to figure out how to live those laws, a task known in the Islamic world as *fiqh*, or jurisprudence. In this sense, the power of God is certainly a subjective power, in that God demonstrates intention toward and consciousness of human life; but, it is not a natural power in the sense of being located in the empirically observable world of the created order.[7]

The theological alternative to Islamic submission to supernatural subjective power is the mode of religious activity commonly understood as petitionary prayer, in which religious actors attempt to engage with supernatural subjective powers and exhort them to actions that are advantageous to the religious actors. In this case, religious people attempt to change the course of "fate" through their religious actions, so as to bring about healing, or wealth, or peace, or whatever material or spiritual goal they desire. An examination of any religious system will likely reveal the presence of both of these religious responses, even though they are theologically self-contradictory. Religions are complex and messy cultural systems and tend to embrace contradictory forms in practice. But in both of these basic religious responses of submission on the one hand and negotiation on the other, we can see that they are a response to the perception of an agency and a subjectivity that are culturally postulated as supernatural.

The sense of an environment as a realm beyond the subjectivity of the individual, therefore, favors two broad cultural responses, which can be divided in the modern social imagination into "technology" and "religion." Bacon best characterizes the idea of technological imperialism, in which the human task is to bring as much of nature's powers under the technological control of human society. The second can basically be characterized as a religious response: either submitting to God's will or attempting to bring the divine realm under the control of the individual agent.

Since the Chinese word *tian* can be characterized as either nature or heaven, this term provides a way to see how nature and religion overlap. An example of this can be found in the preface to Judith Shapiro's book *Mao's War Against Nature*, which opens with a quotation from a Communist revolutionary song: "Let's attack here! Drive away the mountain gods, break down the stone walls, to bring out those 200 million tons of coal."[8] In this song, the goal of bringing out the coal involves an attack on both the physical landscape through mining and on the theological landscape, by destroying the cultural power of the gods to protect the mountains they inhabit. Here, nature and religion are brought together in the struggle of the human will against the subjective powers of heaven/nature that threaten its existence.

The experience of being conditioned by environmental factors that have the power to influence and shape one's life is likely universal across cultures. But, as seen in the previous examples from Chinese and Western history, the precise way that this environmentality is experienced and imagined can vary. Within the modern social imagination, this environmentality can be posited as natural objects or supernatural subjects and can lend itself to the development of technological mastery or religious culture. This leads to two conclusions that are, from the modern perspective, completely obvious. The first is that nature should fundamentally be conceived as our "environment," as the space around us that lies beyond our own sense of self, our own subjectivity. Secondly, the same applies to the supernatural realm of subjective powers: gods, conceived as environmental factors that have some power or influence over human lives, are also external to our own sense of self, our own subjectivity. The Chinese concept of "humans must defeat nature/heaven" (*ren ding sheng tian*), however, demonstrates the way in which the technological and theological realms overlap.

From these examples, we can more easily see how the modern sense of the "natural" environment and the "theological" environment is in fact a social, historical construction. As a result, it is neither necessary nor inevitable that human beings should imagine the natural and supernatural realms as external to the sense of themselves as individual subjects or as fundamentally separate from each other.

To understand how the Daoist tradition has approached this way of imagining nature and heaven requires an investigation of the foundation of the Daoist tradition, namely, the idea of Dao, or Way. The best place to start is the *Daode jing*, the foundational Daoist text whose title is often translated into English as *The Way and Its Power*. Consisting of eighty-one short chapters in aphoristic style, the text records various sayings attributed to a mythical figure known simply as the Old Master, in Chinese, Laozi 老子. Chapter 25 of the standard edition of this text contains perhaps the most famous cosmological statement:

Humans follow earth
Earth follows heaven
Heaven follows Dao
Dao follows its subjective nature.[9]

Here, the three realms of human, nature, and the transcendent cosmos are not understood as absolutely distinct spaces. Rather, they are related in that they follow from or are normatively modeled (the Chinese term is *fa* 法) on one another in a process of hierarchical creativity. The ultimate norm for this process is Dao itself. Dao is not modeled on or dependent upon anything else. Rather, it takes its own self-creativity or self-emergence as its norm. The three "realms" of human, nature, and supernatural are folded into a hierarchy, whose ultimate ground is Dao, which is understood in this text as a recursive process or pattern of creative self-emergence. This Daoist model differs from the modern Western cultural imagination of three distinct spaces to the "world." It proposes first of all that the three dimensions of humans, earth, and heaven are related through a process of "normative modeling," or "following" (*fa*). Secondly, it proposes that all these dimensions are to be understood as following Dao, which does not have any ground or foundation; Dao, rather, is a creative process of self-emergence.

From this Daoist perspective, the modern cultural imagination of humanity, nature, and the supernatural as three distinct, and ideally nonoverlapping realms, is very hard to grasp. Firstly, this text sees that these three realms depend on or follow from one another. They are not truly distinct or separate but share some fundamental pattern or model that relates them. The activity of one domain will thus be significant for the other domains, especially given that what is essential about human life is the way it models or is patterned on natural life, rather than the way it stands out from or distinguishes itself from nature. As a consequence, nature, if we understand this as "the earth" in the terms of the *Daode jing*, is not something that we can grasp objectively. From this perspective, contrary to what our senses tell us, the earth does not lie outside us as an object to be perceived, manipulated, or indeed preserved or "saved." Rather, it is something that patterns, models, or informs us as human beings. And if we understand this patterning or modeling in its ultimate sense as the Dao, then we can say that the Dao is the ground of ultimate subjectivity. This basic meaning of the fourth line of this phrase is that there is nothing to which Dao itself is subject. Instead, Dao is the ground of subjectivity itself: it is the power of things to be autonomous, self-governing, and self-creating.

The classical scientific imagination of nature in modernity is precisely the reverse of this: only human beings possess subjectivity; only human beings are capable of understanding and creating themselves, and of deciding what to do and when. Nature, by contrast, is ideally objective, passively following "laws" and not having any capacity to shape or create itself. The Daoist view presented in the *Daode jing* is basically an alternative to this imagination of nature. The ultimate ground of subjectivity is the Dao; this Dao is the model or pattern for the heavens; the heavens are the model or pattern for the earth; the earth is the model or pattern for humans. The fact that humans possess subjectivity, an individual sense of self, an identity, and a consciousness, is grounded in their emergence from within the world of nature, understood as the earth, heavens, and Dao. That humans possess autonomy and subjectivity is not something that makes them different from nature but rather is precisely what they inherit from the earth. It is "nature itself" that shapes, transforms, and emerges. That humans also shape, transform, and emerge is due to their inheritance of these capacities, not due to their distinction from the "background" of the natural world. Ultimately, human subjectivity, from a Daoist perspective, is rooted in the subjectivity of nature, which is rooted ultimately in the Dao as the recursive process of self-creation.

The modern social imagination focuses on nature as law or pattern in its most "natural" state and is thus forced to come up with a theory to explain how change or transformation within nature takes place (evolution). The Daoist social imagination, by contrast, focuses on nature as subjectivity in its most natural state and conversely is forced to come up with a theory to explain how patterns and regularity take place. The consequence of this basic difference between the classical Daoist and modern Western social imaginations is profound. Whereas the latter regards humans as unique or special precisely because of their subjectivity, consciousness, and individuality, the former regards humans as fundamentally natural (or uninteresting) because of their subjectivity, consciousness,

and individuality. Humans do not stand out from the natural world because of their subjectivity; their subjectivity is precisely derived from or
modeled on (*fa*) "nature" because Dao in itself is subjectivity. Dao is not
subject to any higher law or pattern but is self-generating, spontaneous,
and ultimately free. Inasmuch as humans grasp this subjectivity for
themselves, or, in Daoist terms, "obtain the Dao" (*dedao* 得道), they are
in fact grasping what it means to be rooted in Dao.

As a consequence, the basic model for nature advertised in this text is
not premised on an idea of creation, in which one entity, A, may be said
to "create" another entity, B. Rather, the normative relationship between
different dimensions of the cosmos is that of modeling. The Dao does not
create the world, or human beings, in the way that the Jewish-Christian-
Islamic God is said to have created the world. Instead, it models subjectivity, the power of self-creation. Inasmuch as "nature" models this power
of self-creation, it is "natural." And the same is true for human beings.

The question that arises from this is how we can see this subjectivity
in nature: where is it genuinely evident? The answer lies in understanding nature not as a collection of objects that mechanically follow laws or
patterns that they do not understand. It requires us to understand nature
from the perspective of evolution. That is to say, what is most remarkably
"natural" about "nature" is that it constantly evolves, generating new and
complex forms and species. From the perspective of evolution, nature truly
is subjective. It is a self-generating, creative power, especially when viewed
from the perspective of cosmic evolution. When understood as a process
of emergence over 13.7 billion years, the raw power of nature from the big
bang to the evolution of life on earth can be seen as nothing but sheer,
overwhelming subjectivity. As Swimme and Tucker note, "With our empirical observations expanded by modern science, we are now realizing
that our universe is a single immense energy event that began as a tiny
speck that has unfolded over time to become galaxies and stars, palms
and pelicans, the music of Bach, and each of us alive today."[10] From this
perspective, it is impossible to imagine that humans somehow "stand
out" from nature or are distinguished from nature by their possession of
"consciousness," "feelings," or capacity for self-determination. Rather, their
possession of subjectivity is their natural state.

This argument constitutes something of a challenge not only to the
modern imagination of nature, but also to contemporary discourse regarding the environment. Later Daoist alchemy came to sum up this notion
in a phrase that is quite shocking to the modern imagination. It says,

"My fate lies within me, and not within the heavens/nature" (wo ming zai wo bu zai tian 我命在我不在天). This remarkable phrase calls attention to a Daoist social imagination in which the complex of environmental factors known as "fate" are not to be imagined as being located within the "heavens" or indeed the realm of "nature" but rather within the individual subject (wo 我). That is to say, the "environment" is not external to the self, but located within the self (zai wo 在我). Furthermore, this Daoist concept of "environment," or "fate," encompasses what in modern terms we understand as both "nature" and "gods." In fact, one of the chief characteristics of the Daoist cultural imagination is that both the natural world and the theological world came to be envisioned as interior to the body of the Daoist practitioner.[11]

Nature as Insistence

The environmental character of nature, the notion that nature is all around us acting on us in ways beyond our control was, in the Daoist cultural imagination that emerged in China's middle ages (from the end of the Han dynasty in 220 C.E. to the beginning of the Ming dynasty in 1368 C.E.), replaced with an alternative character that I refer to as nature's "insistence." What I mean by this term is that Daoists developed an understanding as to what we moderns term nature, and also what we moderns term gods, not as beings or spaces that exist beyond the realm of human bodies, as it were, "out there," but rather as subjectivities that "insist" or "dwell within" the space of the body.

From this perspective, to possess some individual subjectivity is not to assert some existential uniqueness over and against an undifferentiated chaotic mass but rather to embody the subjective powers of Dao that have come together to inform each unique being. To be an individual is not to be distinguished from the world by virtue of some unique characteristic that "nature" does not possess. Instead, the subjectivity of nature insists in or informs the subjectivity of the individual; the uniqueness of each individual life, and the uniqueness of the human species, are constituted by how specifically the Dao is configured or constellated within each life.

Up to now, this Daoist view has largely been understood from the perspective of what it has to say about the relationship between human beings and gods. But in fact, this viewpoint has an important consequence for how human beings imagine the natural environment. Rather than providing a neutral backdrop for human life and action, the environment in this Daoist sense is within human beings, not external to them.

An example can be seen in a Daoist visualization text known as the *Scripture on Inner Observation* (*Neiguan jing* 內觀經; DZ841):

> Heaven and earth mingle their essences; yin and yang engage in interchange. Thus myriad beings come to life, each receiving a particular life: yet all are alike in that they have a share in the life-giving Dao.
>
> When a father and mother unite in harmony, man receives life.
>
> In the first month, essence and blood coagulate in the womb.
>
> In the second month, the embryo begins to take shape.
>
> In the third month, the yang spirit arouses the three spirit souls to come to life.
>
> In the fourth month, the yin energy settles the seven material souls as guardians of the body.
>
> In the fifth month, the five phases are distributed to the five orbs to keep their spirit at peace.
>
> In the sixth month, the six pitches are set up in the six intestines nourishing the vital energy.
>
> In the seventh month, the seven essential stars open the body orifices to let the light in.
>
> In the eighth month, the eight luminants descend with their true vital energy.
>
> In the ninth month, the various palaces and chambers are properly arranged to keep the essence safe.
>
> In the tenth month, the energy is strong enough to complete the image.[12]

This passage describes the gestation of the fetus over a period of ten lunar months as an act of infusion, indwelling, or "insistence" of cosmic powers. Very likely, it was used as a form of meditation in which the practitioner aims to create for him- or herself an "immortal body." It describes how the various elements of the body, including both "material" and "spiritual" aspects, are formed not simply by the act of intercourse of the parents, but by the infusion of a whole array of cosmological elements. Yin, yang, stars, the five "phases" or elements, cosmic sounds, and the seven stars of the Big Dipper (Ursa Major) combine to inform the particularity of an individual life. From this perspective, we can say that nature does not surround or exist beyond the subjectivity of human life. Rather, the environment is something that ideally insists within the subjectivity of human lives. In fact, it is precisely because the creative powers of the cosmos insist within human life that human subjectivity is possible. From this Daoist perspective, the creation of life is not to be understood as life coming to "exist" in the sense of stand out or emerge from some background. Instead, life is a process of infusion or insistence in which the subjective powers of the cosmos transform and combine to inform the unique nature of the new individual.

The description of the gestation of the fetus found in this text can be taken as a further explication of the idea of "normative modeling" (*fa*) contained in chapter 25 of the *Daode jing*. The Dao is in essence a self-creating process of self-creation. This process infuses the heavens, the earth, and human life in ever more complex patterns, forming the individual lives, creative possibilities, and self-conscious subjectivities of human beings. Neither the *Daode jing* nor the *Scripture on Inner Observation* views this as a process of creation out of nothing, but rather as a process of "information," or as I term it "insistence." The end of this process is that the ideal individual "completes the image" or is born. But, his or her uniqueness is informed by the process of creative modeling that is supplied by the subjective powers of the cosmos, and it is ultimately grounded in the autonomous self-creative power of the Dao itself.

Texts like the *Scripture on Inner Observation* can be read not only as documenting a unique Daoist religious sensibility. They can also be read as a way to understand the environment not as something that exists objectively outside us, but as something that insists subjectively within us. This way of imagining the environment is deeply transgressive of our modern, scientific understanding of nature, and of our modern sense of human consciousness and subjectivity. Throughout this book, I explain how this sense of nature's subjectivity runs through the Daoist tradition like a deep, creative thread, and I also attempt to explain how this view may be relevant for the contemporary world. For now, however, I turn to explore the second important consequence of this Daoist worldview, which concerns agency.

The Agency of Nature

Thus far I have sketched the outlines of a Daoist theory of nature as subjectivity. This is, in essence, my way of teasing out the implication of the famous Daoist concept of "Dao following its own subjectivity" (Dao fa ziran 道法自然). In the previous section, I explored the surprising notion that emerges from this: that nature should not be grasped principally as an objective world that exists beyond the hermetically sealed walls of the body, but rather grasped subjectively as a world that insists within the body. This sense of subjectivity, or self-mastery of one's fate, might give the impression that Daoism is an egotistical religion devoted to the cultivation of self and a relative disdain of others. In fact, it is a common and quite fundamental misconception of Daoism that it advocates a life of individualism, detached from ethical concern for everyday society or the natural environment. The reason for this misconception has to do with a misunderstanding of the proper relationship between self and world in the Daoist imagination, understood ideally by the term *wuwei* 無為, conventionally translated as "nonaction" or "effortless action."

Nonaction and Catalysis

The concept of *wuwei* is one of the most significant and pervasive motifs within Daoism. It points first and foremost to an ideal way of acting within the world; it is intrinsically connected to the concept of the subjectivity of nature (discussed previously), and it points toward a Daoist theory of religious and ethical action, as I hope to argue in the subsequent chapters. For now I would like to explain the basic meaning of this term, as it appears in a famous passage in the *Daode jing* (chap. 57):

I do nothing
And people transform themselves
I practice tranquility
And people align themselves
I have no involvement in affairs
And people prosper themselves
I have no desires
And people simplify themselves

As this passage makes clear, the *Daode jing* is not here advocating some kind of individualistic detachment from the world of affairs. It is advocating instead an ethic of relationship between the self (*wo* 我) and the people (*min* 民) in which the nonaction of the former facilitates the spontaneous self-transformation of the latter. In each case, "I" do not do something, with the consequence that the "people" of their own accord are spontaneously transformed, governed, and made prosperous and simple, meaning authentic.

The praxis that this passage advocates is best understood by analogy with the process of catalysis. A catalyst is a substance that enables a chemical reaction to take place at a higher rate but does not itself take part in the reaction and is not, as a result, consumed by the reaction. In the case of the previous passage, the work is not performed by the "I" but is something that takes place spontaneously within the people. In each case, the consequence of the (non)activity of the "I" is that the people transform, align, prosper, and simplify themselves (zi 自). The crucial question here is where does the energy come from? By what means does this widespread social transformation take place? The answer is that it does not lie within the subjectivity of the individual self, the wo or ego of the Daoist sage. It is not through that person's "work" that transformation is achieved. Rather, it is through his or her withdrawal from work, or, as the text puts it, through nonaction, that change emerges spontaneously among the other people.

The theory that underlies this way of acting is quite clear: the subjectivity that emerges from the unfathomable Dao is a creative, transformative subjectivity. At its heart, it is the capacity to change, transform, and be creative. It follows from this that in order to facilitate change, transformation, and creativity among the people, and by extension within the world, the mode of praxis for the Daoist should be that of a catalyst rather than a worker, enabling the transformative power of the Dao to work spontaneously and creatively in the multiple subjectivities of the surrounding world.

This ethical dimension to this theory of action comes from the fact that only certain types of work are produced spontaneously by the subjective power grounded in the Dao. In this case, four are mentioned: self-transformation (zihua 自化), self-alignment (zizheng 自正), self-prosperity (zifu 自富), and self-simplicity (zipu 自樸). These four aspects of the subjective agency of the Dao are thus to be understood as the proper goals of Daoist ethical activity and are to be achieved through nonaction by the catalytic agent.

From this passage, we can thus begin to understand that Daoist ethics are derived from an understanding of the basic functioning of the Dao as the ground of subjectivity and agency inherent within things in the natural world. Given that agency does not derive from an ultimate creator figure or divine lawmaker but is rather inherent within the subjectivity of things, the goal of the Daoist is, to put it positively, to catalyze creative transformation within things, in this case, the "people" (*min* 民). Put negatively, the goal of the Daoist is to avoid doing anything that might inhibit the subjective agency inherent within things. This mode of agency, or way of acting (though agency is not, strictly speaking, the right word here), should be understood by contrast to two opposing views.

First, this view of agency is to be distinguished from the concept of conformity with divine laws. In this latter view, ethical action is understood as action that conforms most closely to the laws of a divine creator. From this mode of creation, and this view of nature, come the idea that submission to, or faithful following of, the mandated laws is the best guarantee of ethical action. For this reason it is no surprise that theologies of divine creation entail ethics encoded in divine laws.

At the same time, the Daoist view of ethical action should be distinguished from that of absolute relativism or perspectivalism, in which there is no basis for judging the value of an action except from the perspective of the one making the action. The Daoist tradition advocates clear ethical goals that derive from the view that the subjective agency of the Dao tends toward the creation of ideal states, listed here as the four goals of ethical action: transformation, alignment, prosperity, and simplicity.

Inasmuch as the "nonactions" of the individual tend to further these goals in the world around, they are consistent with Dao itself understood as spontaneous creative power. In this case, they produce transformation rather than stasis, alignment rather than discord, prosperity rather than poverty, and authentic simplicity rather than spurious adornment. These values, grounded in the creative power of the Dao, are natural values in that they derive from the natural power of subjectivity that emerges from the Dao.

How, then, are we to understand the negative characteristic of the Daoist mode of action? Why is it that the catalytic acts of the Daoist are understood as nonaction, and how is the concept of nonaction related to the parallel "no-" concepts of "no-knowledge" (*wuzhi* 無知) or "no-desires" (*wuyu* 無欲)? The answer lies in locating the creative power of transformation. According to a Daoist understanding of the world, this creative power resides in the subjectivities of things themselves. Just as the catalyst does not participate directly in the reaction that it catalyzes, so also the Daoist facilitates transformation without directly participating in the transformation. This can make sense only if we understand the world beyond the ego to be a world of subjectivity and agency rather than a world of objectivity and passivity. In this regard, action is not about imposing the vision of the ego upon an objective world as a passive recipient, but involves unleashing the creative powers of the world understood as a complex of subjective agencies. To do so means, in part, deferring to and responsively channeling those subjectivities rather than subduing them by violence, power, or discipline. The belief of the Daoist is that the way of nonaction amid a world of transformative subjectivity is far more effective than the way of action upon a world of passive matter, at least when it comes to producing transformation, alignment, prosperity, and simplicity.

For this reason, the Daoist mode of agency can best be understood by the term "transaction," rather than "action" or "nonaction." The word "action" suggests that a subjective actor exercises power over an objective world shaping it according to his or her desires; clearly, this is not the view supported by the Daoist text. It would also be unhelpful to call the Daoist mode of praxis "nonaction," because this suggests that no work is produced. As the text from the *Daode jing* makes clear, transformation does take place and work is effectively done. From the perspective of subject ("I"), this seems to be nonaction, and it is not perceived by the world, or people, as the exercise of agency by an other. Rather, it is perceived by them as self-transformation or the spontaneous operation of their own subjectivity.

One approach in the West has been to designate this kind of action as "effortless" action, implying that the actor achieves his goal with the maximum of skill and the minimum of effort.[13] My approach, however, is to think about agency that does not derive from the mind or brain of an individual subject but rather is distributed among the subjectivities of the world that constitute the field of action where transformation takes place. This is the reason for understanding Daoist modes of action, including ritual action and ethical action, fundamentally as types of "transaction." I use this term in two senses. The first sense is that of an exchange in which the activity of A toward B results in the activity of B toward A. There is no such thing here as a one-way action. Actions always entail some kind of reaction. But the more subtle and deeper sense of my use of the term transaction is to undermine the sense of individual subjective agents who project agency onto an objective world. Agency ought to be understood as being distributed among the various subjectivities of the field where action takes place. In this case, it makes little sense to speak of an individual agent or an individual action. Instead, all actions are transactions that mediate among the various subjectivities of the world, enabling the spontaneous creativity of the Dao that insists within all subjectivities.

Here, it may be instructive to refer to Karen Barad's concept of "intra-actions." In Barad's understanding, based on her reading of Bohr's quantum physics, the boundaries between subject and object only become determinate through "specific agential inra-actions."[14] That is to say, the performance of an "agential cut" brings into being the specific, local relations of subjects and objects. These boundaries do not reside a priori in things, but rather are performed by agents. Although I am not able to read into Daoist texts the same level of metaphysical specificity that Barad identifies here, "transaction" and "intra-action" both serve to disrupt modern notions of subjectivity and objectivity, and in particular traditional notions of causality.

In the *Daode jing*, this mode of transaction rather than subjective action over an objective world is further explained in the passage in terms of "practicing tranquility," "no-involvement," and "no-desires." These terms, I believe, are further examples of what Daoist transactional agency entails and are related to the types of meditative activity that the Daoist tradition promotes. "Tranquility" positively denotes a mode of meditative action that repeatedly appears as a core value in Daoist traditions. In this passage, it functions so as to catalyze harmonious alignment (*zheng* 正) among the people. As a consequence of the spontaneous emergence of alignment, it becomes less necessary for the Daoist to manage others through direct involvement or interference in their affairs. As a result, noninvolvement or noninterference in affairs (*wushi* 無事) denotes an ideal way to achieve flourishing or prosperity (*fu* 富) among the people. Finally, the diminishment rather than expansion of desires on the part of the Daoist provides a way to attain an authentic simplicity rather than an unnatural or spurious adornment that adds nothing to the proper flourishing of creativity that lies within the subjective agency of each thing.

Praxis and Cultivation

The Daoist way of transaction, and its emphasis on the cultivation of tranquility, the diminishment of desire, and noninterference in things, should not be interpreted as the withdrawal or detachment from the world as an end in itself. Rather, these nonactions are to be understood as transactions that catalyze transformation in the world around. In the Daoist tradition, this transaction came to be understood through the agricultural metaphor of "cultivation" (*xiu* 修). Just as the farmer does not "cause" his or her crops to grow by projecting subjective agency onto them, but rather by providing them with the environment and nourishment in which their natural potency can flourish, so also the activity of the Daoist can be understood basically as a kind of cultivation.

A typical category for understanding spiritual activity is that of self-cultivation in which the religious person achieves some kind of perfection and growth through participation in various spiritual exercises. This is just as true of Daoism as it is of other religious traditions. But the Daoist tradition also came to understand cultivation practice as "cultivating the Dao" (*xiudao*), which stands as an intriguing alternative to the traditional understanding of religious activity as something that affects principally the subjective religious actor. In this Daoist phrase, the "object" of cultivation is that of the Dao itself, which we can understand as the root of creative self-transformation. In this case, the Daoist who cultivates the Dao only indirectly cultivates his or her own subjectivity. Rather, the Daoist works to enable the transformative power of the Dao itself, just as the farmer works to enable the transformative power that lies within and among the complex of agencies including the crops, soil, water, and so on. In this way, we can begin to see that the Daoist idea of cultivation in fact draws on the concept of nonaction (*wuwei*) in the *Daode jing*. The prototypical Daoist in the *Daode jing* "does nothing" and yet the people "transform themselves." This transaction can be understood as a mode of cultivating the Dao in which the nonactions of the Daoist facilitate the spontaneous self-transformation of the people.

So far, I have attempted to explain Daoism as a framework for understanding the subjectivity of nature, the place of nature, and the way of action that ideally should obtain between the individual and his or her context. It is my contention that this framework provides a way to understand certain key features of Daoist religious actions and also to understand Daoist concerns with place, environment, and cosmos. These approaches to what we moderns consider "religion" and "nature" constitute the basis for an ecological spirituality and an environmental ethic with profound consequences for the contemporary world.

3   Liquid Ecology

To say that the natural world possesses subjectivity, that it should be considered not as a neutral backdrop to human existence, but as informing or indwelling human life, is to draw the outlines of a system of ecological relationships in which the existence of one thing is connected to the existence of other things. This relationship does not necessarily imply a grand metaphysical unity of all creation, but it does imply that the life and livelihood of one thing cannot be considered in absolute isolation. Moreover, if the "insistence" of the world functions as a primary metaphor for considering how things are, then it should be clear that instead of thinking about the way that something is in the world, one should rather think of the way the world is in something. In effect, it is to argue that humans are fundamentally "worlded" beings, not so much in Althusser's sense of being "interpellated" by social forces, but rather in the sense of being "insisted upon" by the vital forces constellated in the local environment and the larger cosmos.[1] This does not mean that human beings are not subjects that act upon the world, but it does mean that human life should principally be considered as something derived from the world that it inhabits, and that the biosphere is ontologically prior to human life. To live with this realization is to live within a profound social imaginary that has the capacity to transform human life if it widely embedded in a culture of sustainability.

The foundation for this imaginary is the concept of a liquid ecology. It is an *ecology* because it is about the systemic relation of things, showing how one kind of life inheres in, or is insisted in, by another kind of life. It is a *liquid* ecology because the way this insistence takes place can best be understood as one kind of vitality "flowing into" another kind of vitality. The four sections that follow trace some of the ways that this concept of liquid ecology can be derived from key theories of human life and human power in the Chinese tradition. Some of these belong particularly to the Daoist cultural world. Others are more widespread in Chinese culture and can be seen in many different strands of tradition.

Liquid Nature

The basis for this understanding of a "liquid ecology" is the Chinese term *qi*, often translated as "breath," "pneuma," or "energy." *Qi* is best understood as a kind of liquid vitality. It is a fluid rather than a solid in the sense articulated by modern fluid mechanics: fluids respond to pressure by flowing; solids respond to pressure by being deformed. The basic character of *qi*, then, is to flow or move. Like a liquid, its direction is largely determined by the physical features of the space that it inhabits: it does not flow randomly or arbitrarily but through channels in the landscape. In this way, *qi* must be considered together with the system in which it flows; it does not make sense to consider *qi* as an absolutely independent variable that somehow "constitutes" or "creates" vitality. Rather, it is the flow of *qi* within a system that can be said to constitute life. In traditional Chinese thought, two distinct but related systems deserve consideration: the first is the physical landscape as a system through which *qi* flows, and the second is the human body. From the interaction of these two systems it is possible to construct an ecological theory of *qi*. This section considers the liquid vitality of the landscape; the next section considers the flow of *qi* within the body.

The most important context for considering the flow of *qi* within the landscape is that of feng shui (literally, wind and water), the geomantic system for siting graves, houses, and other objects within the landscape so as to take advantage of the natural flow of *qi* within the earth. Chris

Coggins discusses the earliest use of the term feng shui in the *Book of Burial* (*Zang shu* 葬書), a commentary from the fourth or fifth century C.E. on an earlier text, no longer extant, called the *Classic of Burial* (*Zang jing* 葬經) by the Daoist scholar Guo Pu 郭璞 (276–374). The commentary describes the flow of *qi* within the landscape as follows:

> The Classic says, Qi rides the wind and scatters, but is retained when encountering water. The ancients collected it to prevent its dissipation, and guided it to assure its retention. Thus it was called feng shui (wind/water). According to the laws of feng shui, the site that attracts water is optimal, followed by the site that catches wind. . . . Terrain resembling a palatial mansion with luxuriant vegetation and towering trees will engender the founder of a state or prefecture.[2]

As the text indicates, the goal here is to "retain" or "collect" *qi* and "prevent its dissipation." When *qi* dissipates, or scatters on the wind, vitality is diminished. By contrast, when *qi* is attracted and retained, there will be "luxuriant vegetation" and "towering trees." The vitality of nature then entails political prosperity: it will "engender the founder of a state or prefecture." In this way, the political vitality of a region is seen to depend on the vitality of its landscape, and the vitality of the landscape depends on the ability of the ancients to collect, retain, and prevent the dissipation of *qi*.

Coggins goes on to make two points that are relevant for the present discussion. The first is that the flow of *qi* is constituted by its "conduits and repositories."[3] That is to say, the understanding of *qi* is chiefly a locative understanding: it depends on knowing the channels through which *qi* flows and the locations where it is stored and collected. The feng shui practitioner is therefore one who possesses the knowledge of how and where *qi* flows within the landscape. Secondly, however, these "conduits and repositories include water, wind, earth, the bodies of the living, the bones of the dead and the growth, fruiting and flowering of trees and other plants." The significance of this is that *qi* is not contained within one dimension of cosmic vitality. Its nature is to pervade the boundaries of what the modern social imagination would consider to be discretely constituted domains of existence. As Coggins further notes, "In vitalist cosmology all things are connected, not metaphorically or symbolically, but physically."[4]

From this early Chinese perspective, therefore, three aspects of *qi* stand out. First, *qi* functions like a liquid that flows through channels and collects in pools. Second, the dissipation of *qi* leads to the loss of vitality within the natural landscape and consequently the loss of political strength. Third, *qi* pervades the boundaries of the landscape, the body, the living, and the dead. For this reason, understanding how and where *qi* flows, through the practice of feng shui, was of supreme significance in regards to the dead. The bones of the dead, properly buried in the correct location, become the site for the reprocessing of this liquid vitality. The text continues: "Life is the condensation of *qi*. That which is coagulated becomes the bone, which remains after death. Therefore, to bury the dead is to obey the principle of returning *qi* to the bones, thus generating life out of yin."[5]

This text reveals another aspect of *qi* that deserves consideration: *qi* can be "dissipated" or alternatively "condensed." When *qi* is condensed or "coagulated" (*ning* 凝), it forms physical substances such as the bones of the body, the interior frame upon and around which bodily life is structured and enacted. In this way, material life, even that which is constituted from seemingly hard substances such as bones, ultimately derives from a more liquid *qi*. Substance, therefore, derives from the coagulation of liquid. In burial, the bones are placed in the ground and the condensed *qi* returns to the ground and can "generate life out of yin [death]." In this way, the *Book of Burial* envisages vitality as fundamentally cyclical in nature. Not only does vitality have a vector or flow to it, it operates within a system of circulation or recycling.

An analogy can be made here with China's hydrological system. China's physical geography is defined by its three main rivers, the Mekong River (Lancangjiang), the Yellow River (Huanghe), and the Yangzi River (Changjiang). These three rivers originate in the Qinghai-Tibetan plateau, flow generally west to east, and empty into the seas to the south and east. In traditional China, the flow of these rivers basically determined the viability of agricultural life, including the ability to grow rice in southern China. Today, these rivers also provide hydroelectric power, through a massive system of dams including especially the Three Gorges Dam across the Yangzi River. They also provide water for the South-North Water Diversion Project, which transfers water from the wetter south to the more arid north.[6] In contemporary China, just as in traditional China, the prosperity of the economy and the health and vitality of the people are dependent on the hydrological cycle and in particular the flow of water along these three main river systems. In the same way, *qi* is understood in the *Book of Burial* as operating in a similarly hydrologic fashion. *Qi* is "caught" and "condensed" into bones that form the material frame upon which human life is based. Burial is the process by which that vitality is recycled.

Water-life, then, should be understood not so much as a material substance, but in terms of its vectored quality: the Chinese word for water, *shui*, can thus be interpreted verbally as *flowing*[7] and water or liquid vitality is that which "streams." Harder substances are "coagulated" or "condensed." They do not flow of their own accord but maintain a fixed structure or "substance." Nonetheless, liquid is prior to substance, and all substance can in principle be "liquified."

The relationship of Daoist thought to this understanding of liquid vitality can be traced back to the *Daode jing*'s basic understanding of Dao as the uncreated source of liquid vitality. Chapter 4 of the *Daode jing* reads:

> The Dao is empty [empties], yet using it it does not need to be refilled.
> A deep spring (*yuan* 淵)—it seems like the ancestor of the myriad living things.[8]

Here, the Dao, or Way, is understood as a kind of watery abyss or deep spring (*yuan*) from which liquid vitality emerges. This liquid vitality is "like the ancestor of the myriad things," that is to say, the source of the various genealogical lineages from which living things emerge. Life is understood not simply as the flow of water from China's west to east, but also as the transmission of vitality from one generation to the next. The function of this vitality is to beget or engender (*sheng* 生) successive generations. These "myriad things," the humans, animals, plants, trees, rocks, and such, are understood as taking place within the flow of biological time, constituted by the liquid vitality flowing from the previous generation into the successive generation. The source of this generative power is unfathomable. It is like an infinitely deep well that is constantly emptied but "does not need to be refilled." This notion itself contrasts with the supposition of contemporary environmentalism that "nature" is something to be "preserved" or safeguarded in some kind of pristine condition. If nature is to be understood as fecundity itself, then the contemporary category of the "Anthropocene" will itself have to be reworked not as the death or end of nature, but as a geological era that will be surpassed.

Liquid Politics

If Dao is the watery abyss from which the liquid vitality of the world constantly flows, then how is this vitality distributed throughout the world? A way of reading the Chinese vitalist tradition is to consider how political power was thought to be distributed. To do so involves discussion of the Chinese term *de* 德, whose fundamental meaning is "power," but which later came to be understood as "ethics" or the way power ought to be wielded. There are basically two approaches to this question in Chinese tradition. One is to consider power or vitality to be constituted genealogically, transmitted from generation to generation through the patriarchal line. This is a dominant position within Confucian culture, and it is the foundation of the Confucian virtue of filial piety. Children owe an obligation to their parents principally because their parents are the source of their own life.[9] The second is to consider that power or vitality is constituted ecologically, that is, by virtue of the network of relations, the context or "environment," in which a thing is located. The more Confucian, genealogical line of interpretation can be considered to emphasize the temporal flow of political power from one generation of a dynasty to the next. The latter, more Daoist line of interpretation emphasizes the spatial arrangement or cosmic disposition of power. Both of these methods for understanding political power rely on an underlying appreciation of the world as constituted by liquid vitality. In this sense, therefore, power ought also to be understood as a kind of liquid force.

Genealogical Transmission

In traditional China, the most important political theory was that of the mandate of heaven (*tianming*). An emperor ruled by virtue of the mandate that was given to him by heaven, with the corresponding awareness that a mandate could be revoked by heaven. At one level, the theory aims to naturalize imperial authority, in the same way that the European concept of the divine right of kings sought to give monarchs an absolute justification for their own power. At the same time, the concept of the mandate of heaven also suggests that the power of the king or emperor can in theory be revoked. To the question of why one particular house was in power, the answer could be given that it was the result of the mandate of heaven. The question for Chinese intellectuals, however, was on what basis heaven conferred power on one dynastic family and not another, and on what basis the mandate could be taken away. Research into early Chinese theories of the mandate of heaven reveals that the notion of the mandate was bound up with the concept of *de*, meaning "virtue" or "power."

The Russian anthropologist Vassili Kryukov has enlightened modern scholars considerably as to the early meanings of the term *de*, through his analysis of Zhou dynasty (1064–256 B.C.E.) bronzes and Shang-Yin (ca. 1600–1064 B.C.E.) oracle bones.[10] In his interpretation there are three basic lines of interpretation that are relevant. (Kryukov's analysis was also significant for Sarah Allan's treatment of *de* as part of her reconstruction of the metaphoric structures underlying Chinese thought.)[11] Kryukov maintains that the inscriptions on oracle bones discovered in Shang-Yin culture reveal an early forerunner of the concept of *de*, which in this case functioned as a verb with the general meaning of "to punish." In the oracle bones, it referred specifically to the prerogative of the ruler to sacrifice human life in an act of ritual violence that established and maintained his power over his subjects. This idea of capital power was related to two other terms, wei 威 (to inspire fear) and *wei* 畏 (fear, be in awe of), and indicated that the basis of royal authority lay in the capacity to generate the respect of others.[12] The sacrifice of human life is essentially an act of liquidation in which the blood of the sacrificial victim is released from his body and spilled on the ground. The spectacle of blood, whether in warfare or in ritual, is essentially a spectacle of the liquid. In war and sacrifice, bodies are revealed to be not as much constituted by their flesh as by their liquid nature. In the Shang dynasty, then, the power or virtue (*de*) by which the ruler established his authority was the power of liquidation, the power to create the spectacle of blood and thereby produce awe and terror in the population.

In the Zhou dynasty, where historical evidence is more reliable, human sacrifice was deprecated, and *de* was not generated by spilling blood, but was sent by heaven as a mandate (*tianming*). *De*, in fact, became a central concept of aristocratic Zhou religion, and it distinguished aristocratic

Oracle bone from
the reign of King
Wu Ding (late
Shang dynasty).
(National Museum of
China [CC BY-SA 3.0
(http://creativecom
mons.org/licenses
/by-sa/3.0)], via
Wikimedia
Commons)

clans from ordinary people. *De* was the privileged possession of the Son
of Heaven (meaning the emperor) and the elite clans, but it was not conferred automatically: it had to be sought through intercession with the
ancestors.[13] Through ritual means it was passed from generation to generation, but this handing on was not so much like the inheritance of a
property, but the re-birth of *de* in the clan leader. Its sociological function, as Allan points out, was to be a hereditary trait particular to each
aristocratic family.[14] In this case, *de*, or virtue, can be understood by analogy with virility (virtue and virility come from the same Latin root, *vir*,
meaning a man). In patriarchal Zhou culture, virtue was passed from one
male to the next through insemination and confirmed through intercession
with the deceased male ancestors.

Allan also cites Roger Ames's research in the Han dynasty *Shuowen* dictionary to show that the character *de* 德 was related to the characters *zhi* 直 (to grow straight), *zhi* 植 (to sow), and *zhi* 植 (to plant).[15] This organic connection is complemented by reference to the description in the *Daodejing* of "superior power (or virtue) like a mountain valley" (*shang de ruo gu*; chap. 41) and "superior goodness like [flowing] water" (*shang shan ruo shui* 上善若水; chap. 11). Putting together the metaphors of water and seed, she concludes that *de* may best be understood as semen (*jing* 精), the physical aspect of vital energy within human beings. Moreover, the nature of *jing* is that it is generated within people by heaven, and, as seed, it causes descendants to be born.

It is evident, therefore, that there is a deep-rooted liquid symbolism at work in the concept of *de*. *De*, or virtue, is a kind of liquid power in the spilled blood of enemies and sacrificial victims, transmitted through sexual fluids, and is manifested as the distinctive genetic traits of particular aristocratic families. *De* is the liquid possibility of being granted the mandate to rule, and, conversely, the mandate *ming* is the possibility of obtaining power. This reciprocity is what Kryukov terms "dynamic mediation."[16] Dynamic mediation can be understood as a transaction of power that takes place through the transmission of liquids: liquid blood, liquid semen, and latterly liquid virtue.

This line of interpretation of "power" thus constitutes the basis for the "genealogical" approach to the disposition of power. It is focused on the concept of a royal family and the transmission of political power through the male line, and it remains to this day a dominant theme of Confucian culture. When contemporary scholar-politicians such as Pan Yue argue that "ecological civilization" is the basis for the rejuvenation of the Chinese nation,[17] they (perhaps unconsciously) invoke deep-seated ethnogenealogies of the Chinese nation as the family of all Chinese people, through whose blood lineages vital power surges forth.

But, this is not the only way that power was envisaged in ancient China, and it is not the only way that ecological vitality can be pursued in contemporary China.

Ecological Disposition

The doctrine of the mandate of heaven was reworked in relation to the theory of the five phases (*wuxing* 五行) developed and systematized by Zou Yan 鄒衍 (ca. 305–240 B.C.E.) at the Jixia Academy. Zou's thesis was that there were five "phases" or "elements" (earth, wood, metal, fire, water) that form a cycle of natural conquest, in which one element naturally "defeats" a previous one in a continuous cycle. This natural philosophy was then applied to the political world to understand how one dynasty came to be replaced by another one. The idea here is that each dynasty ruled by virtue of the mandate of heaven, which was transmitted according to the cycle of the five phases. Thus: "Each of the Five Virtues [de] is followed by the one it cannot conquer. The dynasty of Shun ruled by the virtue of Earth, the Xia ruled by the virtue of Wood, the Shang dynasty ruled by the virtue of Metal, and the Zhou dynasty ruled by the virtue of Fire."[18]

The main achievement of Zou Yan's restructuring of the concept of virtue (de) was that virtue shifted from being something essentially contained within the ruler himself or his clan to something that operated on a more predictable, cosmological basis, that of the "five phases" (wuxing).

The system of five phases is the most important theory of relationship in traditional Chinese culture. It is key to understanding Daoist religious texts, Chinese medicine, and many other arenas of Chinese culture. The basic idea of the five phases is not only that one phase generates or is destroyed by another in a regular cycle, but also that transformations in one domain of the cosmos entail corresponding shifts in other domains of the cosmos. That is to say, the system of five phases is about understanding not simply how one thing takes over from the previous one in a natural cycle of conquest, but also how transformation in the one dimension of existence should also entail a corresponding transformation in another dimension of existence. Here, the sequence of transformations was extended (tui 推) into another area. Historian Sima Qian's description of Zou's method of tui (extension) is as follows:

> First he had to examine small objects, and from these he drew conclusions [tui] about large ones, until he reached what was without limit. First he spoke about modern times, and from this went back to the time of Huang [Di]. . . . Moreover he followed the great events in the rise and fall of ages, and by means of their omens and (an examination into) their systems, extended [tui] his survey (still further) backwards to the time when the heavens and the earth had not yet been born, (in fact) to what was profound and abstruse and impossible to investigate.[19]

The significant difference between the Chinese concept of correlation and the scientific idea of causation is that correlation is essentially a method for the induction of cosmic correspondence, whereas scientific formulae are determinations of causal relationships.[20] This means that the Han cosmologists were more interested in the observation of correspondence between two different situations that are temporally simultaneous than the observation of causality between two temporally successive events in one particular situation. The metaphysical presupposition of a theory of correspondence is that of a continuous cosmic frame rather than a temporal contiguity of discrete objects.

The emphasis on correspondence as a mode of inquiry thus led to the formulation of patterns or rules that related discrete phenomena in an overarching metaphysical system. The *Huainanzi* 淮南子, a comprehensive theory of sociopolitical order compiled at the court of the Liu An 劉安, the Prince of Huainan 淮南, in the second century B.C.E., for instance, states:

> The feelings of men and rulers rise up to penetrate heaven. Thus executions and cruelties give rise to many whirlwinds. Oppressive laws and ordinances give rise to many insect plagues. If the innocent are put to death, then the countryside will redden with drought. If ordinances are not accepted, then there will be many disastrous floods.[21]

The English syntax "if . . . then" automatically implies a temporal causal series: if A happens then B follows. In Modern Standard Chinese it is also possible to express this sequence of causation with the syntax "*ruguo* A *jiu* B" (如果 A 就 B). In Classical Chinese, however, a common way of expressing this relation is in the form "A *ze* B," the character *ze* 則 meaning a rule or a law. In this way, the text is stating that the situation of improper moral behavior by the ruler will entail a corresponding transformation in the patterns of weather, resulting in drought, floods, or other forms of meteorological chaos.

In the language of insurance policies, the most common way to describe such events of climate chaos are "acts of God," a phrase denoting that no individual person is ultimately responsible for what has occurred. In a Biblical theological framework, however, "acts of God," such as the great flood in the story of Noah, are interpreted as acts of judgment by a divine creator over his creation. God flooded the earth because of the wickedness of the people. This is essentially a religious relationship in which human behavior receives divine judgment, and the consequences are visited upon the earth. The view expressed in the *Huainanzi* is not in this sense a religious view. The actions of the ruler are not weighed by a divine creator who then wreaks havoc on the earth. Rather, the ruler's acts are tied to weather patterns through a natural law of correspondence, and his political decisions entail a corresponding transformation in the weather. In this worldview, politics and meteorology are not absolutely discrete disciplines: they are united through a pattern or rule (*ze*), a rule that operates by means of the principle of correspondence (*ganying* 感應) and which can be diagnosed through the system of five phases (*wuxing*). This is important for understanding how we can envisage relationality and ethics from the point of view of "transaction," rather than from a standard understanding of subject, verb, object. Karen Barad notes that her concept of "intra-actions" produces a view of causality that rejects determinism on the one hand and absolute freedom on the other hand.[22] This is also true of systems approaches, like the one detailed here, in which transactions function within an ecosystem that gives context and contour to agential possibility.

The basic correspondences that emphasize aspects of the cosmos related to Daoist medicine and cultivation can be summarized as in the following table.[23]

In describing this kind of table, Louis Komjathy writes:

Here it is important to recognize that these are, from a traditional Chinese and Daoist perspective, actual correspondences and associations. Each element of the column directly relates to, and often may be substituted for, the others. For example, eye problems frequently appear or become exacerbated during spring; heart issues may manifest in problems with arteries; feelings of grief and depression may be more pronounced during autumn; kidney problems may manifest as a groaning voice; and so forth.[24]

This table begs the question of how, or by what principle, these various dimensions of existence can be correlated with each other. From the per-

yin/yang	phase	direction	color	season	organ	emotion	sense
minor yang	wood	east	green	spring	liver	anger	eyes
major yang	fire	south	red	summer	heart	joy	tongue
yin-yang	earth	center	yellow		spleen	worry	lips
minor yin	metal	west	white	fall	lungs	sadness	nose
major yin	water	north	black	winter	kidneys	fear	ears

spective of a metaphysics of substance, and a scientific theory of causation, it seems hard to explain how physiology, emotional nature, colors, and the seasons can be related in a systematic way. Such associations seem "magical" or "superstitious." Indeed, if the only notion of causation that one has is that of the impact of one material object upon another in a temporally contiguous sequence, then of course such correspondences are impossible to grasp. In order for such a table to make sense, a different metaphysics must be operating. It is, in fact, the metaphysics based on the flow of *qi*.

Liquid Bodies

Given that *qi* is to be understood principally as the flow of liquid vitality, a key aspect of this flow needs to be further articulated, and that is the way in which flow is denoted in terms of two phases, yang and yin. These two aspects can be understood as the projection (yang) and reception (yin) of the dynamic of flow. The flow of liquid vitality can thus be understood in terms of this basic, binary dynamic. An analogy can be made with the process of respiration in which air is taken into the chest and then expelled in a constant breathing in and breathing out. This is one reason for translating *qi* as "breath," but we should remember here that the term *qi* does not refer to the material substance that is breathed in and out, but rather denotes the entire process of inspiration and expiration of breath. Abstractly stated, yin and yang are modes of a somatic dynamic, or as Manfred Porkert puts it, "phase energetics," the continuous exchange or transaction of liquid vitality according to a binary structure of reception (yin) and projection (yang).[25] The yinyang process thus denotes the way in which liquid vitality, whether air, water, blood, sexual fluids, or the subtle vitality of *qi*, is constantly pulsing.

Yin and yang should not, therefore, be understood as substances or elements within the cosmos. They are not to be interpreted by analogy with electrons and protons or other similar phenomena in classical physics. As Alfred Forke put it, "Ultimately, yin and yang do not mean anything in themselves at all, being only employed to express a relation; one notion is the opposite of the other, the one is positive, the other negative."[26]

More importantly, Daoist thought regards the physical experience of breathing as the basic pattern of yinyang that is replicated through nature and abstractly the cosmos itself. That is to say, the cosmos itself, inasmuch as it is a process of the projection and reception of liquid vitality, functions as a continuous breath or heartbeat. A common explanation for the origin of the terms yin and yang are that yin refers to the shady side of a mountain and yang refers to the sunny side. As the sun traverses over the mountain during the day, the side that was shady in the morning will become sunny in the afternoon and vice versa. There is no substantial difference between one side and the other; rather, they go through complementary modes as the earth rotates on its axis. The transition from one state to another is thus natural and cyclical just as breathing in and out is the natural, cyclical process by means of which the body maintains its vitality.[27]

Yinyang is also associated with gender: yin is understood as female, dark, and passive; yang is understood as male, bright, and active. From the point of view of gender relations, this gendered understanding of yinyang is complex, as Robin Wang notes.[28] On the one hand, the association of attributes with genders suggests that men and women should undertake fixed roles that overall work toward the dominance of men in Chinese society. At the same time, the fluid nature of the yinyang dynamic suggests that male and female are not absolutely distinct identities but rather blend into each other in a continuous dynamic interchange. There is, from this point of view, no absolute masculinity or femininity in and of itself. Rather, masculinity and femininity blend in a single complex dynamic. Yinyang thinking thus expresses a number of ways of considering the relation between binaries, whether through contradiction, interdependence, complementarity, or other forms of relationship.[29]

Equally important, however, is the way that yinyang not only symbolize the basic pattern of relationships within the body and the cosmos but also the way in which the body and the cosmos interact with each other. This came about most clearly when Zou Yan integrated the system of five phases (wuxing) discussed previously with that of yinyang. As Wang notes, "Before the Han dynasty, the terms yinyang and wuxing were separate and developed out of different contexts. Yinyang originally focused more on the rhythm of time, whereas the wuxing was more attuned to the position and direction of the terrain."[30] With Zou Yan's synthesis, however, the integrated system of five phases and yinyang came to stand as a rich resource that could be used to explain how the various times, spaces, and dimensions of the cosmos were interrelated. A table summarizing this system is as follows:

	South Red Summer Heart Fire	
Yang		
East Green Spring Liver Wood	Center Yellow Late Summer Spleen Earth	West White Fall Lungs Metal
	North Black Winter Kidneys Water	**Yin**

Yinyang and the Five Phases. (Author)

A chief application of this way of thinking lay in the diagnosis of illness. The human body here is viewed as a network of systems of energy transformation, of which breathing, the circulation of blood, digestion, and sexual reproduction are the most obvious physical manifestations. In Chinese medicine, each major *qi* system is understood as the functioning of an "organ," of which there are two kinds: yin systems (*zang*) and yang systems (*fu*). According to the foundational medical text the Huangdi neijing *suwen* 黃帝內經素問 (Simple questions on the *Yellow Emperor's internal classic*; fifth to second centuries B.C.E.), the function of the *zang* systems is to store or collect (*zang*) the "essential *qi*" (*jingqi*). This is defined by Porkert as "structive [structuring] potential."[31] It is the function of the complementary *fu* systems to "transmit or transform things."[32] Thus, the body contains two basic physiological dynamics. The yin systems store the potential energy to maintain the dynamic structuring of the body, and the yang systems transmit this energy.

The nature of this circulation, thus, is to effect a constant cycle of transformations based on the pattern of yinyang. The medical text stresses the cosmic significance of these categories:

The Yellow Emperor spoke: [The two categories] yin and yang are the underlying principle of heaven and earth; they are the web that holds all ten thousand things secure; they are father and mother to all transformations and alterations; they are the source and beginning of all creating and killing; they are the palace of spirit brilliance.

In order to treat illnesses one must penetrate to their source.

Heaven arose out of the accumulation of yang [influences]; the earth arose out of the accumulation of yin [influences]. Yin is tranquility, yang is agitation; yang creates, yin stimulates development; yang kills, yin stores. Yang transforms influences, yin completes form.[33]

The view of the body established in the Huangdi neijing *suwen* is thus one in which health and well-being are structured principally in terms of the dynamic of yinyang. This dynamic is a liquid dynamic in which *qi* flows through the various systems of the body and is stored in and transmitted through the network of organs. As the text makes clear, the diagnosis of illness depends on understanding the pattern of yinyang, but here the diagnosis of illness turns into a cosmological discussion. In this case, human life is framed by the space that human beings occupy, namely, the middle space between heaven (yang) and earth (yin). Human life is thus a product of the dynamic interaction of these forces, which must be kept in vital tension. Too much yang (activity) or too much yin (receptivity) within a given system of the body will produce an inefficient, blocked, or hyperactive circulation of *qi*. Only through the constant mediation of these somatic (and at the same time cosmic) dynamics can the body arrive at a productive equilibrium or homeostasis. From such a systems view, therefore, the notion of an equilibrium can be understood as an ultimate good, indeed, one that has much to contribute to a theory of sustainability. As I later argue, however, the religious view that is built on top of this medical systems view of the body is one that holds transformation, not equilibrium, as an end in itself. For this reason, as chapter 8 argues, a Daoist theory of nature leads toward a dynamic, transformative view of flourishing, rather than stability, as the desired goal.

The relationship between the internal dynamics of the body and those of the cosmos are further revealed when the Yellow Emperor asks about seasonal illnesses. As the Huangdi neijing *taisu* 黃帝內經太素 (Most elementary aspects of the *Yellow Emperor's internal classic*) puts it:

The Yellow Emperor: I should now like to hear why it is that in certain years everyone is struck by a similar illness.

Shao Shi: This is the result of a manifestation [of the winds] of the eight seasonal turning points.[34]

In this case, illness is the product not simply of the internal deficiency or blockage of *qi* within the body, but the failure of the body to respond adequately to the "eight seasonal turning points." At a basic level, then, human health is produced in correlation with the yinyang dynamics of the cosmos, which can here be understood as the framework of the land-scape (space) and the cycle of the seasons (time). The inference here is inescapable: human health cannot be divorced from its environmen-tal (in this case cosmological) context. Health and well-being are not produced internally in the body but are responses to external stimuli or pressures. These pressures on the body do not cause the body necessar-ily to become deformed in a physical way, but they can impact the flow of liquid vitality within the body. Health is first and foremost constituted from this liquidity because human bodies are essentially liquid bodies. As the seasons change, as "winds" or influences flow from the external environment into the body, the internal dynamics of the body are subtly shifted. Although humans may not be able directly to see the effects of this on the material substance of the body, the effects can be felt inter-nally, and this internal effect may produce the symptoms of disease that are visible on the outside of the body, the skin, the eyes, the tongue, the hair, and so on.

The well-being of the physiological systems can be achieved only by harmonizing with the broader macrocosmic dynamics in which they are located. The environment or macrocosm informs or indwells the micro-cosm of the body in a process of "insistence," as described in the previous chapter. A medical text later than the *Huangdi neijing* texts, the *Compre-hensive Treatise on the Regulation of the Spirit in Accord with the Four Seasons* (*Siqi tiaoshen dalun* 四氣調神大論), argues that the most impor-tant course of action to maintain health is to act in concert with the macrocosmic pattern of the seasons. As a result, the enlightened "sage" works not to repair problems that have begun to emerge, but rather to prevent those problems from arising in the first place by paying atten-tion to the microcosmic alignment of the internal dynamics of the body with the macrocosmic rotation of the seasons. Consequently, in this text, the highest activity of the sage is not the treatment of illness but its prevention:

This is the reason the sages do not treat those who have already fallen ill, but rather those who are not yet ill. They do not put [their state] in order when revolt [is under way], but before an insurrection occurs. . . . When medicinal therapy is initiated only after someone has fallen ill, when there is an attempt to restore order only after unrest has broken out, it is as though someone has waited to dig a well until he is already weak with thirst, or as if someone begins to forge a spear when the battle is already underway. Is this not too late?[35]

This activity of the sage is thus summarized in the term *tiaoshen* 調身, or "regulation of the body," which implies the constant coordination of the internal dynamics of the body with the external dynamics of its environment.

The means of coordinating the internal dynamics of the body with that of its cosmic context can be described as a process of "liquid ecology," for it is fundamentally a way in which liquid vitality is exchanged between the world outside the body and the world inside the body. This "world" is understood by Daoists as a world of both time and space. The particular location or environment in which the Daoist practices has to be carefully understood and adjusted. So also the Daoist has to pay attention to the rotation of the seasons, the positions of the stars, and the cycles of the sun and moon. The approach to environmental ethics that ensues from this is not one in which the natural world is viewed objectively as a domain to be preserved free from human influence. Rather, it is a domain whose dynamic transformation demands continuous adaptation from human beings.

Liquid Ecology

The present section explains the foundation for the understanding of coordination in terms of the "liquid ecology" that relates the body to its landscape or environing context, a relationship of microcosm and macrocosm. One of the more distinctive elements of the Daoist tradition is the level of detail with which it portrayed the internal liquid dynamics of the human body by means of the landscape. A key example in this regard is the *Map of Rise and Fall of Yin and Yang in the Human Body*

Map of Rise and Fall
of Yin and Yang in
the Human Body,
*Tixiang yinyang
shengjiang tu*
體象陰陽升降圖.
(Ming Zhengtong,
DZ90, ca. 1226)

(*Tixiang yinyang shengjiang tu* 體象陰陽升降圖; ca. 1226) presented to Emperor Lizong by Xiao Yingsou.[36]

This map accompanies a work of inner alchemy, the Duren jing *neiyi* 度人經內意 (Inner meaning of the *Scripture of Universal Salvation*, DZ90), which states:

The body contains heaven and earth, the furnace and the stove. Its central place is the alchemical cauldron, while it is the great void. Its Qian [heaven trigram] Palace is the sea of marrow; its Kun [earth trigram] Palace is the chamber of essence; its Divine Chamber is the alchemical cauldron. These are called the Three Palaces. Qian and Kun are the warp and woof of heaven and earth with yin and yang circulating through their midst. Heaven and earth are the great forge, yin and yang are the pivots of transformation, and the unified qi is the great medicine. To refine the elixir, use your inner male and female, yang and yin qi and circulate them all around the inner stars until they form the alchemical vessel. The Metal Mother resides right there and through wondrous transformations stimulates the qi of life.

As yin and yang move in response with each other, we speak of refinement. As the yang essence expands daily and perfect spirit transforms, we speak of the holy womb. As yin gradually dissolves and yang comes to reside in utmost purity, we speak of the immortal embryo. This is the Great One embracing perfection, in harmony with emptiness and nonbeing, fully returning to the nonultimate state.[37]

The Daoist tradition of inner alchemy was a system of body cultivation practice in which the internal dynamics of *qi* within the body were transformed through a complex process of meditation and refinement. It drew on earlier "laboratory" or "outer" alchemical practices in which Daoists would refine minerals and other naturally occurring substances to produce an elixir of immortality that would then be ingested to provoke a transformation of the body into that of a "transcendent" or "immortal." The practice of inner alchemy can best be understood as the product of a long system of engaging in *qi* cultivation practices through which communities of Daoists developed very sophisticated experiences of the inner body.[38] They then developed charts or maps to help explain how the inner body was, according to their *qi* cultivation experiences, structured. The *Map of Rise and Fall of Yin and Yang in the Human Body* is the earliest depiction of the inner "landscape" of the body as a mountain.[39]

Anna Hennessey comments that the depiction of the body as a mountain "acts as a representational system that corresponds to the physiological workings of the human body."[40] While it is certainly true that the body here is imaged as a mountain, the title of the text makes it clear that what is of particular significance in this map is the depiction of the yinyang system "rising" and "falling" within the structure itself. That is to say, it is not particularly the mountain itself that is the focus of the map but rather the liquid process of yinyang, the water rising and falling within. From this point of view, the landscape of the mountain is to be understood not as an enormous mass of rock, but as a porous space through which liquid vitality is circulated. The Daoist practitioner, then, is not interested principally in the body as a mountain, that is, as a solid form with a distinctive external appearance and physical structure, but in the body as a mountain-space, as a waterscape, not as a landscape. It is the rise and fall of liquid vitality within the body that is the object of concern here.

This point becomes more significant when we consider the Chinese characters that are carefully arrayed throughout the map. These characters indicate the spaces within the body that are the focus of the Daoist practitioner's internal alchemical practice. Hennessey notes in particular that "the characters 命門 *mingmen* 'Gate of the Vital Force' rest above a stream that flows from an opening in the mountain. In Chinese medical literature, as well as within the context of *neidan*, the term *mingmen* refers also to key points of the human body including the naval [*sic*], the spleen, the space between the kidneys or as a denotation for the right kidney."[41] From this, we can observe that again it is not the structure or physical form that is of particular interest to the Daoist practitioner but rather the spaces through which the liquid vitality of the body flow. The designator "gate," for instance, may denote that this is a place where flow can be regulated, engaged, or directed in some way, as part of the alchemical practice of the Daoist.

Although the function of these maps had nothing to do with what we might call "ecology" in any modern sense, but with the training regimes of Daoist communities, maps such as these take on a new significance in the context of the present ecological crisis, a significance that could never have been intended or even anticipated by their original creators. The significance lies in the way that humans imagine the spaces in which they attribute meaning to their experiences. In the case of the maps of bodies as landscapes, one effect of these depictions of the body is to minimize the bifurcation of experience into what takes place inside the body and what takes place outside the body. The map suggests that the most appropriate way for locating and experience the internal dynamics of *qi* flow within the body is by means of the liquid landscape (or waterscape) of the mountain.

It is hard to underestimate the significance of how Daoists produced and represented space in this way. Perhaps the most important aspect of this is it immediately serves to undermine the construction of an independent internal human subjectivity and an independent external natural objectivity, which is necessary for implementing a social order based on sustainable principles and practices. It suggests that the perception of a fundamental difference between the objective world without and the subjective world within is a way of ordering and experiencing one's imaginative powers that can, and indeed ought to be, overcome. That such imaginative schemas for the inner functioning of the human body were produced as part of a training regimen for Daoist monks suggests also the plasticity and perfectibility of our modes of constructing experience and giving meaning to those experiences. The map of the body as a mountain waterscape indeed suggests that it is the play of water within the form of the mountain that in fact constitutes human vitality. It is the liquidity of human experience flowing through an apparently monolithic corporeal structure that deserves our attention, not the monolithic corporeal structure itself.

In the text that accompanies the picture, the focus is on cultivation as a process of "refinement." The text continues to describe the way in which the yang processes of the body expand and transform to create a "womb." From this an "embryo" is created that "embraces perfection" and returns to a "nonultimate state." It is hard for an outsider to grasp exactly what the alchemical practitioner concretely experienced in order to formulate precisely those words. They speak of rebirth, perfection, and attainment of something that seems to transcend ordinary experience and reach a state of "nonultimate" (*wuji* 無極). In Daoist philosophy, this nonultimate can be understood as the state before which creativity emerges through the bifurcation of yin and yang, a state of nonduality in which the experience of subjectivity and objectivity is dissolved into a single unitary plane. From this point of view, the process of refinement of internal alchemical experience can be understood as a return or "reversion" to a place before the bifurcation of experience, variously described as "perfection" or "transcendence."

The map of the body as a mountain waterscape thus stands not only as an educational tool, describing the spaces within the body where alchemical practice can be focused. It also describes an ideal state in which the body and the waterscape of the mountain become not only imaged but identified as the same kind of reality, a liquid reality enacted through the flow of yinyang vitality. In this sense, the inner form of the body has the same kind of flow dynamic as the waterscape outside the body. An ecological interpretation of Daoist inner alchemy would be the process of the experiential realization of this liquid dynamic.

This brief survey of key themes within Daoist understandings of the body and the landscape points toward an important feature of the Daoist experience, namely, its focus on vitality as a liquid process. The process within the body and the landscape can be understood as a yinyang dynamic involving the flow of liquid vitality from one state to another continuously and naturally. The Daoist experience is also characterized by its attempt to forge an experience of this inner vitality within the body itself, a process that is imaged by means of the mountain waterscape. A Daoist ecology must then be built on the interrelationship between the human body and its environmental context as a fundamentally liquid relationship. The task of the next chapter is to examine more carefully the nature of this flow from body to landscape and back by providing an eco-critical reading of certain Daoist practices. These practices depend on a view of the body as irreducibly porous, open to the world through orifices and membranes, interacting within a queer ecology of cosmic power.

4 The Porosity of the Body

Orifice and Oracle

On a beautiful fall day in 2010, I found myself in the company of a real estate developer in Taiyuan, Shanxi Province, whom I shall refer to as Mrs. Wang. She treated me and a group of her friends to a lunch in the restaurant attached to the high-rise building she owned. It was a simple banquet of cold and hot dishes, tea and fruit juice, with a delicious bowl of noodles at the end. After lunch, she invited us all to visit her hometown, a small village about an hour's drive outside the city. The eight of us fitted comfortably into two SUVs, and we soon arrived at the village. The real estate developer's secretary apologized to me as she ran off to a convenience store, explaining that she needed to buy some cigarettes. No one had smoked at lunchtime, and when she came out of the store with an entire carton of expensive Zhonghua-brand cigarettes, I was intrigued.

Further down the unpaved road, we came to a new building, rather unremarkable on the outside, but when we went inside, it turned out to be a small temple to the bodhisattva Guanyin. We did not remain long in the temple, though, and went to sit down in a side room. It turned out that Mrs. Wang had built the temple with her own funds because she was a spirit medium who since childhood had been possessed by a spirit who lived in her home village. Her parents were strict leftists who were horrified that their daughter had developed this "talent," and she did her best to conceal it. Later in life, when she had become a successful businesswoman, she was able to build a proper temple for the spirit, including the adjoining room where we were now sitting. Here, she could hold consultations. Suddenly, the spirit was present. It possessed her body and began to speak in a local dialect that was unintelligible to me. It also spoke in a deep voice and was a chain smoker. Between sentences, the spirit inhaled vast quantities of smoke, taking only two or three inhalations to devour an entire cigarette. Within half an hour, the pack was empty, and the assistant fumbled quickly to pull the cellophane wrapping off a new one.

Although this story has nothing directly to do with Daoism or ecology, it did put in my mind that the religious experience that I was witnessing could best be interpreted as a transaction. The spirit was inhaling the smoke by possessing Mrs. Wang's body, and presumably without her body it had no way to smoke cigarettes. In return, the spirit made pronouncements for the benefit of those who had come to consult him. People consulted the spirit as a doctor and, having described their ailments to him, the spirit would pronounce a prescription, which would be jotted down by Mrs. Wang's assistant. The prescription would then be taken to the local Chinese medicine pharmacist who would prepare the ingredients according to the spirit's recipe.

The entire routine can be understood as an "orificial" process in which Mrs. Wang's mouth functioned as a chief conduit for the religious encounter. Through her mouth, smoke entered her body and "fed" the spirit who had possessed her. And through her mouth, the spirit exhaled its esoteric knowledge in the form of the prescription. This orificial process should also be understood as the conduit for a communal transaction in which the bodies of the living were kept alive through communication with the spirits of the dead. Through the oracular prescriptions uttered through the mouth of Mrs. Wang, the dead brought life to the living.

During this encounter, I could not help wonder about the toll that this process was taking on Mrs. Wang's own health. Again, it seemed that the smoking, though no doubt beneficial for the community in terms of the prescriptions that it produced, would likely inflict harm on Mrs. Wang over the long term. The transaction produced benefits for the community by risking the physical health of Mrs. Wang, the medium of communication. The entire process brought life and death together through orifice and oracle: the mouth as conduit for the harmful cigarette smoke and health-bringing oracles.

This experience became instructive for my own reflections on Daoist texts, in which the liquid vitality of *qi* serves as the medium of communication between the spirit world and the interior world of the human body, bringing healing and transformation. Earlier, I explained how this form of communication can be understood as a "transaction." In this chapter, I would like to give more concrete examples of what these transactions look like in the context of Daoist religion. I further propose that a network of such transactions constitutes an "ecology of cosmic power," a system in which vital energy is distributed through nodes in the body, the natural landscape, and the cosmos.

An example of such a transaction can be seen in the following excerpt from the *Method of the Nine Perfected* (*Jiuzhen fa* 九真法; fourth century C.E.), a meditation text associated with the medieval Daoist movement known as the Way of Highest Clarity (Shangqing dao).

In the first month, on your fate day, the jiazi day and the jiaxu day at dawn the Five Spirits, the Imperial Lord and Supreme Unity merge together into one great spirit which rests in your heart. His title is the Lord of Celestial Essence, his courtesy title Highest Hero of Soaring Birth, and his appearance is like an infant immediately after birth. On this day at dawn, enter your oratory, clasp your hands together on your knees, keep your breath enclosed and shut your eyes. Look inside and visualize the Lord of Celestial Essence sitting in your heart. He is called a great spirit. Make him spew forth purple *qi* to coil thickly around your heart in nine layers of *qi*. It rushes up into the Mud Pill. Inner and outer [dimensions] are as one. When this is done, clack your teeth nine times, swallow saliva nine times, then recite this prayer:

Great Lord of Celestial Essence,
Highest Hero of Soaring Birth,
Imperial Lord, transform inside me,
Come and visit my heart.

Your body is wrapped in vermilion garb,
Your head is covered with a crimson cap.
On your left you wear the [talisman of the] dragon script;
On your right you carry the [talisman of the] tiger writing.

Harmonize my essence with the threefold path;
Unite my spirit with the [realm of] Upper Prime.
To the Five Numinous [directions] I offer a talisman,
With the Imperial [Lord] may I be wholly identical.

May your mouth spit out purple blossom
To nourish my heart and concentrate my spirit;
As my crimson organ spontaneously becomes alive,
May I become a soaring immortal.[1]

An outstanding feature of this method of meditation is the function of the mouth as the means though which the liquid vitality of *qi* is transmitted from the god to the adept. In the first place, the adept is instructed to visualize the god sitting in the heart, spewing forth purple *qi*. The Chinese text literally says "shi dashen kou chu zi qi" 使大神口出紫氣, "make the great spirit's mouth emit purple *qi*." As the spirit sits inside the adept's heart, it emits a purple-colored breath that emanates from the spirit's mouth and coils around the heart nine times, enveloping it in a protective layer. The function of this orificial emission is to nourish the adept's heart, regenerating it and transforming the adept.

At the end of this visualization process, the adept is instructed to recite the prayer, but before doing so he or she should clack the teeth together nine times and swallow saliva nine times. Swallowing saliva is in fact a standard Daoist practice that may help to activate the *qi* flowing through the body. Saliva is considered a basic form of liquid vitality, one that is self-produced in the mouth and to be ingested by swallowing. Here, the production of saliva marks the transition between the visual meditation and the recitation of the prayer, in which the adept expresses the fervent desire that the god's "mouth spit out purple blossom" ("kou tu zi hua" 口吐紫華). The "spitting" of the purple blossom is the method through which the god transfers vital power to the internal organs of the adept.

The *Method of the Nine Perfected* contains nine such visual meditations together with their accompanying prayers. In each case, a god spits a certain color of *qi* and regenerates a different organ of the body, with the ultimate goal that the body of the adept will gain power over the spirit world and pass through death without suffering the decay of the body.[2]

The significance of this visualization is that it clearly establishes the mouth as orifice through which transactions of cosmic power are mediated. In this case, the mouth of the god produces health-bringing purple *qi* (unlike the chain-smoking spirit featured in the anecdote), and the mouth of the adept produces saliva in preparation for the recitation of prayer. It is hard to say whether this prayer was to be spoken out loud or recited silently to oneself. But assuming that it may have been recited aloud by some devotees, it again constitutes another instance of orality in this tradition: the lips and mouth form the sounds that communicate the adept's deepest desires to the god. The mouth is the space in which the saliva is produced and swallowed. From the lips of the god the liquid purple vitality is passed directly to that of the adept in a kind of "mouth-to-organ" resuscitation.

There is clearly an element of deep intimacy in this transfer of *qi*. The god, dwelling in the heart of the adept, emits his vital fluids and brings renewed vitality not in the form of a pregnancy but in the form of a regenerated life for the adept. It is as though the adept becomes pregnant with herself, engendering a renovated body that has the capacity to survive the trauma of death and become a "soaring immortal."

There is, throughout the Daoist tradition, a minor but persistent engagement with themes relating to sexuality, and in particular the "arts of the bedchamber" (*fangzhongshu* 房中術). In general, though, the attitude of Daoists toward these traditions has been to deprecate them in favor of a more spiritualized understanding of the transactions of liquid vitality. That is to say, the sexual arts are clearly related to Daoist practice but considered a very inferior form of energetic transaction. An example of this attitude of deprecation can be seen in the criticism made by the Daoist scholar Ge Hong (283–343) in his text *The Master Who Embraces Simplicity* (*Baopuzi* 抱朴子). In this book, Ge Hong evaluates the methods that people have used to achieve the goal of immortality. Fabrizio Pregadio presents Ge Hong's arguments regarding sexual energetics practice in the context of a general discussion of the arts of nourishing life (*yangsheng* 養生): "Among the arts of Yin and Yang (i.e., the sexual practices), the best ones can heal the lesser illnesses, and the next ones can prevent one from becoming depleted. Since their principles have inherent bounds . . . how could they confer divine immortality, ward off calamities, and lead one to happiness?"[3] In this case, Ge Hong is clear that sexual practices are insufficient to achieve the religious goal of immortality. They may have some minor efficacy in healing certain illnesses but are not at all what the proper student of immortality should be concerned with. He then corrects what he sees as a common misinterpretation of the legend of the Yellow Emperor, who ascended to heaven accompanied by twelve hundred women. He writes:

> The common people hear that the Yellow Emperor rose to heaven with 1,200 women, and say that he obtained longevity only thanks to this. They do not know that the Yellow Emperor compounded the Nine Elixirs on Lake Ding at the foot of Mount Jing, and then rose to heaven by riding a dragon. He might have had 1,200 women, but it was not for this reason that he was able to do it [i.e., become a transcendent].[4]

As Pregadio goes on to note, in Ge Hong's view the only practices that enable communication with the gods and the ascension to immortality are those of alchemy and meditation.[5] The point, however, is that Ge Hong felt obliged to distinguish what he considered properly effective practices aimed at producing immortality from those lesser practices that may be causing confusion in the mind of the people. Since Ge Hong has to take pains to refute the notion that the transfer of sexual energies can produce transcendence and immortality, this notion was already in the mind of the people.

Ge Hong's separation of the more spiritual goal of transcendence from the more material goal of healing continued the process of differentiating Daoism from popular traditions and cultural practices. As the tradition developed, the laboratory alchemy tradition developed by Ge Hong was itself spiritualized and interiorized into a tradition of inner alchemy. The Highest Clarity tradition that emerged after Ge Hong's death marks a transition point in which Daoist elites began to focus on the interior visualization of gods and the significance of somatic meditation techniques for the effective realization of spiritual goals. As Isabelle Robinet writes:

> Shangqing [Highest Clarity] formed an important link in the evolution from operative or laboratory alchemy to inner alchemy. It caused transformation of physical sexual practices into platonic love relationships with the gods, diminished the bureaucratic, formal, and theurgical spirit of the Celestial Masters in its ritual, and

transmuted the ideal of quasi-physical immortality into one of spiritual salvation.[6]

The tradition began with a series of pronouncements by various "perfected ones" (zhenren 真人), spirit beings living in the Heaven of Highest
Clarity, through the medium Yang Xi 楊羲 (330–386). Significantly, these
pronouncements were originally produced as written sacred scriptures,
not as oral communications that were subsequently transcribed.

In the Shangqing revelations, the orality of the communications process,
evident in its most "vulgar" or "common" form in the widespread Chinese
tradition of spirit mediums (such as Mrs. Wang), takes place completely
in the interiority of Yang Xi's body and then is expressed in stylized form
through the medium of the ink brush. Although these revelations are
noted for the importance they pay to the written texts, the documents that
seal the bond between heaven and earth, it is important to remember
that the process of transmission through which they originally occurred
should be understood nevertheless as an oracular process taking place
in the interiority of the body of the spirit medium Yang Xi. This oral tradition is expressed in Highest Clarity scriptures such as the Method of the
Nine Perfected through the continuing emphasis on the intimate transmission of liquid vitality between the gods and the adept. This transmission
does not occur in a verbal way, but it is nonetheless an oral, orificial,
oracular process, but one that takes place internally, that is to say, through
the internal orifices of the body by means of which the liquid vitality of
the gods circulates within the adept.

A second clue as to the relationship of Highest Clarity texts to the liquid
vitality of the cosmos lies in the Highest Clarity theory about the origin
of these texts. The revelation of the Shangqing scriptures continued, and
extended, the notion that texts of Chinese characters somehow disclose—
and facilitate—the real interaction between humans and their cosmic
environment. The texts of the revelation were said to have preexisted in
heaven, and, indeed, "predate" time itself. The Chinese term for scriptures (jing 經) is also used for the warp of a piece of fabric, and thus the
scriptures can be understood as a thread running through the fabric of
the cosmos. Similarly, the talismans contained within the scriptures
(fu 符) were understood as distillations or coagulations of primal liquid
vitality (qi). Put together, the Highest Clarity texts were regarded as the
media for the transformation of the physical body into a cosmically transfigured one. The characters of the texts, then, were understood not only

as transcripts of heavenly communications, but even as the symbols that permit such communications. Without the texts, the gods would not be able to speak.

The texts of the Shangqing revelation were therefore understood to be clues or icons that interpreted the infinity of cosmic potential to the privileged possessor or reciter of the scripture. In this way, the scriptures constitute a hermeneutic of power in which the texts, the earthly traces of cosmic signification, mediate the universal Dao—not a thing but a creative act of signification—and concrete human actuality. This mediation is in fact a reciprocal fiduciary relationship that is summed up as follows: "It is by leaning upon the Tao that the ching [*jing*] have been constituted; it is by leaning upon the ching that the Tao manifests itself. Tao is substance and the ching are function."[7]

Robinet has pointed out that the Highest Clarity texts revealed by the immortal Lady Wei to the medium Yang Xi "are only the material aspect of texts that were formed from the primordial breath that existed before the origin of the world."[8] The term "material aspect" suggests that the texts are the manifestation of some transcendent substance, which does not precisely capture the meaning of the Chinese terms *ti* 體 (body) and *yong* 用 (functioning). The Chinese philosophical terms in the earlier quotation indicate that the flourishing or activation of the primordial breath cannot in principle be distinguished from that which it infuses. This is, in the end, a process in which the liquid vitality of ultimate cosmic breath is distilled in the liquid ink with which the Chinese characters and talismanic writings were produced. There is a reciprocity to the terms *ti* and *yong* that implies an interactive relationship between the sacred text (the ink on the page) and the cosmic breath from which it originated. This reciprocity is evident in the dual aspects of the text as a seal (*yin* 印) between humans and deities, that is, particular constellations of cosmic power. As humans recite the texts, which are the coagulated traces of the originals in the heavens, deities were said to echo in response. Likewise, sacred treasures (*bao* 寶) are said to be hierogamic unions of divine-earthly shamanic couples; sacred talismans (*fu*) are written in a double or mirror script or in two colors.[9]

In the Highest Clarity system, therefore, human beings are given an extraordinarily privileged role in the evolution of the cosmos. Their sacred texts are active symbols that mediate this creative power. As such, they do not entail a hermeneutic of intellectual comprehension so much as a hermeneutic of the embodied power manifested through the liquids of ink and *qi*. The chief requirement for Highest Clarity adepts, therefore, is to be initiated into the texts and to learn how to use them. Thus, the "body" (*ti*) of the text lies in its use (*yong*): what it truly is, is how it is truly used. Ultimately, then, the "hermeneutical" relationship an adept has with a text is not one of intellect or meaning, but of power and effect entailed through the liquid transmission of cosmic breath to the ink on the page, and the liquid vitality of the gods circulating in the bodies of the adepts. The revelation of the Shangqing texts, therefore, presents the possibility of human-cosmic transformation.

This transformation of human beings within the context of the cosmic frame that defines the horizons of meaning for them can be understood as the cultivation of Dao (*xiudao*). Cultivation is fundamentally an ecological process in that it depends upon the relationship between human beings and their contexts in order to take place. It eschews the radical bifurcation of subjects and objects in favor of a process that takes place within a context. This context is not, as in traditional Confucian readings of Chinese religion, a patriarchal lineage of power and productivity, but rather an environmental context: the space that constitutes the existential location of the practitioner. The implication of this for the contemporary context is that through cultivation it is possible to push beyond the meanings offered by the ideology of modernity in which humans have come to understand themselves as atomized subjects whose meaning is chiefly constituted by their capacity to consume.

Conjunction and Correlation

The Chinese traditions of genealogical lineage and authority imply that the liquid vitality of the cosmos is transmitted genetically, or spermatically, through the patriarchal reproduction of power in Chinese society. Such was the notion of the Shang and Zhou kings who imagined their power to rule (*de* 德) as being transmitted from their ancestors to them and then on to their offspring through the liquids of sexual reproduction.[10]

The Highest Clarity tradition, however, clearly distinguishes itself from such a genealogical concept of the transmission of power, or virtue. While it also emphasizes the liquid nature of power, cosmic breath, and vitality, it construes the transmission of this cosmic power ecologically rather than genealogically. What this means is that the transmission of liquid vitality occurs through the cosmic disposition of the adept, and not because of his or her ancestral lineage. Unlike the popular Chinese (and Confucian) traditions that emphasize the continuous streaming of vitality from ancestors to descendants through the male line, the Highest Clarity revelations point to a higher disposition of liquid vitality through the correlation of the body of the adept with the natural cycles of the heavens, the positions of the stars, and the rotation of the seasons. That is to say, it is the spatial or environmental disposition of the adept that secures his or her religious transformation and not the power of deceased ancestors. The liquid vitality of the cosmos is transacted in moments of correlation, conjugation, and conjunction between the adept and nature.

This process of conjunction can be understood more clearly in the way that the Way of Highest Clarity specified the importance of times and dates in the performance of visual meditations such as the one detailed previously, from the *Method of the Nine Perfected*. This method, contained within the scripture known as the *Central Scripture of the Nine Perfected*, a key text of the Way of Highest Clarity, is accompanied by a second, similar method, the "Eight Secret Sayings of the Dao" ("Badao miyan" 八道祕言). These texts are translated and studied in my previous book, *The Way of Highest Clarity*.[11] The interpretation that follows builds on the one that I presented there but emphasizes an ecocritical dimension to these Daoist practices.

Both cultivation methods can be understood from within the broad framework of "visualization practices." The Chinese term for this, one especially prevalent in the Highest Clarity scriptures, is *cun* 存, whose more common meaning is "to exist." In modern Chinese, it is commonly paired with the character *zai* 在 (to be in a place) to mean "to exist" or "to be present." In the Highest Clarity texts, *cun* means "to visualize" in the sense of "to cause something to be present." In particular, it means to cause the gods to be present within the body through an act of internal vision (*neishi* 內視) or internal observation (*neiguan* 內觀). The important thing to note, however, is that Daoist adepts cannot simply will visions of the gods into existence by dint of their own mental efforts. Rather, the process of visualization must pay close attention to the cosmological context, in particular the times of the year and the directions in which the meditation takes place.

In the case of the *Method of the Nine Perfected*, each of the nine stages of the visualization process must take place on a particular date specified according to the sixty-day cycle of the Chinese calendar. On those specific dates, certain gods are to be visualized in certain organs of the body. The key information that the text contains, therefore, is which gods are to be visualized in which organs of the body on which dates. The text, therefore, functions like a combination lock in which the various cycles of the body, the gods, and the calendar are brought into alignment. When this conjunction of cycles occurs, the transformative energy of the god is released and the body of the adept is mystically transformed. In the case of the text previously cited, the purple *qi* coils around the adept's heart and a process of unitive fusion occurs, described in the text as "inner and outer are as one" ("nei wai ru yi" 內外如一).

In previous readings of this text, I emphasized what I termed the "reciprocal" nature of this fusion. That is to say, it seemed to me that the process of biospiritual transformation that the text aimed to produce was neither the product of the Daoist adepts themselves, nor the product of the gods: it was, rather, a reciprocal process in which the individual and the gods came together to produce a religious transformation. It seems to me now, however, that a more accurate way to describe the framework in which the transformation occurs is that of a cosmic ecology. It is a cosmic framework in that it involves a range of dimensions that together function to provide the context of meaning for the life of the adept. These dimensions include the internal physiology of the individual, the calendrical cycle as dictated by the rotation of the sun and planets, the gods themselves, who were thought to descend from the Heaven of Highest Clarity, and also the text of the prayer and the talismans offered to the gods (the distillations of primal *qi* "coagulated" in the precious ink transmitted from master to disciple). This framework should also be understood, however, as an ecological framework, because all these various dimensions function as interlocking cycles of liquid vitality (*qi*). The organs of the body are not simply the physical material of the heart or lungs, but rather the energy cycles that they regulate, the circulation of liquid vitality within the body. The dates of the calendar, moreover, are abstractions derived from the cycling of the sun around the earth, the stars in the heavens, the planets, and the moon. These heavenly objects can also be understood as systems of energy transformation in which liquid vitality transforms through a predictable yinyang cycle, waxing and waning on daily (sun), monthly (moon), and sixty-year phases (as determined by the cycle of the planet Jupiter). At the same time, the appearance of the gods themselves, the color of *qi* that they spit out, and the texts, talismans, and prayers recited to them also follow a cycle as set out in the *Method of the*

Nine Perfected. As a result, the process of biospiritual transformation is not simply to be understood as the "fusion" of human and heavenly worlds. Rather, the process involves the interlocking of complex cycles of energy transformation that operate on yinyang principles of waxing and waning with various frequencies or periodicities. In this sense, the framework for religious transformation is a complex network or ecology of relations that obtains within multiple overlapping dimensions of a cosmic frame: the internal physiological frame; the heavenly frame of natural transformations as determined by the sun, moon, planets, and stars; and the wholly religious dimension of culturally postulated super human realities, the visual imagination of the gods themselves.

The *Eight Secret Sayings of the Dao* reveals a similar pattern, though the method of religious transformation is quite different. Like the *Method of the Nine Perfected*, it involves a sequence of prayers that takes place over a year, in this case following eight of the twenty-four "solar terms," the main nodes of the solar calendar beginning with the day *lichun* 立春 (start of spring), usually February 4 in the Gregorian calendar (the text also specifies other times when these rituals may be performed). On these days, the adept is to face a certain direction, look for clouds of certain colors, and then he or she will see a Daoist deity riding on a carriage through the skies to visit the Jade Emperor, the highest deity in the pantheon. At this point, the adept is to engage in a visualization in which he makes a petition to the Jade Emperor, with the hope that the adept will have the chance to be transformed into one of the perfected immortals.[12]

This formula differs from the *Method of the Nine Perfected* in that it does not directly involve the visualization of liquid vitality being transmitted from the mouth of the god to the body systems of the adept. Rather, it involves visualizing in one's heart-mind (*xincun* 心存) a courtly audience in which the adept kowtows to the Jade Emperor and makes his formal request to become one of the perfected. This text thus follows a formal, bureaucratic religious process in which spiritual power is transacted through ritual obeisances and by conveying oral requests to the highest god of the pantheon.[13]

Nonetheless, the outstanding feature of this sequence of prayers is the formal system of conjunctions and correlations that it follows. Like in the *Method of the Nine Perfected*, the external observation of the clouds and the internal visualization of the gods are to take place in accordance with the solar calendar and are to follow a strict cosmological pattern. On different solar terms, the adept should face different directions, observe different colored clouds and different intermediary gods, and offer prayers to a different high god. Like the *Method of the Nine Perfected*, the text's key information is the details of the various combinations of cycles that must be precisely observed so as to unlock the power of religious transformation. Both texts depend on the system of correlations and correspondences, themselves underwritten by the fundamental binary transformation of energy cycles according to an overall process of yinyang.

In both these cases, therefore, the religious process is built upon and determined by the yinyang pattern. Even the gods themselves function in accordance with the natural cycles of the sun, stars, and planets. Indeed, the very definition of their divinity may be said to lie in their perfect coordination with these cycles. The uneducated human does not naturally understand how these cycles function together so as to unlock transformative power. Such people live in ignorance of these powerful rhythms and as a result do not have the chance to experience radical biospiritual transformation within the interiority of the physical frame. The privileged Daoist adept, on the contrary, is given the key that unlocks the mystery of these combinations. The Daoist adept knows how all the various natural cycles function together to produce transformative power that can be absorbed in the somatic liquidity of the bodyscape.

Pervasion and Penetration

Komjathy notes what he terms a famous Daoist saying, "Out of step with the times, but not with the seasons," which he interprets as meaning that the values and experiences of the Daoist adherent may not be those of the "dominant society."[14] Put in more positive light, the Daoist, as noted in the previous section, should act in concert with the seasons, the shifting patterns of time and circumstance in his or her context or environment; moreover, this should be his or her overriding concern, not what is dictated by external social forces. Komjathy mentions this saying in the context of a discussion of Complete Perfection (Quanzhen 全真) Daoist mediation practice and, specifically, the way in which the Daoist community noted several "boons along the way," or signs of the acquisition of spiritual powers. Such powers are termed "numinous abilities" or "numinous pervasions" (*lingtong* 靈通). He writes:

The "Lun liutong jue" (Instructions on the Six Pervasions), a Yuan dynasty internal alchemy text, provides a clear description:

(1) Pervasion of Heart-mind Conditions, involving the ability to experience unified nature as distinct from the ordinary body;

(2) Pervasion of Spirit Conditions, involving the ability to know things beyond ordinary perception;

(3) Pervasion of Celestial Vision, involving the ability to perceive internal landscapes within the body;

(4) Pervasion of Celestial Hearing, involving the ability to hear the subtle communications of spirits and humans;

(5) Pervasion of Past Occurrences, involving the ability to understand the karmic causes and effects relating to the Three Worlds of desire, form, and formlessness;

(6) Pervasion of the Heart-minds of Others, involving the ability to manifest the body-beyond-the-body. (Neidan jiyao, DZ1258, 3.12a–14a)[15]

These "supernatural" abilities are described as "pervasions," an unusual term that requires some explanation. The Chinese term is *tong* 通, and it goes back as far as the early Daoist work of mystical philosophy, the *Zhuangzi* 莊子, where the scholar Yan Hui describes his wishes to make himself "identical with the Great Thoroughfare" or "Great Pervasion" ("tong yu da tong" 同於大通). This is usually taken to denote a state of mystical realization in which the individual's subjectivity is merged with the ultimate reality of the Dao.

In the text cited by Komjathy, this mystical realization, however, is specified as six specific instances of pervasion, typically involving the ability to see or perceive things that lie beyond the common sensory powers of the ordinary person. These superhuman abilities go back also to the earlier descriptions of the abilities of "immortals" or "transcendents." Here, it is important to note that such people did not merely prolong life within their existing bodies, but rather gained new abilities as part of the transformation toward immortality or transcendence. Benjamin Penny lists several sets of abilities, including the ability to travel and exist in the world in a seemingly superhuman way: "They can walk great distances in a day, run at great speeds, possess great strength and are impervious to extreme temperatures. . . . Like the perfected in the *Zhuangzi*, they can 'enter water without getting wet and fire without getting burnt'—an almost proverbial statement in the texts."[16] What unites the abilities described in this paragraph with those pervasions cited by Komjathy is the seeming transparency or porosity between the individual and his or her environment. For instance, the ability to enter water without getting wet, or fire without getting burned, suggests that the body of the individual functions like that of a chameleon, adapting itself perfectly to its environment and not suffering the normal range of environmental harms that water or fire would inflict on an ordinary body. At the same time, Komjathy's list also suggests that the "gap" between the individual and the environment is diminished to an absolute minimum, allowing that person to know more, hear more, and see more. In this way, the transformed body is supremely sensitive, able to absorb more perceptions of the world than an ordinary person can.

The tradition came to describe such abilities not in the language of "magic" or "the supernatural" but with the term *tong*, which is conventionally translated as "pervasion." The basic meaning of this term is "to go through" from one place to another. It denotes "connection" or "interpenetration" in the way that a tunnel "pervades" a hill by connecting one side with the other. In modern Chinese, it appears in the binome *jiao-tong*, meaning "traffic" or "communication."

An ecocritical reading of this term suggests that the experience of "pervasion" or "signs of pervasion" should not be treated as the acquisition of supernatural powers, in the sense that these powers enable the adept to wield some magical ability over the natural world. That is to say, these pervasions do not mean that the adept has somehow acquired transcendental or superhuman powers. Rather, these signs should be treated as the special ways that a transformed Daoist body is able to perceive and integrate with its natural environment. The reason for this transformation is that the fully realized, subtle body of the experienced Daoist practitioner is an absolutely porous body, one that is fully open to its environmental context, enabling the "heart-mind" of the practitioner to fully engage with and respond to its context.

The notion of pervasion as an ideal is one that is relatively widespread in Chinese culture. For instance, in *Analects* 2.4, Confucius described his own process of self-cultivation in terms that suggest the increasing integration of the self and its context: "The master said: 'At fifteen I set my heart on learning; at thirty I took my place; at forty I became free of doubts; at fifty I knew the will of heaven; at sixty my ear was attuned; at seventy I could follow my heart's desires without overstepping the mark.'"

Although he did not describe this in terms of pervasion, the key idea here concerns the relationship between the individual, his own will and desires, and those of "heaven," a term that can equally be used to refer to "nature" and denotes the basic existential context in which the individual lives.[17] When Confucius was young, he was keen to "learn" and to "take his place." When he was older, he came to know the "will of heaven," which is to say, the ultimate disposition of things in the cosmos. He learned to become "attuned" to this disposition and eventually was able to fully align his own will or personality with that of his ultimate context (the will of heaven) "without overstepping the mark." This is a classic description of pervasion as a sagely ideal; it denotes the full adaptation of the individual within the "ecosystem" or network of meanings and ultimate ordering of things.

For Confucius, this is ultimately a psychological process involving the "heart-mind," the organ of affect and rationality that, according to Confucian moral philosophy, can be trained through a systematic process of "teaching" (*jiao* 教) and "learning" (*xue* 學); note here that education as learning is far more important than education as teaching). While Zhuangzi and other Daoists may have had some similar ideas about the goal of the cultivation process, they strongly disagreed with the Confucians that the means to achieve this should be through a focus on "learning" (*xue*) or that the most important organ of the body should be the heart-mind (*xin*). Rather, for the Daoist tradition as a whole, the process of cultivation toward the attainment of "pervasion" is one that is thoroughly somatic, taking place in and through the body, conceived not simply as a heart-mind directing inert "matter" but rather as a network of yinyang processes of liquid vitality. In this regard, as noted in the previous chapter, the bodyscape is no different, ultimately, from the landscape that it inhabits. From the perspective of a Daoist ecology, therefore, it is not the particular cognitive capacities of the heart-mind that enable the self to be fully attuned to the cosmos it inhabits, but rather the underlying symmetry of the body with its environment.

This underlying symmetry, however, is obscured by the density of the skin, which prevents humans from observing the ways their bodies function as liquid landscapes. Only through a learned process of "interior vision" or "visualization" does it become possible to fully realize the underlying similarity of the bodyscape with the landscape. Here, it is useful to relate an episode in the biography of a Daoist perfected, born Zhou Yishan 周義山 in 80 B.C.E. His "esoteric" or "inner" biography presents the story of how he progressed from being a misunderstood young man, whose natural affinity with the Dao mystified his father, to a Daoist transcendent of the highest rank, given the title "Perfected Purple Yang."[18] Two features of his early biography stand out. The first is that as a young man he practiced the daily worship of the sun, in which he would get up at dawn, face east, and absorb the sunlight:

> As a rule, right after first light and before the sun had come up, he stood facing due east. He rinsed his mouth, swallowed saliva, absorbed [the solar] qi one hundred times and made a double bow to the sun. He did this dawn after dawn for a number of years. His father thought this was odd and asked him what kind of activity it was. Lord Zhou made a full-length genuflection then replied: "I, Yishan, deep in my heart love the splendor of the sunlight and its eternal radiance. This is the only reason why I bow before it."[19]

The text does not give any further explanation for this practice, but it brings to mind the phrase noted by Komjathy (discussed earlier) in which the Daoist is one who is attuned to the rhythm of the seasons rather than the fashion of the times. In this case, Zhou's life is oriented around the sunrise, and he persists in his morning practice even though his father, who represents patriarchal power and social normativity, cannot grasp why he is doing it. Of note here is that Zhou's practice involves the ritual worship of the sun, absorbing its *qi* and at the same time absorbing the saliva produced in his mouth. He is thereby achieving a correspondence between the *qi* systems of his body (as manifested in saliva) and the *qi* systems of the wider world (as manifested in sunlight). He simultaneously absorbs the external *qi* of the sun and the internal *qi* of the saliva.

The second feature of his early biography that stands out is the elixir of immortality that Zhou received from Su Lin. The text records that the elixir, compounded from various roots and herbs, is to be taken at dawn when facing east. This recalls the practice that Zhou had undertaken as a young man, but it is here presented in an intensified, alchemical form. Zhou is instructed to gradually increase the dosage until he is taking about a dozen pills a day, and that "this will cause your body to become light and possess a radiant glow."[20] Zhou carries out this practice for five years. The result was that "his body produced a transparent glow so that it was possible to see right through to his five [*zang*] organs."[21]

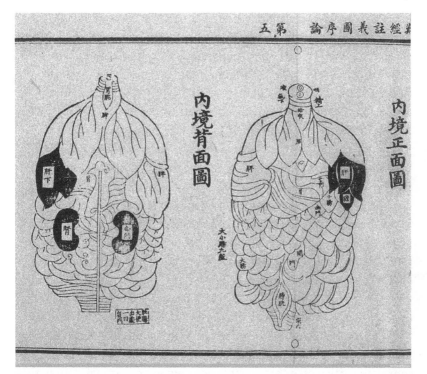

Woodblock illustration from the Zhengtong daozang (Daoist canon compiled during the Zhengtong reign period [1436–1449] of the Ming dynasty), depicting the "internal topography" (neijing) of the human body from the front and back view. (Wellcome Library, London, Creative Commons Attribution only licence C BY 4.0)

Whether understood literally or metaphorically, the significance of this practice is clear: the goal of this set of Daoist practices is to achieve a pervasion of the body by the energy of the sun, and the result of this pervasion is the increased transparency, radiance, and porosity of the skin itself. What Zhou achieves by absorbing the sunlight through ritual practice and alchemy is the transparency of his own skin. The ecological significance of this transformation deserves careful consideration. While I am in no way claiming that what Zhou was engaged in was something that he understood from the perspective of "ecological" thought, I am claiming that this practice of absorbing the vitality of the sun and the concomitant increasing transparency of the skin reveals an important point for ecocritical thinking. The point is that when the skin is understood first and foremost as a barrier between the outer landscape and the inner bodyscape, the result is a practical reluctance to grasp how the liquid vitalities of the landscape pervade and circulate within the inner bodyscape of the individual. Consequently, it is difficult to understand how environmental devastation has a direct effect on the health of the body. If the health of the body is something that apparently functions wholly autonomously and independently from its external environment, then it is easy to poison the world outside without realizing that this is also poisoning the world within the body.

The effect of Zhou's practice, then, is to arrive at the realization that his skin is more of a porous membrane than a physical barrier. In so doing, he is able to see for himself the "internal organs" of his body. But here we must remember that the *zang* organs do not refer simply to the physical flesh of the heart, liver, and the like but rather to the organs as nodes within the networks of vitality that flow within the body. The full revelation of this practice, then, is to see how the liquid vitality of the bodyscape functions in correlation with the liquid vitality of the landscape. In this way, the skin itself becomes an even more sensitive organ of sensation, a mode of perception and integration between the inner world of the body and the outer world of light and air. Understanding the skin as a mode of ecological relationship is not something that is commonly articulated in discourse on religion and ecology. Often, this discussion takes place in the context of moral theories, cosmological ideas, or discussions of science and religion. But the notion that this set of Daoist practices points toward is far more immediate and in a sense practical: to understand how human health and social relationships are embedded in the health of the environment and networks of ecological relationships, one should focus on the skin as the porous membrane through which the world pervades the body and the body pervades the world.

Queer Ecology

The headings of the previous sections have aimed to emphasize, perhaps provocatively so, the seemingly sexual nature of the transmission of fluids within the overall ecology of liquid vitality that permeates the worldview of Highest Clarity Daoism. The reason for this is not to suggest that these meditations took place within a heteronormative framework of the sexual body. In fact, as I argued earlier, the ecocritical reading of these texts emphasizes quite the contrary: that whereas other Chinese models of power and authority derive from or relate to the genealogical transmission of "virtue" through the male line, the ecocritical reading that I offer here emphasizes that such "virtue" is to be transacted cosmologically, through correlation with the seasons, directions, colors, and so on. In employing the sexualized language of conjunction, orifice, and penetration, my goal has been to suggest a sexual undertone that suffuses the Highest Clarity techniques of transformation, in fact a queer sexuality that is not oriented toward heteronormative sexual reproduction. It is also an ecological sexuality in that the body is oriented toward the cosmos itself.

Before turning to a queer ecocritical reading of Daoist praxis, it may be useful to define and examine standard ways in which religious studies has approached Daoist sexology. This topic has attracted considerable commentary and debate, partly as a result of a natural fascination with matters of sexuality in their relationship to religion, but also as a matter of internal debate within the Daoist tradition and argument between Buddhists and Daoists.

Gil Raz begins his discussion of Daoist sexual practices with a quotation from an anti-Daoist polemical text written by a convert to Buddhism, Zhen Luan 甄鸞 (535–566): "Husbands were instructed to exchange wives merely for carnal pleasure. Practitioners had no shame, even before the eyes of their fathers and elder brothers. This they called the 'perfect method of concentrating pneuma.' At present, Daoists regularly engage in these practices, in order thereby to attain the Way."[22] Given that this discussion of Daoist sexual practices occurs in such a polemical text, it is difficult to know how widespread such practices were or how accurate Zhen Luan's characterization of them was. Nonetheless, it does seem clear that Daoists engaged in ritualized forms of sexual intercourse in which the liquid vitality of men and women were exchanged. Corroboration comes from the fact that such practices were also condemned within the tradition, not just by Buddhist outsiders.[23] This suggests that although the practices were generally understood within a heterosexual framework, they did not reproduce the heteronormative patriarchy that Buddhist or other scholars championed. That is to say, the condemnation arose because such practices were seen to be defying socially normative mores regarding sexuality, mores that favored either single-sex Buddhist abstinence or Confucian patriarchy. It is also entirely possible that homoerotic versions of such practices may have taken place in single-sex monasteries, though of course given the hidden nature of such practices, it is impossible to know what may have taken place.

The key issue in the interpretation of such practices, as Raz notes, has been the relationship between sexuality and cosmology, that is to say, the way in which the pairing of yin and yang vitality mirrors or reenacts the fundamental cosmological pattern of yinyang. In this line of thinking the transaction of sexual energies should not, in the first place, be read in terms of erotic power (which is the anti-Daoist claim articulated by Zhen Luan), but in terms of spiritual and cosmological transformation.

As an instance of such a transformation, Kristofer Schipper discusses one ritual in which sexual intercourse between a husband and wife takes place in the context of their ordination into a higher rank of the Celestial Master's tradition.[24] The uniting of their sexual vitality here performed a religious, cosmological, and socially transformative function. It was not framed as a lewd erotic act, except by the rite's detractors. The interpretations of Catherine Despeux and Livia Kohn focus on the rites for the union of *qi* between men and women as rehearsals or reenactments of the primordial patterning of yinyang.[25] Raz, however, focuses not on the idea that such rituals reproduced cosmic patterns of yin and yang, but rather that they produced a somatic transformation within the body of the adepts.[26] For the adepts, in Raz's view, the significance of ritualized sexual intercourse is not about the reproductive sexuality itself, the merging of yin and yang, but about the nature of transformation that it, like any other Daoist practice, produces in the practitioner. This reading is altogether more subversive than perhaps Raz realizes. It suggests that Daoist sexuality, even Daoist heterosexuality, need not function in service of patriarchal genealogical reproduction, but should ideally serve to produce a radical spiritual transformation of the participants.

In the Highest Clarity tradition, the practice of sexual transformation is queered even further. Firstly, this tradition takes on an interiorized, spiritualized form in the hierogamies or "sacred marriages" between the adept and a god (usually of the opposite sex). Secondly, the tradition advocated visualization practices in which adepts individually engaged in the production of spiritual rebirth without needing to engage physically with any other person. As Raz quotes:

There is no need to bother about techniques performed by man and woman together for cycling and augmenting essences. Moreover, intercourse with a woman for the purpose of rising to the heavens and recycling pneumas [*qi*] in order to become a Celestial Transcendent are methods more treacherous than fire and water.[27]

As a historian, Raz wants to make clear that his interpretation of these practices proceeds by putting them in the historical context of contemporaneous Daoist practices, rather than within the whole body of literature both Daoist and non-Daoist, that concerns the "arts of the bedroom." My goal, by contrast, is to understand these practices from the perspective of the fundamental relationship between cosmic vitality and sexual vitality.

To read these practices from the perspective of a Daoist ecology, oriented around the concept of "pervasion," means to understand from a vitalistic, ecological framework that crosses the boundaries between the human and nonhuman worlds. The fundamental porosity of this boundary is symbolized by metaphors of pervasion or the translucence of the skin; here, the overwriting of cosmic and sexual, heavenly and earthly patterns of engagement in a fluid discourse suggests that both human sexuality and cosmic vitality are transacted within an overall ecology of cosmic power, namely, the flourishing of the Dao. As such, the goal is not preservation or conservation of the status quo or the reproduction of patriarchal genealogies, but rather the performance of somatic transformation, a process that I describe as "transfiguration."

The Daoist texts and practices discussed here function so as to effect a transfiguration of the body, a somatic rewriting of the mode of engagement between the adept and his or her context. Crucially, this engagement is not produced by virtue of the subjective agency of the individual, but by correlation between the individual and the cosmic context that frames the individual's location. The process of transfiguration is thus irreducibly local, occurring within the materiality of the practitioner, but also reaches out to immediate horizons of meaning and cosmic vitality that frame that person, and extends ultimately to everyone within the world. It is most definitely not a heteronormative, genealogical process of the sustainability or continuity of the status quo, but rather a queer ecological one. It is queer in that it fails to reproduce heteronormative genealogy and instead approaches Judith Butler's notion of resistance to heterosexist gender performance. In her argument, the performance of heternormativity is founded upon the ideological supposition of absolute boundaries between self and world, male and female, inside and outside.[28] Daoist sexual anthropology shares a queer sensibility in which yang and yin are not construed as absolute categories whose function is principally oriented toward sexual reproduction, but rather as processes that take place within a body that is engaged with the world around in a process of continuous transformation. In this sense, Daoist sexual anthropology can also be viewed as ecological in character, in that it arises from the transaction of liquid vitality of the body in the context of an overall ecology of cosmic power, an ecology mediated or transacted through the radical penetrability, porosity, and permeability of the flesh in its relation to the cosmos. It is a celebration of a radically queer ecology.

The next chapter considers this ecological relationship from the perspective not of the individual practitioner but rather the physical spaces in and through which such transactions take place. For now, however, the important characteristic that this gives to any Daoist ecological discourse is that the transfiguration of the body is seen as the inevitable functioning of the Dao within the world. As a consequence, the goal of any ecological ethic that may derive from such a view cannot focus solely on environmental conservation or the preservation of some natural space in an absolutely wild state. The Daoist focus on transformation within nature (*bianhua* 變化) and the concomitant transfiguration of the body through the porosity of the flesh suggests a radical process of continuous cultivation (*xiudao*) as the best mode of engagement between the individual and his or her environmental context. In such a context, the individual, the social world, and the cosmos are locked together in a process of coevolution and mutual interpenetration. Subjectivity is distributed radically throughout such an ecological matrix, dissolving the boundaries between self and other in favor of a continuous ecology of transfiguration. Such a transfiguration is, in the traditions of Daoism articulated here, an act that takes place in specific locations and requires an understanding of the Daoist construction of space and place.

5 The Locative Imagination

Early in my academic career, I was introduced to a Daoist lay practitioner who had spent a lifetime in the vicinity of Mt. Wudang, one of Daoism's most famous holy mountains today. I had been introduced to her as a scholar of Daoism in the West and, in a familiar ritual of inspection, she proceeded to interrogate me as to the extent of my knowledge about the Daoist tradition. Her first question, however, differed radically from any other opening question that I had previously been asked by scholars and colleagues within the field of Daoist studies. She asked how many mountains I had visited. She was, of course, referring to Daoist holy mountains, home to monasteries and temples, hermits, and seekers of immortality. Such mountains have played a central role in the Daoist religious landscape for centuries. Their sacred status is marked by inscriptions improbably etched into cliff faces, pavilions perched on lofty eyries, and temples carved out of caves. This book is, in part, an attempt to explain how and why knowledge of a religious tradition can be measured not by the numbers of texts read, nor by the depth of theological reasoning, but by experience of specific places, and their particular topographies, ecosystems, and environments.

All religions, of course, have their sacred spaces: they are typically places where significant events occurred in the lives of religious heroes.

View from a Daoist
temple at Mt.
Qingcheng. (Author)

The great pilgrimage sites of the world's religions testify to the importance of these sacred sites and their accompanying stories in the religious imagination of countless masses of individuals. As a young theology student at Cambridge University, I had the great experience of walking the Camino de Santiago in northern Spain, arriving in Santiago de Compostela in time for the July 25 celebration of the Feast of Saint James. For a week I walked with hundreds of other pilgrims, both religious and secular, who were drawn by the power of shared experience and long history of pilgrimage. Our route traversed the stunning hillsides of northern Spain, threading its way through now-deserted villages. Day after day we rose before dawn, anxious to arrive at our next resting place before the pulsating heat of the summer sun overwhelmed us. It was as though the power of Saint James's bones exerted a transformative effect not only on the pilgrims but on the natural landscape, paved and trodden for hundreds of years by thousands of devotees.

Although similar pilgrimage experiences have doubtless occurred over many centuries of Chinese history, this is not the power of sacred space that I explore here. That is to say, this chapter is not concerned with the social history of Daoist mountains, or even the way that social history has interacted with China's physical environment. Rather, the aim of this chapter is to highlight what I believe to be a key feature of the Daoist religious experience that has been only partially grasped up to this point. This feature I term the "transfigurative power of nature." By this, I mean, first, that Daoist religious experience can be understood as an experience of transfiguration, a transformation or restructuring of one's form as the approach to immortality, and, second, that this transfiguration is achieved by the encounter of human beings with the subjectivity of nature as located in particular topographies, spaces, and configurations.

Transfiguration is a significant, but little researched, cross-cultural religious category. It refers to a transformation in one's physical appearance, a shift in form, often invoking a play of light and color. Transfigurations denote a moment in the divinization or sacralization of the individual, a moment that can be understood as a shift in the identity of the religious practitioner. After the transfigurative moment, with its change in form or light or color, the religious individual is qualitatively different than before. He or she has been transformed.

We might wonder what causes this transformation to take place. An ecocritical reading of Daoist texts suggests that it is the subjectivity of nature itself, configured in the particular spaces, topographies, and environments of the physical landscape, that brings about this transfiguration of the religious practitioner. Here, a key point emerges that relates to the general scholarly discourse on religion and ecology. Although Daoism is a universal religious tradition, one that makes general theoretical claims about human anthropology and understands the Dao as the underlying source of generative vitality for the cosmos, it is also a tradition that philosophically and practically defers to the specific engagements of Daoist practitioners with their immediate contexts, lineages, and locales.[1] That is to say, although the tradition posits general theoretical conceptions of humanity, and offers general moral principles for human conduct, it also acknowledges that such principles are always and inevitably mediated through the specific encounters of individuals with their communities, places, and lineages. In this sense, the tradition takes into consideration the specific locations (temporal and spatial) in which religious practice and training take place.

This aspect of Daoist practice I term the "locative imagination": it is only through the immediate, local context (meaning sites, lineages, and communities) that one has the possibility of engaging in transfigurative practice. This is because the ecology of cosmic power, as noted in the previous chapter, takes place through somatic transactions in the bodies of Daoist practitioners. To put it another way, the only way toward transcendent encounter with the Dao is through the immediacy of the lived, material experience of the body. But, the materiality of the body naturally entails that it occupies a specific place and forms its experience through the encounter of the body with its environing context. For this reason, just as much as the Daoist tradition focuses on the body as the matrix for transformation, it also focuses on the environment, the space in which the somatic transformations of the adept take place. As Robert Campany concludes from his study of Ge Hong: "All of the tracks leading beyond this world are to be found in this world; the only way to get There is from Here."[2]

This discussion of the locative character of Daoist religion is also important for the discussion of a Daoist ecology. Too often, writing about religion and ecology has viewed the engagement of "religion" with "nature" in terms of the meeting of two abstract concepts in the overlapping field of "cosmology." Willis Jenkins describes such an approach (at least a Christian version of it) as follows:

A cosmological strategy creates an imaginative field for moral agency by using theological beliefs and symbols to interpret social reality and its problems from a Christian point of view. . . . The ethicist thus confronts social problems by investigating the cultural imaginary in which they appear and by uncovering the reality-shaping goals and values that have lead to a crisis. She can then propose alternative moral symbols by which to reshape the worldview through which agents determine fitting action.[3]

His criticism of such an approach is that the task of reshaping worldviews is simply too ambitious to drive practical moral action when it is needed now. He writes, "A cosmological strategy risks that long interval of ideological debate in order to achieve the deep cultural transformation that it holds necessary to address problems whose roots lie in moral consciousness."[4] When the problems of climate change are exacerbated with each year of inaction, then such a strategy of long-term cultural change seems not only foolish, but practically wicked, as it effectively defers concrete action to the time after the cultural imaginary has transformed.

A second problem, noted by Dana Phillips, is that humanities scholars who advocate the methods of ecocriticism uncritically appeal to science as a justification for their own ideological discourse.[5] One example she gives is that of a scholar who implies that "unity" is in and of itself an "ecological" value.[6] In the field of Chinese religions and ecology, a similar argument can be made that the Confucian value of the "unity of heaven and earth" ("tian ren he yi") is self-evidently an ecological value, because it underscores the fundamental interdependence of human life with that of the cosmos above and the materiality of the earth below.

Any conflation of a sense of cosmic "unity" with that of "ecology" fails to recognize the way in which ecological theory itself draws on metaphorical accounts of scientific reality. Indeed, Phillips cites the environmental historian Donald Worster, who argues that the notion of an "ecosystem" as a model of "order and equilibrium" is no longer supported by much scientific thinking about ecosystems: "Nature . . . should be regarded as a landscape of patches of all sizes, textures, and colors, changing continually through time and space, responding to an unceasing barrage of perturbations."[7] Phillips continues her argument with a reference to Joel B. Hagen, who similarly writes that the "new ecology emphasizes indeterminism, instability, and constant change."[8] Her conclusion, following Worster, is that "nature" provides "no model of development for human society to emulate."[9]

The arguments of Jenkins, Worster, Hagen, and Phillips direct any understanding of "religion" and "ecology" away from a broad metaethical cosmology in which the unity of the cosmos and humanity serves as the ground for practical action as regards the natural environment. In the first place, "religion" is itself the product of a cultural, scholarly, and theoretical construction that draws on and is partly defined by the historical situation of modernity. It cannot be defined above all else as a "worldview" or "cosmology," as though those aspects of religious traditions were foundational, and their ethical, practical orientations secondary. Secondly, "ecology" does not necessarily imply an overarching theoretical or practical unity to the natural world, but rather may equally imply a view of the "cosmos" as constituted by overlapping and perhaps mutually inconsistent networks of relationship. While evolution may function as a single, overarching metanarrative, the encounter of species with their habitats, predators, and food, which together constitute an ecosystem, may function at a practical level completely differently than any overarching metanarrative of "ecology." Thus, while "religion" or "worldview" in some broad sense may well be brought into dialogue with "nature" or "evolution" in some equally broad sense, such conversations do not necessarily, immediately, or unidirectionally translate into the practical encounters of species with their habitats and local environments, the threat of climate change, the extinction of species, or climate injustice.

Nevertheless, there are at least three reasons for retaining a focus on cosmology as a key element of the nexus of religion and ecology. The first is, as Jenkins himself argues, that new ideas, cosmologies, and values can at least be useful as "ways for arguing for new strategies of action that seem to better meet contextual problems."[10] Here, the role of a cosmology is not to portray a philosophically "true" description of the relation of human beings with their natural environment, but to play a pragmatically useful role in displacing conventional ideas that are considered to be ineffective or dangerous (however long-term such a strategy may be).

The second reason is that cosmologies are significant because they provide the overall framework for orientating moral values, describing the parameters within which practical moral reasoning takes place, and articulating sites of importance regarding such moral values. Given that responsibility for misaligned ecological relations lies not so much with individuals or corporations but rather with the structuring power of social and cultural systems that orient and organize human behavior, religions should then address ecological issues at the symbolic level, the orienting signs and categories of ordering by which we deem our experience of the world to be significant, and which also structure our moral priorities.[11]

Thirdly, however, the distinction that Jenkins makes between a "cosmological" view and a practical "environmental" approach suggests that these two arenas, the "cosmos" and the "oikos," are perceived as distinct rather than conjoint dimensions. This distinction itself trades on an important metaphysical claim about the relationship between the ultimate reality of the cosmos and the provisional, practical reality of the environment. Rather than following Jenkins's approach that sees these as a dichotomy (a view that prevails within the Christian ontological framework that Jenkins is using), I propose a Daoist framework that sees these two realms (the cosmos and the environment, or the universal and the particular) as a continuum.

In the following section, I analyze one Daoist approach to providing an operative set of symbols that bring together the human body with its natural and cosmological context into an overall network of relationship. From this, it will be possible in subsequent chapters to derive an aesthetic, ethical, political, and ultimately spiritual approach to the contemporary problem of unsustainability.

Space

> The perfected one said: "The [part of] heaven [where there is] nothing is called space. The [part of] a mountain [where there is] nothing is called a grotto. The [part of] a human [body where there is] nothing is called a [grotto] chamber. The empty spaces in the mountains and organs of the body are called grotto courts. The empty spaces in human heads are called grotto chambers. This is how the perfected take up residence in the heavens, the mountains and human beings."[12]

This quotation comes from a sermon given by the Daoist saint Zhou Yishan at the culmination of his quest for transcendence, in which he receives the title Perfected Purple Yang and is installed among the rank of the Daoist perfected. The esoteric biography ends with this record of his teachings, summarizing his knowledge of the Dao after he has attained the highest wisdom. As the next two sections detail, this quest for knowledge is built up from his encounter with Daoist masters and texts in various specific locations. The culmination of this knowledge, however, is a general theoretical cosmology that unites human beings, the natural environment, and the cosmos.

The uniting factor of this cosmology is the term wu無, which is usually translated as "nonbeing" or "emptiness." The quotation relates three kinds of wu: the emptiness of heaven, or the skies; the emptiness of the mountain; and the emptiness of the body. An ecocritical reading of this text should note two things. The first is that these three dimensions of existence—the sky, the mountain, and the body—can be read fundamentally as locations. This is emphasized in the final sentence of the quotation in which the perfected beings "take up residence in" (*chu*) these various spaces. For this Daoist, therefore, the most significant cosmological detail is that these three dimensions of the cosmos—the body, the mountain, and the sky—are to be understood fundamentally as locations in which things take place, most notably the encounter with gods or perfected beings, who "take up residence" in the sky, the mountains, and the body. In order for them to do so, they require an "empty space" in which they can be located. The key aspect of this Daoist cosmology, therefore, is that it is the interior emptiness of things that constitutes their ultimate significance. This notion goes back to the *Daode jing*, which refers to the usefulness of the window or a room being the emptiness that is constituted by the frame or window.[13]

The kind of emptiness that is significant in this text, therefore, is a locative emptiness: the Daoist relates the body, the mountain, and the sky together because of their foundational spatiality. The body is significant because it contains spaces in which the gods can take up residence and be encountered. The mountains are significant because they contain caves where the gods can take up residence and be encountered. The same is true for the sky, which is also constituted largely by empty space.

The second element of an ecocritical reading of this text would be that this very locative emptiness is what brings together these three dimensions of the cosmos in profound interrelationship. That is to say, because the body, the mountains, and the sky are pervaded by the same "emptiness," they are ultimately related to one another. In their interior spaces, the Daoist finds the same *wu*, or empty space. This thus points to the fundamental ecological and cosmological nature of human beings. Humans are pervaded by spaces in which vital energy flows and in which gods take up residence. It is precisely this interior emptiness and accompanying porosity that also deems human bodies to be at the same time landscape bodies. Human bodies are ineluctably constituted and pervaded by the same emptiness that lies within the mountains. In this sense, although the exterior form of human bodies is in appearance fundamentally different from that of mountains, in terms of the internal disposition of bodyscapes and landscapes, humans and mountains are exactly the same. The empty spaces of our bodies are the same as the empty spaces of the mountains.

The same can also be said in terms of the relationship between the human body and the far reaches of the cosmos, namely, the stars that occupy "outer space" and the "outer space" that divides the stars from one another. In the Daoist imagination, these stars were understood to be palaces for perfected spirits, occupying the vast "emptiness" or "nonbeing" (*wu*) of the sky. Just as human bodies are in their interior emptiness identical with the mountainscapes that they inhabit, so also, says Perfected Purple Yang, are human bodies identical with the skyscape of the heavens. In other words, human bodies are not simply the product of their fleshy frames, skeletons, and cells. They are also the product of the emptiness within, an emptiness that is identical with that of the natural world, and with that of the heavenly world. Human bodies are, at the level of their being empty spaces, at the same time ecological bodies and heavenly bodies. Their emptiness is the emptiness of their ecological relatedness, a relatedness not constituted by matter but by emptiness.

The emphasis on "empty space" draws on a tradition of Chinese religious practice known variously as "pacing the void" or "flight beyond the world." This in turn drew on an earlier substrate of shamanic practices of astral voyage in which the "sky traveller projects his soul over the rainbow and beyond the clouds."[14] Accounts of such practices can be found most famously in the collection of shamanic songs from southern China known as the *Chuci* (Songs of Chu), dated to around 200 B.C.E. The most famous of these, known as "Yuanyou," or "The Far-off Journey," describes how the shamanic traveler encounters a variety of spirits in his journey through the cosmos:

Asking the Xiang [river] goddesses to play their zithers for me,
I bid the Sea God dance with the River God.
They pull up water monsters to step forward with them,
Their bodies coiling and writhing in ever swaying motion!
Gracefully the Lady Rainbow circles all around them,
The phoenixes soar up, stay hovering above—
The music swells ever higher, into infinity.
At this point I leave to wander yet again.
With my entourage, I gallop far away.[15]

Of specific interest in the heavens were the stars of the Dipper, the seven stars that point toward the north star, Polaris, around which the heavens were said to rotate. To these seven stars, the Daoists added two more, to create a collection of nine stars that were correlated with the grotto chambers of the body. Such stars were invoked by Daoists either through internal visualization techniques or by meditatively tracing out the constellation through a ritual movement known as the "Pace of Yu." In either case, the Daoist is invoking the power of the stars by ritually appropriating their power inside his or her body. One such technique, for instance, required the adept to "repose himself at night on a diagram of the dipper laid out on his bed, with its bowl-like canopy over his head, and his hands and feet pointed at major stars."[16] The symbolism could not be clearer: the body of the adept is a constellation of points of light, here mapped out literally upon his own frame.

The biography of the founding figure of the Way of Highest Clarity describes this mapping of the stars onto the body in a bejeweled description of Wei Huacun's own physical appearance:

Empyreal phosphor, glistening high;
Round-eye lenses doubly lit;
Phoenix frame and dragon bone;
Brain colors as jewel-planetoids;
Five viscera of purple webbings;
Heart holding feathered scripts.[17]

As Schafer notes in his commentary, her vital organs are "plainly displayed" in a characterization that "yields a transparent effigy, a goddess of crystal, lit from within."[18] Such a text was not intended simply to dazzle, but to recall the way in which the human body is in its ultimate sense a space body: transparent, crystalline, and dazzling.

For Perfected Purple Yang, however, the relation of the human body with the space body lies not so much in the brilliance of the stars as nodes of energy, but rather in the dark, empty spaces that function as conduits relating the gods of the body with the gods of the mountains and the gods of the stars. Without such "space," there could be no visions of transfiguration such as those recorded in the biography of Wei Huacun seen here.

As regards the stars, however, it should be noted that the locative imagination of the Highest Clarity Daoist served to map the specific spaces of the body with those of the specific nodes of outer space. Although Perfected Purple Yang's sermon notes a general theoretical correspondence through the experience of emptiness or nonbeing, the transaction of a correspondence between the body and the cosmos within an economy of cosmic power took place through specific encounters in specific locations with specific gods. In this sense, the ecology of spiritual relationships fostered within the tradition was defiantly local: specific gods could be encountered only in specific places and at specific times.

Mountain Spaces

The focus on specific places and specific ritual encounters can be seen most clearly in the encounters between Daoists and spirits that take place in specific mountain sites. The nature of these encounters trades in part on a long-standing distinction between what Gai Jianmin terms "urban" (*dushi* 都市) Daoism and "mountainforest" (*shanlin* 山林) Daoism. This distinction between the urban, civilized, domesticated areas of China and the forested, wilder, and more remote areas of China plays an important role in the popular cultural appreciation of Daoism in China. There are two reasons for distinguishing the mountainous areas. The first is a positive appreciation of the vitality of the mountain as affording something that cannot be found in the ordinary world. The second is a desire to disassociate oneself from the common traditions of "civilization" that have produced an unhealthy environment for the cultivation of the Dao.

The latter of these two themes is emphasized in the following statement by Ge Hong in his book *The Master Who Embraces Simplicity*: "The completion of the cinnabar [*he dan*] must take place at a famous mountain where no people live, not more than three people may follow. First purify [yourself] for one hundred days, clean yourself with the five fragrances. . . . Do not go near dirty and unclean environments, and [do not go] where ordinary people go."[19]

Here, the value of the mountain seems to be located in the fact that the mountains contain very few people. The process of ascending the mountain is also preceded by an extensive ritual of purification and an insistence that the adept steer clear of the places where "ordinary people" go. In this case, the significance of the mountain as a natural site is precisely that it is not a place where the "dirty" and "common" people live. The mountain is here associated with a separation from the ordinariness of life and, more specifically, the pursuit of a hierarchical distinction between the elite Daoist and the common folk. The mountain is elusive, remote, high, and pure, characteristics to be adopted by the elite Daoist. In this tradition, therefore, it seems that the chief significance of the mountain is that it functions as a marker of social difference.

At the same time, this statement also raises the question of why the lives of ordinary people should seem "dirty" or require "purification." At a basic level, it cannot be denied that urban life produces squalor, filth, and disease that is not immediately conducive to long life, well-being, and happiness. This is by no means simply a feature of the modern megalopolis but was clearly a concern in ancient China. The primitivist strain of the *Daode jing* also emphasizes a desire to produce human civilization on a small scale.[20] In this sense, therefore, the mountains constitute both a refuge from conventional social organizations where the Daoist may enter into seclusion away from the "common people" and also a metaphorical and literal place of purification. The high mountains in ancient China, just as today, were valued as places of clean air, pure water, and rare flora and fauna.

This then leads to an understanding of why the mountain should be viewed not simply as a marker of elite seclusion but also as the producer of a vitality that was keenly sought by the Daoist. Ge Hong himself acknowledges this in his discussion of the rare "vegetable and mineral substances" that could be useful in concocting an elixir of immortality. Campany contains an important discussion of a particular "stony honey exudation" (*shimizhi*) produced by a set of stalactites in a cave on the peak of Mt. Song, the central of China's five sacred mountains.[21] Ge writes:

> Many Daoists have given long thought to this place but feel that it is unapproachable. Perhaps only by affixing a bowl to the end of a bamboo or wooden pole, and stretching it across, might one catch and collect some [of the *zhi* as it drips down]; but no one has been able to do even this. But, judging by the inscription in the rock over the chamber, someone in an earlier age must have been able to procure some.[22]

Campany comments: "The link between inaccessibility and efficacy is here nicely captured by the inscription, promising untold benefits yet carved in a seemingly unattainable spot: the reach required to get the transcendence-inducing mineral nectar just exceeds the grasp of all but the most fortunate and best qualified aspirants."[23] As this makes clear, the remoteness and inaccessibility of the place is also related to the power and efficacy of the substance that it produces. Just as the physical landscape is not flat but punctuated by high mountains and low valleys, inaccessible peaks, and fertile plains, so also the liquid vitality of the Dao is distributed unevenly across the natural world. Remote and inaccessible places harbor more powerful "exudations" or "perspirations" of the Dao, condensations of liquid vitality that have the power to bring health and long life to those who are able to obtain these substances. Ge Hong's hagiography of Wang Lie, for instance, notes that Wang "happens upon a rice-flavored 'green mud' oozing 'like bone marrow' from an avalanche-induced rock crevice."[24] This description of the natural world "oozing" or "transpiring" rare and vital liquids is a perfect example of the way the vital power of the Dao was conceptualized in early China.

Although the landscape produced such rare liquids naturally, if not universally, the Daoist religious tradition continuously developed processes that overlaid religious meaning on to such natural exudations. A chief example of this is the way in which mountains proved to be the location of divine revelations. Indeed, when the Daoist scholar Lu Xiujing (406–477) went to compile the first collection of Daoist books, he divided them into three "caves" or "grottoes": the Grotto of Mystery, the Grotto of Perfection, and the Grotto of Spirit. These grottoes were imagined to have heavenly counterparts, spiritual libraries presided over by the gods who had transmitted the texts to earth from time to time.

The sacred connection between the mountain and the text was mentioned by Ge Hong, who wrote:

All noted mountains and the Five Marchmounts [the Five Sacred Mountains] harbor books of this sort, but they are hidden in stone chambers and inaccessible places. When one who is fit to receive the Dao enters the mountain and meditates on them with utmost sincerity, the mountain spirits will respond by opening the mountain, allowing him to see them.[25]

Here, like the natural exudations noted previously, Ge emphasizes the inaccessibility of these books or texts; but in this case, he also specifies that the Daoist requires the intervention of the spirits to make them accessible. The mountain is understood, like the body, to be a porous system whose interior transpirations are of particular interest to the Daoist. It takes genuine faith on the part of the individual for these interior texts to become accessible.

Entrance to a cave
temple in Shandong
Province. (Author)

Just as the texts written by spirit mediums could be understood as condensed liquefactions of primal vitality emanating from the Dao itself, so also the texts found in the interiority of the mountains should be understood as condensations of liquid vitality. The Chinese characters and talismans that they contain, whether painted in ink on paper or etched by water upon rock face, are the "symbolic condensations" of the natural "oozings" noted in the alchemical tradition. Although such mountain texts could be copied and transmitted universally through printing, like the texts revealed through the spirit medium, they have an originating point, a specific location from which they emanated.

The importance of these specific locations is revealed in the *Esoteric Biography of Perfected Purple Yang*, which recounts how Zhou Yishan, on his quest to become a perfected person, took part in a pilgrimage through twenty-four of China's sacred mountains. The text details each of these places following the same formula. The first three are as follows:

He left and climbed Mt. Qi. He met Zang Yanfu and received the *Pure Formulas of the Songs of Sadness and Happiness.*

He took his leave and next climbed Mt. Liang. He met Zicheng of Huainan and received the *Three Diagrams of the Celestial Pass.*

Next he left and climbed Mt. Niushou. He met Zhang Zifang and received the *Scriptures of Great Clarity.*[26]

The text continues in a similar vein, detailing the names of all twenty-four mountains, the gods Zhou encounters, and the texts he receives. The purpose of this enumeration of places, gods, and texts is likely to demonstrate how Zhou incorporates within his own journey the earlier traditions and texts that were deemed significant by the Highest Clarity tradition.[27] Texts that were not listed here may be assumed to be of relatively little interest to the compiler of this biography. But from an eco-critical, rather than a social-historical perspective, the key detail here is that Zhou's method for incorporating these previous traditions into his own religious journey is a peripatetic one: he must move from one location to another in order to encounter the specific deities and receive the specific texts.

Although Daoism may be considered to be a universal religious tradition that makes universal claims about human anthropology, texts such as these also reveal Daoism's ineluctably locative character. Gods and texts, though in principal universally accessible, are nonetheless tied to specific locations. The approach to the universal power of the Dao is thus always mediated by specific places, texts, and gods, each with its own history, lineage, and community.

The second point that an ecocritical reading of this text can make is that these locations are not within cities but within the relatively undomesticated spaces of the mountains. This reinforces the argument that the encounters with the gods and the texts should be understood by analogy with the encounters with rare flora, minerals, and other "condensations" of liquid vitality. They are in principle alchemical encounters in which the somatic vitality of the adept is transfigured by engagement with the vitality of the mountain, thematized in the encounters with the gods and their texts. My argument here, therefore, is that an important strand within the Daoist religious tradition, including its textual corpora, with attendant gods, and lineages, should be understood as the "textual condensations" of transfigurative encounters between humans and the distributed liquid vitality of the natural landscape. That is to say, this strand of the Daoist textual tradition is itself contingent upon the experience of the transfigurative power of nature's subjectivity distributed throughout the landscape.[28]

Further evidence for this argument can be seen in the way in which the Daoist ritual tradition functioned as a way to access the mountains. One example is cited by John Lagerwey:

> Before taking a walk in the mountains, the adept must clasp his teeth nine times, close his eyes and visualize five-colored clouds which rise all about him and completely cover the mountain; after a long while the immortal officials of the five sacred peaks (wuyue xianguan) and all the animals and plants of the mountain come to place themselves at his service. Then he lifts his head and pronounces an incantation.[29]

In this text, the adept must go through a physiological preparation (clasping his teeth together and closing his eyes) and then an interior visualization process. The result of this is that the spirit officials of the mountains are summoned to the adept's service and grant access to the mountain, placing all its animals and plants at his service. The goal of this religious ritual is not to worship gods, beg for forgiveness, or bring salvation to humankind, but rather to gain access to the mountain itself. Here, the gods are best understood as tutelary spirits: they exercise power over the animals and plants on the mountain, and their function is to facilitate the encounter between the adept and the mountain. Through the religious process, the adept "ritually domesticates" the mountain's animals and plants, rendering the space of the mountain and its natural vitality accessible in a way that would not be the case for the ordinary human being.

Again, the purpose for the Daoist of walking in the mountains is to encounter the specific configurations of liquid vitality that are present in that specific space. Although the general principles of this process might apply equally to all such encounters, the Esoteric Biography of Perfected Purple Yang suggests that such encounters are significant precisely because of their differences, not their similarities. That is, it is the unique features of each place that are religiously meaningful for the Daoist, not the general features of the mountain as a high place, with topography, flora, and fauna similar to other high places.

Body Spaces

The Daoist body is, then, not just an interior somatic process, but an ecological process connected through the porosity of the skin to the wider contexts and environments in which the liquid vitality of the cosmos is distributed. When scholars make the argument that Daoism is a tradition that is supremely focused on the body as the location of religious experience,[30] they are also inadvertently making the argument that the Daoist experience is an ecological experience. This is simply to make the general ecocritical point that if one considers experience to be generated within the body, the fact that the body is a porous substance, defined by porous skin, orifices, and vital organs that are "empty spaces" for the residence of gods, then the body is also an ecological body. It is an ecological body because somatic experience is produced by interaction between the body and the spaces or environments that it inhabits, and there can be no "biosprituality" without a contextual "ecospirituality."

In the Daoist religious experience, however, the ecological body is also the matrix that produces the transfiguration of the body, because the contexts and environments in which the body lives serve as points of mediation between the body and its ultimate horizon of meaning, namely, the cosmos itself. That is to say, the precise configurations through which the body engages and transforms the physical landscape (and vice versa) form the basis of the Daoist's encounter with the Dao itself. The specific location of the Daoist body in the physical environment is the way the Daoist practitioner encounters the ultimate horizons of the cosmos in an act of spiritual transfiguration.

The question here is, what is the relationship between the immediate practical concerns of the environment and the ultimate context of the cosmos? Earlier in this chapter, I summarized Jenkins's argument that (Christian) ecological ethics should abandon a quest to reorient humanity's ultimate value system, grounded in the cosmologies of the world's religious and cultural traditions, in favor of a more small-scale, practical approach to dealing with environmental issues on a local basis. This distinction between the local and the ultimate itself reflects the Christian framework within which Jenkins is operating. Within such a Christian framework,

the ultimate is in a profound sense the negation of the particular. Especially in evangelical Protestant traditions of thought, God stands as the
ultimate judge of his creation and wields final authority and power over
the world that he created ex nihilo. The gap between cosmology and ecology, the transcendent and the material, the sacred and the profane is, in
the Protestant Christian world, an infinite one, to be bridged only in the
person of Jesus Christ.

In the Daoist worldview that I have been explaining here, however, the
relation between the ultimate and the particular is not that of infinite
difference. To recall Campany's summary of Ge Hong's philosophy,
the "only way to There is from Here." In the Daoist tradition, or at least the
strand that I have been exploring in this book, the "here" is not a person
but rather a place, and it is not one place, but many places. The biography of
Perfected Purple Yang reveals that the attaining of perfection, or the ultimate transfiguration of the body, takes place incrementally and locatively,
by pursuing the gradual integration of bodyscape and landscape.

This integration is consummated in the final event of Perfected
Purple Yang's biography, in which the protagonist is advised by the gods
he encounters to "go back and look inside [his] own grotto chamber."[31]
Having spent many years traveling through the mountains, he is now
instructed to engaged in an interior visualization in which he encounters
gods in grottoes that are not inside the mountains, but inside his own
body. These "grotto chambers" in the Highest Clarity tradition are nine
"residences" or spaces within the brain in which the highest level of spiritual encounter could take place. By visualizing the gods inside his own
grotto chambers, Zhou Yishan engages the highest level of visualization
in which he makes the gods present within his own body. When Zhou
conducts his visualization inside the "cave rooms" of his brain, he makes
the final step on his journey toward becoming a perfected person. He
meets two high-ranked deities and receives the most sacred text of the
Highest Clarity tradition, the *Scripture of the Great Grotto* (*Dadong zhen-
jing* 大洞真經; ca. fourth century C.E.). In this moment, the physiological,
locative, and cosmological worlds are fused together in an act of ultimate
integration of self, environmental context, and cosmos.

This process of inner observation (*neiguan*) or visualization (*cun*) is a
highlight of the Highest Clarity tradition of meditation. Often, it is regarded as a transition between the more physical, or material, alchemical
tradition that Ge Hong favors and the subsequent traditions of inner
alchemy, in which the alchemical process is conducted entirely within

the space of the practitioner's body. A way of explaining this might be to suggest that the Daoist tradition was in the process of "internalizing" the quest for the physically transformative powers of nature that were distributed throughout the natural landscape. According to this interpretation, earlier traditions, such as those of Ge Hong, saw this transformation as a wholly material process, but later traditions engaged in the quest for transformation in a wholly internal way regardless of the material properties of the natural landscape in which the adept was located. But such a transformation of the Daoist tradition could equally be read as the "ecologizing" of the body, a process by which the body increasingly came to be thematized as a landscape with "grotto chambers" or "cave rooms" in which the Daoist could encounter spiritual power. In this ecocritical reading of the development of the tradition, it is not that the body of the Daoist replaces the mountain as the location of spiritual transformation, but that the mountain replaces the body of the Daoist.

Given the fact that the Daoist tradition is, overall, a tradition focused on ultimate matters, it is reasonable to suggest that of these three frames, the body, the environment, and the heavens or cosmos, the last is truly the most significant in terms of its ultimacy. But just as there are many features to the body, and many features to the landscape, so also there are many features to the cosmos. In the Highest Clarity imagination, the heavens are not an abstract, featureless place, but a constellation of power and vitality, focused on the stars and the planets. The perfected Daoist, whose body is perfectly at ease in a multiplicity of environmental contexts, will eventually leave this world either in death or through a process of ascension and attain a higher location in the heavens. The *Esoteric Biography of Perfected Purple Yang* records the final words of a middle-ranked immortal, Juanzi, who was said to have spent 2,700 years on earth before finally departing:

I have wandered throughout the famous mountains, I have gazed upon the eight seas and wandered through the five sacred mountains. I have rested in grotto halls. I have delighted in the drooping fronds of vegetation and have enjoyed the call of animals, the streams gushing forth their essence, the hills lush with forests, the elegance of the hundred creatures and the rhythm of winter and summer. I have fished the long waters and roamed the mystical rapids. I have stilled my mind on mountain peaks, meditated on perfection and cultivated energy.[32]

Finally, however, Juanzi is able to depart the "present world" and take his place in the heavens as a transcendent being. In this regard, the Daoist religious tradition is, like many religious traditions, one that ultimately favors the heavenly world over the earthly world. The Daoist distinction, however, is that it is the earthly world that furnishes all the materials to enable the Daoist to progress on his religious quest. Without the "Here," there would be no way to get to "There." Without the locative imagination, and without the many subjective powers of nature distributed throughout the natural landscape, there would be no way for the Daoist to transcend them.

This points, then, to a distinct feature of the Daoist religious imagination that has important consequences for thinking about the relationship between cosmology and ecology. For the Daoist, cosmology is in an important sense predicated on the specific forms of the spaces that it produces. The cosmos is always constellated in particular forms and spaces: it is never completely abstract. For this reason, the way the cosmos is symbolized bears directly on the way that the landscape is deemed significant, and also the way that the bodyscape is thematized. The heavens, the earth, and the body are constellations of empty spaces, with liquid vitality circulating within these three dimensions.

The ethical frameworks that flow from this picture will necessarily be different from the ones portrayed by Jenkins, which are predicated on a disjunction between ultimate values and practical problems. In the Daoist imagination that I am attempting to construct and articulate here, such a dichotomy must be false. The natural world is not simply a realm of "problems" to be solved: it is a world of significations, a world of subjectivities, and a world of agencies that pervade the human body, open up the body's "grotto chambers," and enable the continuous transfiguration of the human form. It derives those powers, in the same way that the body and the heavens derive their powers, from the fecundity of liquid vitality flowing in ceaseless patterns of transformation in and among these three dimensions of existence.

This Daoist framework that I am constructing here would surely agree with Jenkins's argument that environmental ethics should focus on practical, immediate problems. But, it would not view those problems as constituting a different field of inquiry than the question of cosmology. The ultimate values and significations that humans attribute to the cosmos are also interwoven in the proximate values and significations that are attached to the specific fields and locations of engagement, as they are in the field of somatic experience. Without the body and without the land-scape, there could be no cosmos. All three realms are mutually implicated and coconstituting fields of vital power. It follows, therefore, that the "problem of the environment" is at some level a problem of the body and a problem of the cosmos. The distinctive feature of a Daoist approach to ecology, as I am attempting to construct here, is to regard environmental problems as simultaneously problems of the landscape, problems of the bodyscape, and problems of cosmology. Inasmuch as ecological problems are thematized only at the level of physical environment, such a themati-zation must remain inadequate. Ecological problems are perforce questions of ultimate value (or cosmological problems), and they are also questions of human health and vitality (or somatic problems).

Kuang-ming Wu, in his massive philosophy of Chinese body think-ing, summarizes this philosophical approach as follows: "My body is this systematic experiential totality of constituting the world."[33] The body does not "take place" in the "space" of the environment or world, but rather "the body is the subject's being-in-the-world and to-the-world."[34] If we construe this "world" as both the immediate lived experience of the body and also the ultimate horizons of meaning produced by the body's encounter with the world, then this must transform the approach to understanding "environmental" problems and "environmental" ethics. It also demands a transformation in how we think about religion and the engagement of religion with nature.

6 The Political Ecology of the Daoist Body

If nature and the self are coconstituting subjective agents, grounded together in the Dao, what does this mean for ethics in regard to the natural world? Such a question must be considered from two levels: that of the individual actor, and that of the system in which the actor functions. As the emphasis on understanding Daoist praxis under the category of transaction indicates, these two dimensions must in practice be considered together as constituting the Daoist world of distributed subjectivities. The Daoist experience of cultivation that is outlined in this book can make two distinct contributions to this discussion. The first is to consider the way in which the aesthetic experience of the world produces sensitivities that can influence practical moral decision-making. The second is to consider the way in which moral rules and social or political systems are ordered to be most suited to dealing with the range of environmental problems that the world faces.

One possible approach to the problem of ethics in regard to the natural world can be developed from the basis of the Daoist concept of "pervasion" in which the world floods into the porous body, insisting within it, informing it, and transforming it. This approach, one might say, is chiefly an aesthetic or a phenomenological approach, which focusses on the way that the body and world are phenomenologically correlated in the experience of "worlding the body" and "embodying the world." In this chapter, I consider how such an experience can be trained, and what the moral effects of such an experience may be. The concept of pervasion is thus rooted in an aesthetic experience but one that has clear moral consequences. The second approach, examined in further detail in the next chapter, is denoted by the term "affect," which will be used to explore the way that cultural sensibilities construct the broad normative parameters for the general range of feelings that people experience in the world.

As Tim Ingold notes, British social anthropology, following Durkheim, made a sharp distinction between these two approaches to the question of perception, distinguishing on the one hand between personal, private sensations, and on the other hand the collective social representations of those sensations.[1] Ingold traces the way that this distinction has played out in terms of separating psychological approaches from sociological approaches to the way humans experience and enact the world and, more, recently to the development of cognitive science approaches to perception. This bifurcated approach itself rests on the long-standing Cartesian distinction between self and world, or subject and object. Ingold, however, shares with many other contemporary theorists an approach that considers the subject not as an isolated entity but as an "agent-in-an-environment."[2] This approach he traces back to Heidegger's argument that the perceiving subject does not simply receive the "brute facticity" of experience and then proceed to make sense of that experience through a process of categorization; rather, the world presents itself to the subject already in a certain "availableness." In this sense, "self and world merge in the activity of dwelling."[3] To be, is always to be dwelling in a world that constitutes the lived reality of one's own experience.

Ingold then draws on Jacob von Uexkull's biological studies to make a further distinction between the natural environment as is objectively studied by scientists and the *Umwelt*, or environment that constitutes the "living-world" of the animal. Although a scientist may objectively understand the former, she cannot experience the *Umwelt* of the animals she is studying; this latter world is constituted by the interactions of the animal with the natural environment and is a world made out of experience that cannot be shared directly by the scientist. Following von Uexkull, then, one might say that the human social world constitutes a shared *Umwelt*, in which human actors create a "living-world" for themselves and others through the network of symbols that define human cultures. The capacity for language and symbol-making enables animals to create shared worlds of experience, that is to say, cultures. From this perspective, it is possible to consider the contribution that a Daoist sensibility could make both to critiquing the shared cultural world of modernity and also to constructing the symbols and values that could produce the optimal mutual flourishing of the human social world and the biophysical reality upon which it is ultimately predicated. One reason for the world's current ecological crisis is that the shared cultural world of human beings is producing a deteroriation in the objective biophysical reality that is studied by climate scientists. For a culture to be sustainable in the long run, the physical world and the cultural world must be brought into closer alignment.

Phenomenology of Perception

Understanding the function of human bodies in constructing human perceptions of the world has been the major project of Maurice Merleau-Ponty and other philosophers who were convinced that the Heideggerian emphasis on lived experience should point us toward the body not simply as the container for experience but as the generative matrix of those experiences. According to this way of thinking about perception, it is not simply that the body functionally generates an "experience" of an external "world" but rather that the body's interaction with the world provides the spatial construction that is the condition for the possibility of any perception of the world. Without a body there could be no experience of the world as it is given to us, and without a world there could be no body. Merleau-Ponty writes: "My body is not an object, but a means, an organization. In perception I organize with my body an association with the world. With my body and through my body, I inhabit the world. The body is the field in which perceptions localize themselves."[4]

Merleau-Ponty thus regards the body as the fundamental building block of human beings' lived experience of the world. In *The Visible and the Invisible*, he develops his understanding of perception with the notion of reversibility, by which he means that when perception is understood as being constituted in the flesh, then to perceive the world is also to be perceived by the world. One cannot touch without being touched; one cannot see without simultaneously presenting oneself to be seen by the world. In contrast to Descartes's *cogito ergo sum*, one might say *tango et tangor* (I touch and I am touched). The crucial idea here is that whatever humans touch, perceive, and even think, they do so from within a world, not from outside it. There is no ultimate Archimedean vantage point from which the subject can be fully isolated from the objective world that he or she is observing. Rather, the world and the perceiving body are constituted together in an act of perception.

Merleau-Ponty's approach to phenomenology has furthermore been instrumental in generating what has been termed the "enactive approach" of embodied cognitive science.[5] According to Giovanna Colombetti and Evan Thompson, this "dynamical systems approach" has challenged the idea that "cognition is the manipulation of abstract representations according to syntactic rules."[6] Rather, it proposes that cognition develops from the interactions of the brain, body, and environment. This approach is, moreover, challenging the dominant tradition of cognitive science that draws on Cartesian understandings of the mind/body dualism. Colombetti and Thompson describe this new field as follows: "In summary, according to the enactive approach, the human mind is embodied in our entire organism and embedded in the world, and hence is not reducible to structures inside the head. Meaning and experience are created by, or enacted through, the continuous reciprocal interaction of the brain, the body, and the world."[7]

A similar approach is taken by Mark Rowlands, who argues that "it is not possible to understand the nature of cognitive processes by focusing exclusively on what is occurring inside the skins of cognizing organisms."[8] This approach is based on the work of the philosopher Hillary Putnam, who claimed that the world cannot be understood simply as something that is external to the mind.[9] Rowlands develops this epistemological argument into a deeper position in which cognitive processes themselves are not located exclusively within the body; rather, the cognitive process itself involves the manipulation of one's environment. For Rowlands, cognition is a hybrid process in which individual bodies engage with and manipulate the environment in which they are located. Rowlands uses an analogy from psychotectonics (the study of how to build minds) that a mind is not like a computer but rather a robot, that is, a machine that interacts with and manipulates its environment in order to process information about it.[10]

Rowlands argues for this theory of cognition by examining perception, memory, thought, and language. In terms of perception, Rowlands defends James Gibson's theory that visual perception takes place through an optical array. This means that the optical system of the perceiving person manipulates a spatial pattern of light and does not simply process information collected by the retina and delivered to the optic nerve. Instead, the total system of visual perception is one in which eyes move and focus, heads turn, and bodies move, thus manipulating the structure of the optic array in its environment.[11] Any comprehensive understanding of perception, Gibson claims, cannot be understood unless it involves the total "ecosystem" of manipulating and processing information. Humans do not acquire visual knowledge simply by internally processing information acquired from external sources, but, rather, "in certain circumstances, acting upon, or manipulating, external structures is a form of information processing."[12] From examples such as this, Rowlands argues that Putnam's epistemological claims must also be supplemented by an ontological claim—that some forms of cognition involve the manipulation of structures in one's environment.

A second example of how this works is given in Rowlands's examination of memory. In this example, he distinguishes between biological working memory and external working memory, and argues that memory, like perception, is a hybrid of internal and environmental elements. He cites as an example David C. Rubin's theory of memory in oral traditions.[13] In his book, Rubin argues that oral memory, for instance remembering a poem, is constructed out of the sequence of sounds that is involved in the performance of the poem. Specifically, the rules of rhythm and rhyme severely limit the quantity of information that must be remembered. Provided that one can remember the beginning word of the poem, each word functions as a phonetic cue for the next word: "Eenie" leads to "Meenie" leads to "Miney" leads to "Mo."[14] Rowlands likes this example because it shows that the patterns of ambient sound located outside the remembering mind help constitute the memory process. The manipulation of one's aural environment (by voicing the first word of the poem) is not only the first stage in the performance of the poem, but also the first stage in the remembering of the poem.

Such developments in understanding how cognition may be constructed out of the engagement between individuals and the worlds they inhabit have been significant both for reshaping cognitive science and also for thinking about the lived world that is generated through the process of cognition. Indeed, his work has been instrumental for a new line of ecological phenomenology that seeks to explore the value of phenomenology for contributing to a holistic, ecological, systemic view of the relationship between the body and the world. One of the chief proponents of this movement, David Abram, first alluded to the ecological possibilities of Merleau-Ponty's phenomenology in an early essay published in 1988:

His work suggests a rigorous way to approach and to speak of the myriad ecosystems without positing our immediate selves outside of them. Unlike the language of information processing and cybernetics, Merleau-Ponty's phenomenology of the flesh provides a way to describe and disclose the living fields of integration from our experienced place within them. The convergence of Merleau-Ponty's aims with those of a genuine philosophical ecology cannot be too greatly stressed.[15]

In short, Merleau-Ponty's approach to phenomenology has been taken up by people on both sides of the self/world divide. Ecophenomenology has emphasized the way that the material world presents itself to the self through the materiality of the body with which it constantly interacts. Embodied cognition stresses the other side of this coin, namely, the way that cognition cannot itself be grasped from within the mind alone, that it depends on a material body inhabiting a material world.

The approaches of phenomenology and embodied cognitive science are important because they demonstrate the way in which Western philosophical and modern scientific approaches to the idea of the body are already engaging with similar ideas to those generated in the Daoist tradition. Nevertheless, despite the work that has been done to recuperate the body as the foundation for the human experience of the world, such work remains remarkably abstract. Two criticisms are readily apparent. The first is that made by the American pragmatist philosopher Richard Shusterman, who criticizes Merleau-Ponty for emphasizing the way in which somatic perception operates spontaneously. Most people most of the time do not need to think about or reflect upon how precisely they are constructing their bodily experiences of the lived world. The marvel of perception is that humans do not have to consciously think about how to navigate a crowded party without bumping into a waiter carrying a trayful of cocktails: they just do it. But Shusterman wants more than simply being able to be successful in ordinary pursuits. He advocates what he calls "somaesthetics," or training the body's perceptual engagement with the world so as to achieve greater pragmatic benefits. He writes:

While I share Merleau-Ponty's appreciation of our inexplicit, unreflective somatic perception, I think we should also recognize that it is often painfully inaccurate and dysfunctional. I may think I am keeping my head down when swinging a golf club, though an observer will easily see I do not. Disciplines of somatic education deploy exercises of representational awareness to treat such problems of misperception and misuse of our bodies in the spontaneous and habitual behavior that Merleau-Ponty identifies as primal and celebrates as miraculously flawless in normal performance.[16]

The problem, as Shusterman sees it, is that if perception is somatic, then it can and should be trained somatically so as to create pragmatically better representations of our place in the world. The value of such representations, however, may extend beyond purely physical activities such as tennis and golf. Theoretically, at least, it should be possible to engage in training so as to produce a better engagement between the body and the world it inhabits. In this regard, it is worth bearing in mind that the Daoist tradition was allied to a whole range of cultivation practices that sought to do precisely that: to train the body to engage the world in ever more deft and skillful ways, through martial arts, dance, and other disciplines of the body.

The Western tradition has not, by and large, placed a great deal of emphasis on the notion of training the body's perception of the world, except perhaps in sports. This leads to the second criticism that has been leveled at Merleau-Ponty's phenomenology, namely, his seeming reluctance to speak about the depth of the inner body where the material experience of the world is actually generated. While his philosophy makes it perfectly clear that perception depends on a depth of field for experience, he does not consider that this depth, or experience of dimensionality, can also be applied to the perception of the inner body. The philosopher Sundar Sarukkai writes:

But nowhere in these discussions do we find any detailed attempt to explicate the idea of the "inner" body. The lack of such a discussion suggests that these writers view the body as a homogeneous entity, because of which there is little possibility of articulating a phenomenology of the inner body. I believe that the most important reason for this continued ambiguity regarding the notion of inner with respect to the body is to be found in the absence of a tradition of lived experience of the inner body in the West, one that could have been used by Merleau-Ponty in a manner similar to the case histories of Schneider [Schneider suffered head injuries and consequently many mental disorders. Merleau-Ponty used his case notes as evidence to refute empiricist and intellectualist theories of perception]. In contrast, the phenomenological experiences of yoga strongly suggest the possibility of a lived experience of the inner body.[17]

Before discussing yoga, Sarukkai gives the example of eating in order to argue for the phenomenological experience of dimensionality or depth within the inner body. He writes:

The body experience of eating is equivalent to the phenomenological experience of dimensionality and thus is intertwined with the notion of "inside." The process of eating is never visible to us. Further actions related to eating, such as mashing the food, swallowing, and so on, are all events in the "dark side" of the body. We can never "see" ourselves eating, but we experience it all the time. We experience swallowing the food; we experience its passage through the food pipe into the region of the stomach. These experiences all constitute an experience of dimensionality, an expression of the "inside" of the body. We are usually unaware of these processes except in times of pain and distress of the inner body. But practices like yoga allow us a continuous, conscious grasp of the inner body.[18]

Sarukkai's approach is instructive in that it opens up a new aspect of embodied experience. Disciplines of body cultivation practice such as Yoga, Tantra, and Daoist inner alchemy train the ways in which people can experience the world within their bodies. At their simplest level, these traditions focus on paying attention to breathing. At a more advanced level, they train people to develop complex experiences of energies flowing in and through the body, experiences that most people ignore most of the time. Such traditions of body cultivation can be understood as nondiscursive somatic disciplines that inscribe the body within the world and the world within the body. As such, they may be fruitfully illuminated by Merleau-Ponty's analysis of the reversibility of phenomenal perception. From this follows the hypothesis that training in these somatic disciplines can overcome the experience of the world as other and can provide the aesthetic or sensory foundation for ecologically sensitive patterns of behavior. In short, the visual and sensual experience of the body inside the world and the world inside the body can constitute the proper aesthetic grounds for ecologically sensitive praxis. This praxis derives not directly from a worldview or ethical theory, but rather from the experience of the world and the states of feeling that such an experience produces.

Permeable Skin

To rediscover the porosity of the flesh is more than simply an aesthetic endeavor; it also produces new ethical and political paradigms based not on individual agency derived from an isolated rational actor, but on the bodies as sites in which multiple levels of agency are subjectively felt to interact. In the classical Chinese tradition, the body of the emperor was the one that was most significant. In Confucius's terms, all that was required of the emperor was to "govern by means of virtue," and then he would be "like the north star, which keeps its place and all the stars turn around it" (*Analects* 2.1). In this sense, the question of governance was one of the proper disposition of things within the overall ecology of relations, with the emperor at the center, and all other elements properly arranging themselves around him.

This notion is interesting for considering moral relations within an ecosystem because it minimally suggests that one effect of proper moral action is to produce the proper alignment of things within a network. That is to say, if the emperor produces proper virtue within his own body, the effect will be to induce the proper alignment of things within his court. It suggests that the emperor cannot be properly effective on his own: he needs the support of all the political actors within his system of government. His goal is not to produce effective action of his own accord, but rather to produce this within the system as a whole. This suggests that if the emperor disposes himself correctly through the manifestation of virtue, then the result will be to properly align the network of political relations so as to induce the optimal flourishing of the network as a whole. What is of interest here is if we take the community of actors not only as the imperial court, but also more broadly as the ecosystems and cosmic frameworks in which human decision-making takes place. It is then possible to imagine an ethical and even a political system that takes into account that actions are not simply the product of the individual actor but of the system as a whole.

Here, it is useful to draw on the approach outlined by Jane Bennett, who considers the extent to which participants in an ecosystem can also be participants in a political system. Bennett herself bases her argument on *The Public and Its Problems* by John Dewey, which considers "publics" in relation to the "problems" around which they form. Social experiences of harm (such as the experience of ecological crisis) produce publics that focus on a problem and aim to effect change in response to it. Bennett writes: "When diverse bodies suddenly draw near and form a public, they have been provoked to do so by a problem, that is, by the 'indirect, serious and enduring' consequences of 'conjoint action.' Problems are effects of the phenomenon of conjoint action."[19] Bennett is here trying to produce a political theory that is adequate to an understanding of the world as a complex network of ecosystems in which agency is distributed throughout the whole system. In such a network, there is no easily identifiable efficient cause of actions, and therefore it is equally difficult to pinpoint who exactly is responsible for problems or ill health that occurs within the ecosystem as a whole.

The question that arises from this is how ethical decisions can be produced when there is a reduced sense of individual agency. If events happen as constellations of processes interacting on various scales, resonating with each other in possibly chaotic and unpredictable ways, in what sense can moral responsibility be similarly distributed across the various bodies that are interacting? In such a situation, can there be any longer a sense of individual moral responsibility for the effect of one's decisions on such a complex system of interacting events? To answer this question, it is helpful to look at the ways that Daoists have formulated ethical principles and codes historically.

Far from being a tradition characterized by skepticism or radical individualism, the Daoist tradition has produced a rich collection of community rules, precepts, and ethical texts. Livia Kohn's book *Cosmos and Community* provides a compendium of such texts that can serve as a guideline for thinking about what a Daoist approach to environmental ethics might look like. As her title indicates, one fruitful avenue of inquiry is to consider the way that ethics relate the values and demands of the community to the flourishing of the overall context in which it finds itself. That is to say, how ought the community be located within its cosmological (and indeed environmental) context?

As she explains in the opening of her book, however, the most fundamental form of ethical rule in Chinese tradition is the precept (*jie* 戒), which has the basic meaning of guarding against something.[20] It is essentially a precautionary principle that seeks to restrain human beings from behavior that is in some way detrimental to their own well-being. Kohn introduces her examination of such precepts with a quotation from Confucius's *Analects*:

The Master said: The gentleman has three things to be cautious about [*jie*; abstain from]: In his youth, when his blood and energy are not yet settled, he must be cautious about sex. In his middle years, when his blood and energy are just strong, he must be cautious about fighting. In his old age, when his blood and energy are already weak, he must be cautious about greed [gain]. (16.7)[21]

The nature of Confucius's concern is that the physical disposition of the body, driven by liquid vitality of blood and energy (*qi*), is one that changes over time and which produces certain emotional states that must be guarded against. This approach of Confucius reveals a moral framework whose goal is the preservation of social harmony, but which links that harmony to the physiological disposition of the man. The turbulent or unsettled nature of liquid vitality in young men suggests that they need to be particularly careful about sexual relations. It is the responsibility of men to restrain themselves and not fall prey to socially disruptive temptations. The same is true in middle age regarding fighting, and in old age regarding greed for power. Although Kohn does not mention this in her analysis of the text, it could be noted that this ethical framework of self-restraint depends on a sense that human physiology is constituted by forces over which the individual does not have direct control. That is to say, it already recognizes that human beings are embodied creatures in which a complex ecology of liquid forces (manifested in blood and *qi*) together constitute agential powers. The task of the morally educated human being, therefore, is to discipline himself by guarding against the excessive power of those forces within his own body. It is already to recognize a deep relationship between moral behavior and the complexity of human physiology. Morality is, in this Confucian framework, the product of the heart-mind (*xin*) disciplining the various forces of the body.

The second point is that the primary mode of ethical concern here is self-restraint. It recognizes that without self-restraint the social body can become the victim of the excessive depredations of the unruly individual. Within Confucian virtue ethics, social ills are to be solved by promoting individual virtue, focusing most especially on those with the highest degree of political power.[22] Whether or not one agrees with this approach to ethical issues, at the very least one can see that the goal is best described as "regulation." The individual must regulate the complex of forces within his own body so as to contribute to overall social harmony.

The later Daoist tradition continued this note of caution or restraint found in early Confucian moral theory and developed many collections of texts focused on precepts whose overall aim is to help guard against circumstances that may negatively affect the community or the individual. This strain of moral reasoning, though seemingly negative in its outlook, should in fact be viewed in a more positive light. The goal of self-restraint is to achieve the maximum degree of flourishing for the individual or community; it is, so to speak, advice not to shoot oneself in the foot. The crucial element here is that when one recognizes a plurality of subjective powers within the body of the individual, and within the vitality of the natural environment, the goal is to blend, harmonize, and regulate such powers so that the maximal positive effect is produced. The moral question here is not what one should aim to accomplish as a subjective individual, but rather how by restraining oneself and others from certain practices, a greater overall flourishing will be produced.

A classic example of this way of thinking is in a set of precepts extensively studied by Daoist scholars called *The 180 Precepts of Lord Lao* (*Laojun yibaibashi jie* 老君一百八十戒), the earliest extant version of which appears in a sixth-century collection of texts called the *Scriptural Statutes of the Lord Lao* (*Laojun jinglü* 老君經律).[23] As Kristofer Schipper notes, over twenty of these have to do with what we might anachronistically refer to as "environmental ethics."[24] Examples of these are admonitions against polluting wells, urinating on plants, lighting fires on plains, and bathing in rivers, in which cases the natural environment would be polluted by human activity. Another set of injunctions warns against caging birds, startling animals, wantonly whipping domestic animals, and eating meat, which would today be regarded as injunctions for the welfare of animals.

The question here is why Daoist communities would advocate self-restraint in the area of animals and the natural environment. The answer given by Schipper is that each of these injunctions implies some greater harm that will befall the individual or community if the injunctions are not followed.[25] That is to say, if one pollutes the natural environment, then it will no longer be able to function for the benefit of the human community, and this will, in effect, be counter-productive from a human point of view. Similarly, one may also infer that mistreating animals, including raising them for consumption, also produces negative effects for the individual and communal body.

The notion that these are precepts of restraint also suggests that the fundamental moral problem that human beings face is that they are incapable of properly exercising restraint and modesty, and the result is excessive violence and destruction. The precepts may be read, therefore, as documentation of what Daoists of the fifth to sixth centuries saw as fundamental problems in the world that were brought about by the lack of human self-restraint. All these issues may be read as problems that derive from the porous connections between the body and the world. They are, in that sense, ecological problems, for they are structured around how the wealth of forces inside the body produce negative effects for the community outside the body.

It is also interesting to note that in the social imagination of the fifth century the reverse was also true: the porosity of the body opened it up to potential threats from the environment. The penultimate precept reads: "During travels, if you do not have proper lodging or family, you can take shelter under trees and rocks; then recite the 180 precepts, and the spirits will come to stand guard over you, three layers deep. No soldier, brigand, demon, or tiger will dare to come close."[26] The emphasis here is on guarding one's body from predators that roam the natural world, and the text demonstrates a sense of danger as regards the impact of the world upon human beings, whether conceived as dangerous humans, spirits, or animals. It is worthwhile noting, however, that of the 180 precepts, only two are focused on protecting the individual from the environment.

The precepts, therefore, are designed for a world in which the body was seen as a complex of forces that could have negative effects upon the world; and, similarly, but to a lesser extent, the world outside was a potential realm of powers that had the capacity to harm the individual. This ethical framework paints a picture of a world in which subjectivity is not bound up in the rational, autonomous mind but distributed throughout the world and inside the body. The goal of such an ethical system could in part be characterized as defending the world outside the body from the world inside the body, and vice versa. It is an ethical system based on mutual interpenetration of the body, the community, and the landscape.

What can we learn from this Daoist ethical framework for making responsible decisions in a world that increasingly is felt as insisting its way into human bodies, social worlds, and built environments? Can the Daoist precepts give some guidance for a world of superbugs and climate instability? Although I do not wish to turn the clock back, I do think it worth exploring, on the surface at least, the idea that an ethical framework derived from a social world deeply affected by a sense of the porosity of the body to the world could be valuable for considering a posthumanist ethics where porosity is once again a key category of the social imagination.

One salient feature of the Daoist framework is that the model of what is good must be produced at the level of the health and well-being of the various bodies involved. That is to say, *The 180 Precepts* takes the maximization of human vitality as a good toward which ethical decisions should be taken. The precepts are not organized around the legalistic principle of defining harmful actions in an abstract way, but rather list prescriptions for minimizing violence to the optimal flourishing of the community. The fact that the precepts are described in the negative suggests that the chief problem facing human beings in that period was not a deficit of positive activity in the world but rather an excess of violent activity, and that in order to promote the proper degree of interactive engagement to produce the flourishing of communities, it is necessary above all else for individuals to practice some self-restraint.

The question for the present day, therefore, is not only how to encourage modesty and frugality among individuals, but rather to produce social systems that naturally favor the well-being of large-scale communities rather than individual actors. That is to say, if action is understood to be always in some sense transaction, then the scale at which moral decisions are made must be broadened to include the various elements that are functioning together to produce events. This a problem for all bodies, whether individual bodies, corporate bodies, or political bodies. The key here is to recognize that the sustainability of one of these bodies depends on the sustainability of other dimensions: human health, social-economic health, political health, and ecological health are in a fundamental way interdependent.

While it is perfectly possible for these various bodies to make rational decisions about how to maximize their own advantage in the world, it is harder to enter into the imaginative world in which one body sees its own sustainability as being embedded in that of another body. As an example of this, the effects of pollution are regularly transferred from one area of the world to another, so that, for instance, the consumer society of the West is powered by pollution created in China that compromises the health and well-being of Chinese people. Alternatively, consider the way that the worldwide battle for access to coltan, a mineral used extensively in computer networking technology, has exacerbated violent conflict in the Democratic Republic of Congo.[27] These global disasters are the accumulated effects of the failures of ethical interaction at many different levels of various bodies, whether individual, corporate, or political. They are also the consequence of the radical porosity of those bodies, in which a set of decisions taken in one place has effects not only linearly within that system over a period of time, but also more broadly across other systems and in other parts of the world.

Embodied Landscapes

The Daoist emphasis on an ethic of restraint is partially based on a sense that subjectivity emerges from the natural world and insists within human bodies. The Highest Clarity tradition of cultivation can be understood as the quest to materialize the perception of the self in the world and the world in the self. In this tradition of visualization, meditation is first and foremost an aesthetic cultivation in which the adept learns how to "see" the gods become present within the body. It is also a transformative experience in which the adept undergoes an experience of transfiguration that exposes the radical porosity of the body to the world in a positive way. As I have argued, this is a function of the locative experience of the body within the specific features of an environmental or, in this case, cosmic context.

In the modern social imagination, human beings rarely experience the porosity of the body, and rarely experience the interior dimensions of the body, except when they are sick. In these instances, the perception of a deep interiority to the body and the perception of the thinness of the skin in separating that interior from the external environment are pathologized. The aim of medicine is to restore the "thickness" of the skin and remove the sense of the depth of the interiority of the body and its vulnerability to the external environment.

The corollary of this is that it is relatively difficult to imagine how the body of the earth is itself a porous entity capable of being made ill through an excess of certain kinds of human activity. But the radical porosity of the body to the world and the world to the body means that it is possible to construct an ecological sensitivity based not only on the world pervading the body but also the human body pervading the world. Just as the Daoist tradition imagined the way in which the body functions by analogy with a mountain landscape or a cosmos, so also it is possible to imagine, and become sensitive to, the way the earth functions like a body.[28]

Rod Giblett traces expressions of this way of thinking in early modern Western views of the world as body. He quotes Leonardo da Vinci as follows:

While man [sic] has within himself bones as a stay and framework for the flesh, the world has stones which are supports of earth. While man has within him a pool of blood wherein the lungs as he breathes expand and contract, so the body of the earth has its ocean, which also rises and falls every six hours with the breathing of the world; as from the said pool of blood proceed the veins which spread their branches through the human body, so the ocean fills the body of the earth with an infinite number of veins of water. . . . In this body of the earth is lacking, however, the nerves, and these are absent because nerves are made for the purpose of movement; and as the world is perpetually stable, and no movement takes place here, nerves are not necessary. But in all other things man and the earth are very much alike.[29]

Da Vinci's goal here, Giblett argues, is not to produce a Romantic view of nature as living, breathing organism, but rather to reduce nature to its constituent parts so that it can be understood as a machine. The fact that the earth has no nervous system means that, unlike the human body, it possesses no subjectivity or consciousness, and it does not move. Giblett contrasts this approach to understanding the world as body with that of Thoreau's description of a swamp as the place where the earth gives birth to itself:

That central meadow and pool in Gowing's Swamp is its very navel, omphalos, where the umbilical cord was cut that bound it to creation's womb. Methinks every swamp tends to have or suggests such an interior tender spot. The sphagnous crust that surrounds the pool is pliant and quaking, like the skin or muscles of the abdomen; you seem to be slumping into the very bowels of the swamp.[30]

Unlike da Vinci's attempt to understand the whole of the earth by breaking it down into its constituent parts, Thoreau's description of one specific place adds layers of meaning suggesting that it is more than a single spot, but something that is pregnant with life. Giblett's argument leads to a discussion of what it means to imagine the parts of the earth like a living body from within a Chinese cultural framework. He writes:

> In Chinese cosmology and medicine the kidneys are associated with water. . . . The kidneys are the place or organ where ch'i [qi] is generated and stored. . . . Correspondingly, wetlands as the "kidneys" of the earth are the site or "organ" where the life-giving vitality of water is generated and stored. Both are places of the life-giving flow of water, not of foul stagnancy.[31]

Although Giblett does not elaborate on this observation, his approach to understanding the natural landscape from the perspective of Chinese medicine at least begins the process of developing a sensitivity to the earth by means of its analogy with the body. Like Thoreau, and unlike da Vinci, this approach produces a bond between the human body and the natural environment, a bond that is, in the first instance, affective. Thoreau describes the swamp as "tender," "pliant," and "quaking" like the living skin of the abdomen; he induces a sensitivity to the swamp by means of anthropomorphic language. Similarly understanding the wetlands in terms of the kidneys suggests that they are essential components of the whole landscape, and that to lose wetlands is like losing kidneys, producing sickness and death in the body of the earth as a whole.

Disembodied Landscapes

This empathetic approach to understanding environmental issues in terms of body stands in marked contrast to the scientific language used in wetland conservation projects in China today. For instance, the World Wildlife Foundation's project on Wetland Conservation and Resto-

Xixi National Wetland Park. (By Yoshi Canopus (own work) [CC BY-SA 3.0 (http://creative commons.org/licenses/by-sa/3.0)], via Wikimedia Commons)

ration makes no attempt to induce any sensitivity toward the loss of wetlands in China. Their website explains that "under the pressure of population growth and economic development of the last 40 years, some 13% of China's lakes have disappeared, half of China's coastal wetlands have been lost to reclamation and 50% of China's cities have no drinking water that meets acceptable hygiene standards."[32] This explanation implies that the loss of wetlands is a cost that accompanies economic development, and the reader may well conclude that such a loss is perhaps an acceptable side effect of modernization. There is no attempt here to connect the loss of wetland to the failing health of the earth as a whole, nor to the failing health of humans and other animals who depend on fresh water for their survival.

The website further describes the benefits of the wetlands in purely ecological and economic terms: "Wetlands are not only essential for ecological functions such as maintaining biodiversity, controlling floods, and the removal of pollutants, but also serve necessary economic functions in rice and fish production, transport, and hydropower energy." This language maintains the sense that human life and wetland life are connected instrumentally rather than ontologically. It suggests that the wetlands produce goods that humans need, but does not intimately or immediately connect the life of one to the life of another. It is language that extends the radical isolation of human life from that of its environmental context, rather than inscribing the one directly within the other. It presents the need for wetland conservation within the rational, bureaucratic calculus of modernity, thereby failing to recognize that it is precisely this calculus that desensitizes people to the value of the wetlands. By treating the wetlands as the producers of goods for human life, the website gives the impression that the wetlands are parts of a global supply chain providing the materials that humans need to survive, rather than something without which the earth cannot function. Wetlands cannot be transplanted from another planet. They are not simply "parts" to be replaced when worn out, but rather embody the whole of the vitality of the landscape, and by extension human health, within them. They are, in Thoreau's words, the navel connecting the world to the source of life on which it depends, or, in the language of Chinese medicine, the kidneys from which the liquid vitality of the body is generated.

Within the modern Chinese social imaginary, however, such a view of the natural world is far from dominant. In 2005, for instance, He Zuoxiu 何祚庥, a famous theoretical physicist with a high position and strong links to the government, railed against the popularity of Chinese medicine, declaring it to be unscientific. In the same year, he engaged in debate with environmentalists over the concept of "revering nature" (jingwei ziran 敬畏自然). In his modern scientific way of thinking, reverence or awe for nature was not only unscientific, but even antiscientific. He wrote:

> I want to challenge the contention that people ought to respect and hold nature in awe, advanced by one professor. He asserts that mankind should not use science and technology to transform nature, but maintain an attitude of respect and awe. Such an attitude is "anti-science," especially when we are confronting natural disasters like the tsunami or epidemic outbreaks. I hold the opposite view. We human beings should try our best to prevent and reduce losses incurred in natural disasters. Reverence and awe make no sense.[33]

The person in question was Liang Congjie 梁從誡, the head of Friends of Nature, China's leading environmental organization. Liang's response was to invoke China's traditional values, arguing that "numerous Chinese classical works have shown that we have always placed great value on nature, far more than just being a tool."[34] The invocation of traditional culture as a nationalistic argument is ultimately an unhelpful one as it reinforces the notion that traditional values are useful largely because of their being ethnically Chinese.[35] Nevertheless, it is clear that there is a debate in China about how and whether to develop a sympathetic or affective basis for the engagement of human beings and the natural world. The affective position would doubtless be strengthened if it were presented not as an argument against the rational calculus of modernity but within a posthumanist transactional framework of energetic interaction, as I have argued can be constructed from a Daoist philosophical orientation.

Further evidence of the way that the modern social imagination of nature in China reinforces the separation of humans from the natural world can be seen in the development of national parks or other protected spaces. The move to create national parks was accompanied, in the West at least, by the creation of legal frameworks akin to trust funds, in which the decisions about how to make use of a resource would be made by a committee, or "trust," rather than by an individual. These aimed to ensure that the trustees consider the long-term interests of the trust from a dispassionate perspective and were designed to forestall short-term thinking, personal corruption, or other hindrances to ethical decision-making.[36] In this way, the trust "preserves the environment" by effectively placing responsibility for it in the hands of a committee. The problem with this approach is that it "has the effect of forestalling more radical considerations of the relationship between humans and the environment because it accepts the basic premise that nature is to be preserved in some authentic state."[37] In the modern social imaginary, the key value of nature is that in its "natural state" it is authentic to itself, and that human engagement with the natural world must in and of itself be regarded as inauthentic or corrupting in some way.

Evidence for the strength of this view in China can be found in Robert Weller's discussion of the formation of national parks in China.[38] China's first nature reserve was founded in 1956, but the emphasis was placed almost completely on "scientific research rather than conservation, education or tourism."[39] More recently, however, China has established nature reserves following models of UNESCO's biosphere reserve project and the World Conservation Union's model for nature reserves. As Weller notes, these models tend not to follow the U.S. model of protecting large areas of land by designating them as wilderness areas free from human habitation. Rather, they allow for various levels of human engagement with nature. The biosphere reserve system, for instance, designates a core area where no human activity except for scientific research and monitoring is allowed, a buffer zone where some tourism and economic activities consistent with environmental goals are permitted, and an outer zone where "local inhabitants, governments, and all others work together for sustainable development."[40] As Weller notes, however, none of these systems share the traditional Chinese idea of seeing humans and nature together as part of a single anthropocosmic vision. Rather, they deploy the modern idea of protecting nature from human beings, albeit to varying degrees. The notion of a core area where humans are not permitted at all, and a buffer zone where limited activity takes place, precisely materializes in spatial form the modern notion that humans and the natural world are ideally to be kept separate from each other and should engage in only limited ways.

An example of this modern social imagination of the environment can be found in the Xixi National Wetland Park, just 5 kilometers from Hangzhou's West Lake. The wetlands area was previously home to several small villages containing traditional thatched-roof houses, where locals practiced sericulture and fishing along the many streams that traverse the wetland area. Today, all the locals have been moved out of the area, and this traditional complex of culture, ecology, and economy has been thoroughly modernized. In this process, the housing has been carefully preserved so that people can see how the locals used to live, and traditional opera performances are put on in the village squares for the benefit of tourists. Small restaurants serve traditional dishes to tourists in disposable plastic bowls. A complex of modern hotels stands at the edge of the park, next to a modern shopping plaza and a wetlands museum. The several small Buddhist and ancestral temples patronized by the former villagers have been turned into museums to "preserve" the ancient way of life that formerly took place in the environment. The wetlands park is also host to an aquatic ecological reserve, which, aside from conserving many species of fish, other water creatures, and plants, also serves as a bird sanctuary. In many ways, the Xixi National Wetland Park is a modern ecological success story, but it reveals much about the position of nature and traditional culture in the social imagination of modern China.

The continuity of culture, ecology, and economy that previously constituted the space can no longer be seen. Instead, the wetlands have been transformed by the modern social imagination under a new paradigm of ecological ordering. The area is physically fenced off from the "real world," and tourists must pay a hefty fee to enter. Once inside, it is clear that "tradition" and "nature" are no longer valued as operative categories that shape human lives and livelihoods but are "preserved" as in a museum. China's new middle class thus has a chance to observe how in former times tradition, nature, and culture functioned together. Thus preserved, nature and culture can be observed by all, made profitable by entrepreneurs, and enjoyed as a new leisure activity.

This modern social imagination can also have particularly difficult political implications, as Qi Jinyu notes in his study of the Sanjiangyuan Nature Reserve, located at the headwaters of China's three major rivers systems, the Mekong, Yangzi, and Yellow.[41] This area, which occupies 363,100 square kilometers of the Qinghai-Tibetan plateau, supplies 25% of the Yangzi's water, 49% of the Yellow River's, and 11% of the Mekong's. It thus plays a key role in supplying fresh water for drinking and also for hydroelectric power upon which China's economic development depends. The ecological condition of this area has been severely depleted in recent years, leading to its designation as a national nature reserve with the official approval of the State Council in 2002.

Given the national significance of this area for China's ecology and economy, the decision was taken to relocate the nomadic Tibetan herders who have traditionally lived in this area. Although there was no strong evidence that their activities were responsible for the degradation of the ecosystem, the designation of this area as a national nature reserve provided the justification for the euphemistically titled "ecological migration" in which the tribespeople were forcibly relocated and urbanized. The goal was both the social and economic development of the Tibetans and also the ecological protection of the nature reserve. From within the modern Chinese imagination, these two activities could be completed only by separating the one from the other. That is to say, human economic activity and the protection of the environment are understood to be mutually incompatible. Rather than trying to find a creative way in which the goals could be served together, in which the Tibetans could contribute through their activities to the protection of the nature reserve, the government took the decision in 2005 to separate these two activities completely, with a plan to force forty thousand Tibetans off their traditional land, disrupting their traditional nomadic lifestyle, and resettling them in towns, at a cost of some 243 million RMB.[42] Anthropologist Jinyu Qi writes:

In the popular Chinese social imagination, most people pursue wealth and status, are keen to blend into modern life, and look forward to escaping from the countryside in order to participate in modern urban life. This may explain why many scholars and experts thought that setting up the Sanjiangyuan Reserve and implementing a programme of ecological migration would be a good way to deal with the ecological crisis and also help local herdsmen attain a comfortable standard of living.[43]

As can be seen here, the logic of this social imagination makes it difficult to consider that there may be other alternatives, and that what is good for one group of people may not necessarily be good for another. Rather than creatively imagining the natural landscape and its inhabitants in localized terms, and considering how the two may function together to promote the flourishing of both, the modern Chinese social imagination produces human activity and the natural world as mutually exclusive others, and produces a totalizing view of each, refusing to admit cultural or environmental differences. In such a logic, the ideal is to protect the one from the other, whether through forced migration such as in Qinghai, or in the ecotourism areas such as the Xixi National Wetland Park. In contrast to the ethics of restraint, resonance, and mutual relationship, the modern Chinese imagination of nature reinforces the disconnection of the modern middle classes from nature by producing it along with traditional culture as a world to be consumed in carefully managed ways. Traditional complexes of culture and ecology, whether in China's wealthy east or its poorer west, are displaced in favor of modern strategies of management, consumption, and administration.

7 From Modernity to Sustainability

Having examined some particular ways in which religion, culture, nature, and environment have been framed together in the Chinese experience, we now return to the theoretical questions posed in chapter 1, and in particular to think about the alternatives going forward. This chapter focuses on the question of how to rethink Daoism from the perspective of an emergent paradigm of sustainability. The next chapter focuses on the question of how to rethink sustainability from the perspective of Daoism.

Given the way that religion and nature have been framed from the perspective of modernity, it is hardly surprising that modern Western scholarship on Daoism has largely ignored the significance of Daoism as a culture relevant to the construction of ecologically sustainable societies. Rather, it has been dominated by thoroughly modern discussions regarding the differences between science, philosophy, religion, and theology. When Sinologists attempted to explain what Daoism "is," they naturally deployed these kinds of categories, derived from the modern Western cultural imagination, to analyze and debate Daoist thought and practice. Joseph Needham, for instance, dedicated his life to understanding the way science developed in China, and how this development was related to fundamental Chinese understandings of "nature" and its "laws." This necessarily involved extensive historical investigations into Daoist philosophy, religion, and cultivation practices, but his operating goal was to understand Daoism (and other aspects of Chinese civilization) from the perspective of their contribution to scientific development. In so doing, he produced an enormous body of valuable work, but his question was how Chinese civilization contributed to the development of science, and the ways that it did not. It is clear that this very powerful and highly productive mode of scholarship involved interpreting Daoism and other Chinese traditions from the perspective of categories within Western culture. This is not to imply any sort of negative value judgment about the scholarship produced in this way, but simply to acknowledge that a dominant mode of historical scholarship about Daoist culture and civilization has been from the perspective of modern Western theoretical frameworks. Those frameworks permit scholars to ask certain kinds of questions and to produce valuable knowledge, but this mode of scholarship does not always contain within itself the ability to question the assumptions that underpin the questions it asks.

Daoism and Modernity

The first modern attempts to translate Daoist texts into English were undertaken by James Legge, a Scottish missionary who later became the first professor of Chinese at Oxford University.[1] He is responsible for creating the dominant paradigm by which Daoism has come to be understood in the English-speaking world, as a tradition made of both "philosophy" and "religion." Of course, many religious traditions contain with themselves aspects that could be classified as philosophy. The important point about the way that Daoism has come to be framed, however, lies in what Louis Komjathy refers to as a "bifurcated interpretation."[2] In this interpretation, the dimensions of "philosophy" and "religion" that are found within the Daoist tradition are separated into two distinct strands that can be given separate histories, separate terminologies, and separate interpretations. This is, on the face of it, rather odd, as it would be clear to Legge and his contemporaries that Christian history, for instance, is replete with examples of the integration of philosophical and religious thinking. Augustine and Thomas Aquinas, for example, produced profound philosophical work from within the framework of their self-identification as Christians. Other examples could doubtless be given from Islam,

Buddhism, and Hinduism, all of which have stimulated deep philosophical inquiry that has complemented the self-understanding of religious
practitioners. Why should Daoism be different? Why should Daoism be
understood as containing two distinct threads, one a philosophical tradition and one a religious tradition?

The answer to this question lies in the way that the religious traditions
of Judaism, Islam, and Christianity frame religion as a belief system that
originates in a book. In one sense, the chief difference among those three
religions is that each possesses a different understanding of where and
when divine revelation came to an end. With Judaism it is the Torah,
with Christianity it is with Jesus, and with Islam it is with Mohammed
and the Koran. These three traditions distinguish themselves by reference to what they regard as canonical religious revelations. Given this
basic framing of how to understand religious identity not in terms of religious practice, but of scriptural authority, Legge's quest to understand
China similarly led him to translate what he regarded as the classic works
of Chinese civilization. As a result, the earliest body of scholarship about
Daoism was built upon understanding Daoism from the perspective of
just two early classics, the Daode jing and the Zhuangzi. These two texts
do not look like religious texts in the way that the Koran or the Bible looks
like a religious text because they do not purport to be the product of
divine revelation from a unique creator god. Nor do they contain instructions for how to manage relationships between a self-evidently "human"
world of creatures and a self-evidently "divine" world inhabited by an
eternal, uncreated deity. From this perspective, they are not "religious"
texts in the way that Legge or his coreligionists could have understood
"religion."

At the same time, when it comes to the practical functioning of Daoism, it is immediately clear that Daoism "looks like" a religion in the sense
that it has temples, priests, monks, rituals, gods, and altars. Daoism was
thus from the very beginning a perplexing tradition for Western scholars.
How could it be that something that did not originate with a sacred text
like the Bible could become something that in its ordinary operations
looks a lot like Catholicism? The answer that Komjathy gives is that "the
conventional presentation suggests that so-called 'philosophical Daoism,'
associated with the Daode jing and the Zhuangzi, is 'original' or 'pure
Daoism,' while so-called 'religious Daoism' is a 'degenerate' and 'superstitious' adjunct to the former."[3] In other words, the categories by which
Daoism originally came to be framed conceptually were reinforced and

materialized through a historical explanation: Daoism, it would appear, began as one thing, philosophy, and transformed into another, religion. It is hard to underestimate the power of this framing, because once these categories were fixed in the scholarly mind, it then became desirable to look for historical "evidence" to fit in with and reinforce this explanation.

In this regard, two pieces of evidence are regularly adduced, one conceptual and one material. The conceptual evidence draws on the fact that there are two terms regularly used in Chinese to denote what we in English term "Daoism." These are "Daojia" 道家 and "Daojiao" 道教. The term *jia* means "family" or "school," and the term *jiao* means "tradition" or "lineage." Neither of these terms self-evidently means what in English is termed "philosophy" or "religion," and there is no evidence to suggest that until very recently there was a strong categoreal distinction between the two in the way that there is between philosophy and religion. As Komjathy notes, the term Daojiao was deployed by the Daoist scholar Lu Xiujing 陸修靜 (406–477) not to distinguish Daoist "religion" from Daoist "philosophy," but to establish Daoism (Daojiao, the tradition of the Dao) as an equal alternative to Buddhism (Fojiao, the tradition of the Buddha).[4] In articulating Daoism as a *jiao*, Lu Xiujing was making the claim that the Daoist tradition was capable of meeting, engaging with, and standing as an alternative to Buddhism, which was, at this time, establishing itself strongly in China. The category was deployed not for reasons of internal self-identification but over and against a perceived other, namely, Buddhism. In this sense, therefore, one can say that Buddhism provided the first reason for Daoism to define and identify itself as something like a "religion." But this does not mean at all that before this period Daoism did not function like a religion, only that with the arrival of Buddhism as a foreign religious tradition in China, it became necessary for Daoists to redefine and rearticulate their own sense of identity and religious belonging. Of course, this caused a transformation within Daoism as it more strongly adopted the outward form of Buddhist religious traditions such as organized, single-sex monasteries, but there is no evidence to suggest that there was nothing like religion before Daoists articulated their tradition as a *jiao*.

The historical argument that is often made regarding the relationship between Daoist "philosophy" and "religion" is that there is no material evidence of formal Daoist religious organizations until the Later Han dynasty, which saw the arising of two religious movements, the Way of Great Peace (Taiping dao) and the Way of the Orthodox Unity (Zhengyi dao) in the middle of the second century c.e. The latter movement was established, according to tradition, by one Zhang Ling, later known as Zhang Daoling, who claimed to have received a revelation from a now divinized Laozi, the purported author of the earlier "philosophical" text, the *Daode jing*. On the basis of this revelation, Zhang declared that a covenant between the gods and humankind was now established, in which humans would be given some power over the spirit world and would be able to cure diseases in exchange for the ritual confession of sins. To this date, one main tradition of Daoism traces its lineage back to Zhang Daoling and claims to perpetuate the covenantal authority originally given to Zhang by the god Laozi.

Given that this religious tradition bears a strong similarity to Christian and Jewish concepts of a covenant between god and the people, and a strong similarity to the tradition of papal authority passing down from St. Peter onward generation after generation, it is not surprising that Western scholars should be quick to identify this as a religious tradition. It so obviously parallels Western religions in its concept of a covenant between a god and humans, in its ritual emphasis on the forgiveness of sins, and in the claims to divine authority for priestly power. No wonder scholars quickly identified this as clear evidence of Daoism as a historical religion.[5] But if these three characteristics (a covenant, the forgiveness of sins, and a priesthood) become essentialized as necessary characteristics for what defines a religion, then it becomes impossible to regard earlier Daoist traditions as self-evidently religious. Since Zhang claimed to be the originator of these religious claims, it follows that before Zhang there could be nothing like this religion in Chinese history. Of course, while this may be true, it does not mean that there was nothing religious about Daoism, only that there was nothing religious in precisely the same ways that Zhang's movement could be understood to be religion.

From this discussion it would seem that arguing about what Daoism is or is not is like playing a game of football where the goalposts are constantly being moved. That is to say, religion is itself a category that has no immediately self-evident definition but is the product of scholarly creation, or the internal efforts of religious practitioners to define their identity in relation to what they perceive as challenges from outside, such as Lu Xiujing's response to the emergence of Buddhism as a powerful cultural force in China.

When we turn to Daoism in modern China, the situation is even clearer. In the nineteenth century, Chinese scholars first learned about the Western concept of religion. The term for this, *zongjiao*, was first invented in Japan, and then brought to China. It is a term that is quite negative-sounding to Chinese ears, meaning something like "sectarian teachings." The emphasis here is not on "religion" in the singular as a unifying concept to be found within many different civilizations, but rather on "religions" in the plural: sectarian teachings, vying for adherents and social power. As Prasenjit Duara made clear over twenty years ago, the status of such teachings came into conflict with the nascent modern Chinese state.[6] Some teachings were deemed to be local traditions focused on local gods and therefore a potential threat to the establishment of the modern nation-state, which was desperately trying to assert its authority in the face of external colonial threats and internal regional factionalism. Other teachings were deemed to be "superstitions" and at odds with the project of building China as a modern "scientific" country.[7] At the same time, the whole notion of religion as tradition ran counter to the ideology of modernizers, both Communist and Republican, who sought to overturn the old imperial order and the sociocultural apparatus that invested it with authority and meaning.

After the Communist Revolution of 1949, the state took the project of modernizing religions to its logical conclusion, administratively defining, classifying, and structuring legitimate religions and legitimate religious activities. Protestant sects were forcibly ecumenized under the banner of a single patriotic association. Daoist traditions were brought under the guidance of a single, national Chinese Daoist Association, in which the more organized, monastic tradition of Quanzhen Daoism was favored over local, communal traditions. Community temples with no formal Daoist religious association, but which were previously the location for many rituals performed by Daoist priests, were often closed or turned into schools or other cultural sites. In such cases, it is easy to see the power of the modern classification of religion, drawing ultimately on the Western experience of, construction of, and classification of religious identity.

Ironically, the project begun by missionaries over a hundred years ago to understand, identify, and classify Chinese religious activity came to be most fully realized by a formally atheist Communist Party. In adopting a Western-derived framework for understanding religion and especially religion in relation to the state, China embarked on a project to deny its own cultural heritage and perpetuate, albeit in a transformed way, an ideological project that was conceived by European missionaries and allied to the colonial ideologies of Western powers.

The issue here is that to raise in China the question of Daoism in relation to the question of sustainability is to invoke as profound a perplexity and befuddlement as faced early European interpreters of Daoism. Daoism, defined by the state as a sectarian tradition (*zongjiao*), operates within controlled limits, at specific sites, and under guidance from the State Administration for Religious Affairs (Guojia zongjiao shuwuju 國家宗教事務局). The notion that it might have social power, transformational ideas, or even a positive role in contemporary society is hard for many people to comprehend. The only way to do so would be to decolonize China's own understanding of itself and its own religious traditions. This puts any outsider in a difficult position, because decolonization is not something to be carried out from the outside. Chinese Daoists, however, operate within the limits established by the state and are able to carry out their own religious activities in historically valid ways, but they have little room to maneuver in terms of questioning the framework within which they operate. But this is the task of intellectuals whether insiders or outsiders, and from this point of view it hardly matters whether one is Chinese or not. My approach to constructing Daoism as an intellectual tradition depends on a kind of internal dialog between my reading of the tradition and my concern for contemporary environmental issues. In this regard, it is quite idiosyncractic, but I hope nonetheless it produces insights that resonate with people both inside and outside China. The project of undoing modernity's powerful construction of normative social orders across the world is one that demands the participation of people everywhere.

Despite the overwhelming evidence of China's massive environmental problems, contemporary Sinology has paid relatively little attention either to understanding the nature of this problem or to understanding how China is attempting to chart a new model of economic and social development, largely through massive urbanization projects, that will enable it to survive the coming ecological challenges.[8] One reason for this is that although there are many scholars of China in Western universities, their training has largely been dominated by the traditional Sinological concern to understand China from the perspective of the past: to understand the core motifs, values, and concepts that have driven Chinese civilization and defined its unique characteristics.[9] One could also argue that this project has, in turn, been adopted in China through its rehabilitation of Confucius as the icon par excellence of Chinese civilization who, in the Axial Age 2,500 years ago, is said to have defined the overarching trajectory that Chinese civilization would take even to the present day.[10]

Sinology and Sustainability

Two problems immediately ensue from a traditional approach to the study of China. The first is to regard Confucius and Confucian values as the dominant beat driving the rhythm of Chinese society and culture. Of course, Confucius, or more importantly the tradition that was invented in his name, is a key element of the Chinese cultural DNA; but, so are Buddhism and Daoism, the other two of China's "three teachings." Confucius has been given a paramount position by the government because he is associated with a humanistic, pragmatic tradition that does not directly challenge the atheistic values of Marxism. The second, and greater, problem is not to do with Confucius himself, but rather the broader Sinological tendency to theorize China from the perspective of the past rather than the future, to understand China today in terms of the key values and concepts from the "classics." Put together, this produces an understanding of China as a "traditional" culture seasoned in "Confucian values," albeit one whose traditions were ruptured by a modernity imported in part from the West. This historical framework thus produces such questions as "how do traditional Chinese values continue to influence modern Chinese society?" or "in what sense is China a nation founded upon a civilization?"[11]

The concept of sustainability, however, has the power to radically transform this mode of scholarly enquiry into history, tradition, and modernity, and the basic cultural pattern of thinking it inspires in the wealth of popular books about China. When sustainability becomes the orienting question for a culture, no longer can that culture be focused on the past as the origin and source of its identity. Rather, in an age characterized by the evident unsustainability of contemporary social, cultural, and economic patterns, the basic orienting framework must perforce come from the future, from the perspective of an era that does not yet exist but which one hopes will. Sustainability, then, is a paradigm driven by unimagined hope for the existence of a future world.

To produce religion from the perspective of sustainability is therefore to produce a radical transformation in how to think about religion in its fundamental relationship to the category of modernity. Gone are the questions of "tradition" or "innovation." Gone too are the fundamental questions of the relationship of religion to the state, the preeminent political ordering produced by modernity. Both these sets of questions are transcended by the larger orienting question of the capacity of cultural frames to produce sustainable modes of living. Questions of ecology and economy thus come to the fore.

From this perspective, the skills of traditional Sinological scholarship seem less relevant to the task of imagining a sustainable future for China. Traditional Sinological methods train scholars to produce interpretations of classical Chinese civilization, its art, culture, literature, history, and philosophy. Such scholars are not immediately prepared to grasp the significance of their areas of scholarship as regards the contemporary issue of sustainability. Nor are moderns, habituated into an imagination of cultural and religious traditions as legacies from the past, useful chiefly for the production of nationalistic values, or as sources of moral training that can protect children from the wealth of choices that modern consumer society has to offer.

The question of the relationship of cultural traditions to sustainability is one that is not immediately obvious within the logic of modernity, and it is not one that traditional scholarship is organized so as to grasp. Duara gives a clue as to the scale of rethinking that is required in his discussion of the relationship among transcendence, globalization, and modernity in Asian civilizations.[12] There, he argues that the classic Weberian question of why modernity was produced in the West and not in Chinese or Indian civilizations should be stood on its head. Given that modernity has produced an "*overreach* in the conquest by man of nature," the important question should now be what moderns can learn from Asian civilizations in order "to examine whether they allow a more viable cosmological foundation for sustainability."[13]

From such a perspective, therefore, the reason for examining China's cultural traditions is not to study Daoism for the sake of Daoism or China for the sake of China, but to theorize Daoism from the future perspective of sustainability: to imagine how future scholars will rewrite the discourse of tradition, including the discourse of Daoist studies, from the vantage point of a culture of sustainability that does not yet exist, and to imagine how cultures and religions will be produced not from the perspective of a dichotomy between tradition and modernity but from the perspective of a paradigm of sustainability.

Scholars of China, and Asia more broadly, know that the twenty-first century is already an Asian century, a century of Shanghai or Seoul or Bangalore or Jakarta. But they also know that while the forces of urbanization, modernization, technology, and globalization produce seismic shifts in society, they do not necessarily reproduce the values of modern secular Western culture. Religion and other distinct cultural traditions continue to thrive in Asia, all the while reinventing themselves, and in the process rewriting the discourse of modernity, from multiple perspectives and from beyond the hegemony of the West. From this perspective, the narrative of modernity in relation to tradition is already shown to be deficient, or, in Duara's terms, an "overreach." As China invents new forms of modernity, and even eschews modernity as an organizing paradigm in favor of other transcendent values and principles of self-identification such as "harmony" or "civilization" or even "sustainability," it increasingly rejects being framed by the questions that have driven classic academic scholarship, and in particular Western approaches to Sinology.

Perhaps the best example of recent Sinological writing on religion in China can be found in Vincent Goossaert and David Palmer's book, *The Religious Question in Modern China*, which explores religion from the perspective of its shifting place in Chinese society under the process of modernization.[14] As this excellent book makes clear, modernity in fact produces religion as a question, as a problem that appears under the gaze of scholars. The idea that modern scholarship in a real way "invents" or "creates" religions as a problem to be articulated and theorized is a position most forcefully articulated by the American scholar J. Z. Smith.[15] But from the perspective of sustainability, the fact of religion is not necessarily a question or a problem to be solved. Sustainability, as an overarching cultural paradigm, does not "produce" religion in the same way that modernity, as an overarching cultural paradigm, does. Rather, the paradigm of sustainability asks what worldviews, values, and social networks can produce the continuity of the human species together with the ecological systems of the planetary biosphere.

For Daoist studies to participate in the construction of a new discourse that integrates Sinology and sustainability it must ask two basic questions: to what extent can Daoism be construed together as both "green" and "religion"; and in what sense can this construction of Daoism be helpful in theorizing and enacting a sustainable future for China and beyond? To construct this new discourse involves two different modes of scholarship that have been woven together throughout the book, but it is useful to distinguish them here.

The first mode of scholarship can broadly be called "ecotheory" in that it attempts to provide a theoretical orientation for scholarship that integrates the study of Daoism, nature, and religion. This approach not only concerns Daoism, but more generally how the study of religion and nature can profit from a Daoist theoretical approach to the world. In so doing, it diverges from the majority of existing scholarship on Daoism in that it does not reproduce the same orienting questions that have historically prevailed in Sinological scholarship. It does not aim to produce a historically nuanced understanding of Daoism as one of China's great cultural traditions; it does not aim to show how Daoism functioned within Chinese society so as to reproduce or authorize certain normative social hierarchies; and it does not aim to produce new historical knowledge about China that can further cultural relations between West and East.

Rather, this approach aims to articulate a theory: a way of seeing the world that is pragmatically useful for the construction of a social, economic, political, and spiritual ordering of the relationships between human beings and their natural environment. It does so by constructing a normative argument through a process of theoretical inquiry, ecocritical readings of Daoist texts, and ethical construction. It is "Daoist" in the sense that it draws on, interprets, and reimagines some of the core motifs and values of Daoist tradition. In this way, Sinology from the perspective of sustainability functions like applied philosophy explaining how the values and concepts of a tradition can be applied to a contemporary situation that was not previously experienced or encountered.

Accompanying this theoretical framework for theorizing Daoism and sustainability have been new, ecocritical readings of Daoist practices, texts, and contexts. The goal of this ecocriticism is to produce new readings of the Daoist tradition, ones that have not previously occurred in Sinology or religious studies as traditionally conceived in the modern West. The aim of such an approach in the past was to elucidate what scholars see as the "essence" of "religion," and if not the "essence" then at least the "features" or "elements" that jointly or severally characterize religious traditions. A typical example of this approach is that of Ninian Smart, who articulates "seven dimensions of religion":

The seven are as follows (the order is rather random):

1. The ritual or practical dimension . . .
2. The doctrinal or philosophical dimension . . .
3. The mythic or narrative dimension . . .
4. The experiential or emotional dimension . . .
5. The ethical or legal dimension . . .
6. The organizational or social dimension . . .
7. The artistic or material dimension.[16]

There is much to be commended in the way that Smart highlights dimensions of religious life that are of interest to him, and the multifaceted way in which he approaches the phenomenon of religion allows him to bring a wide array of cultural practices under the rubric of "religion." The point of this approach is to establish a framework for producing religion as an object of study. This is eminently useful for first-year world religions classes. It enables people to see "narrative" as a key element of religion and thus to compare the way that narrative functions in Hindu or Babylonian creation myth. It allows students to examine religious organizations from the perspective of the unique ways in which religious communities order themselves over and against dominant social systems for distributing labor and economic activity.

This approach, however helpful it may be in the production of religious studies as a discipline, is not helpful in producing the kinds of ecocritical readings of Daoism that I have been attempting in this book. Ecocriticism, as conventionally understood, involves producing understandings of texts that highlight the representation of nature. On a more engaged level, it also involves producing critical discourse oriented toward effecting change in the relationship between humans and the natural world. As Simon Estok writes: "Ecocriticism is any theory that is committed to effecting change by analyzing the function—thematic, artistic, social, historical, ideological, theoretical, or otherwise—of the natural environment, or aspects of it, represented in documents (literary or other) that contribute to material practices in material worlds."[17]

There is, on the face of it, no reason why religious texts should not be subject to the same critical reading as other literary texts, except insofar as the critic feels a burden of deference to religious traditions and organizations as communities of practice and belief who produce what they regard as authoritative interpretations of their own religious texts. As an academic scholar of religion, while I remain cognizant of the power of

religious readings of religious texts, I do not view such internally produced religious interpretations as definitive or in principle superior to
alternate readings of such texts. Religious texts are not necessarily the
exclusive property of religious insiders. Moreover, the framework articulated in the previous section functions as a motivation and also a structure by means of which to read such religious texts, regardless of how
religious people of their time may have read them, and regardless of how
contemporary religious leaders may read them. This does not, however,
grant me, or anyone else, free license to read texts in any way. Rather, all
readings are to be argued and articulated according to clearly expressed
principles.

For this reason, it is helpful to be clear as to the purpose of such
ecocritical readings. They are not an attempt to link "religion" with "nature" as though these were two distinct dimensions of reality. I am not
interested in seeing how Daoist texts "portray" nature or help us to
"appreciate" nature as a phenomenon that somehow stands beyond the
production of texts. My argument is that an ecocritical reading of Daoist
texts and practices documents how Daoist texts and their accompanying
worldviews in fact function to produce a view of nature at the same time
as they produce a view of Daoist religion. What is at stake here is not simply how we read texts, but how we can reorient the way in which we see
the relation between texts and nature, signs and reality.

In discussing Lawrence Buell's seminal text, *The Environmental Imagination*, Dana Phillips notes:

> Buell like other ecocritics falls prey to the false hope that there is
> some beyond of literature, call it nature or wilderness or ecological
> community or ecosystem or environment, where deliverance from
> the constraints of culture, particularly that constraint known as
> "theory," might be found. Do not get me wrong: I think there is a
> beyond of literature. There is, for example, nature. I just think that
> nature cannot deliver one from the constraints of culture, any more
> than culture can deliver one from the constraints of nature.[18]

I share with Estok and Buell the notion that ecocritical readings of literary texts should aim not simply toward the goal of "reading" but also
toward the goal of "effecting" action or change as regards the human
engagement with the natural world. But, I also share with Phillips the
wariness that this way of phrasing ecocriticism might falsely suggest

that "nature" is something beyond the world of "theory" or "criticism," to be "saved" or "preserved" as the material substrate upon which our literary or religious imaginings are projected. Rather, the purpose of my ecocritical readings of Daoist practices, texts, and contexts has been to show how such texts in fact "produced" nature in the experience of Daoists. That is to say, although such practices and texts may not have been directly concerned with the way in which nature was produced and represented, nevertheless, this is in fact what they did. Previous readings of such texts, including my own, have focused on elucidating the religious meaning or theological dimension of such texts, or their social-historical context, and have focused on explaining Daoism as a religious system of belief and practice. My argument here is that at the same time as Daoists produced religious visions of gods, transcendence, and spiritual ideals, they at the same time produced nature as a sphere of activity within which (whether or not they consciously or thematically grasped it) they functioned.

In this way, my ecocritical reading of Daoist practices, texts, and contexts has aimed to show how exactly nature was produced in the Daoist imagination, how it was engaged, and how this production was directly correlated with the production of religious experience. This new approach to Daoist texts and practices reveals what I believe has been a relatively overlooked analysis of Daoism in particular, and religion in general. Such readings have focused on understanding Daoism from the perspective of "religion" as a "supernatural" category because Daoism has been, as it were, pretheorized by the Western bifurcation of nature and supernatural, or material reality and religious ideology. As a result, scholars of religion have not sought to examine the way in which Daoism produces visions of and engagements with the natural world.

At the same time, my hope is that in demonstrating how Daoism theorized the supernatural and the natural together as part of the overall functioning of the subjective agency of the Dao, an alternative, practical reading of human engagement with nature can emerge from this, one that need not be limited to Daoism or Chinese approaches to sustainability but one that can inform the environmental humanities more broadly.

8   From Sustainability to Flourishing

Anyone who has spent time in China over the past decade inevitably alights on one adjective to describe the experience: fast. Whether looking at China's dizzying economic growth that has lifted some five hundred million people out of poverty in the past decades, or China's ever-expanding network of bullet trains carrying millions of people across the country at speeds of 300 kilometers per hour, or China's plan to move four hundred million people from the countryside to the city, it seems that China's headlong dash toward an unrealizable utopian modernity is taking place at breakneck speed. Set against this stunning and rapid social transformation, the question of nature and religion seems somewhat quaint. What place does the natural world really have, except as a location of poverty to be fled, or as a destination for rich Shanghainese ecotourists? What place could religion or tradition have, except as a form of conservative nostalgia for a world that no longer exists? As I indicate in this final chapter, the value of thinking nature through Daoism, and Daoism through nature, lies in part in the ability to construct new ways of thinking sustainability and then new ways of conceiving environmentalism as a social and political movement. My hope is that this new discourse can play a role in shaping China's conception of an "ecological civilization" in a way that has relevance not just for China but for the global environmental movement.

Despite the phenomenal growth in scientific understanding about ecological systems, the human impact on the environment, and global warming, all the data suggest that we are exceeding even the worst predictions of scientists ten years ago. If one were to assess the carbon emissions caused by environmentalists, politicians, and academics flying round the world to discuss sustainability, one might even say that the environmental movement has made a step in the wrong direction. Why is this the case? Why has sustainability not become embedded in contemporary society in the face of overwhelming scientific evidence in its favor? Reading Daoism from the perspective of nature and nature from the perspective of Daoism takes on all the more significance because the environmental movement in the West has by and large been a failure.

Ecomodernists such as Michael Shellenberger and Ted Nordhaus were perhaps the first to argue that the environmental movement was incapable of addressing the depth of the environmental crisis.[1] They strongly criticized the strategy of "saving the planet" and argued forcefully that it should be replaced by one of massive technological innovation, social development, and environmental adaptation. In 2015, they joined forces with other scholars to publish their "Ecomodernist Manifesto,"[2] which argues that since the human domination of the natural world is inevitable, the only reasonable course of action is to make this domination as viable as possible for all concerned. They quote approvingly the notion that the earth has entered the age of the Anthropocene, a term given by earth scientists to denote a new geological era in which the actions of human beings are the determining factor in the future evolution of life on the planet. In such a situation, they argue, the ideal that humans must somehow "harmonize" with nature is impossible to uphold. Rather, they argue that humans should "use their growing social, economic and technological prowess to make life better for people, stabilize the climate and protect the natural world."

An alternative approach to the recognition of the failure of environmentalism is spelled out by Gus Speth, the former dean of Yale University's School of Forestry. In 2008, he argued that the environmental movement requires, more than anything else, a new broad-based politics in order to reverse the tide of failure. He writes:

This will require major efforts at grassroots organizing; strengthening groups working at the state and community levels; and developing motivational messages and appeals—indeed, writing a new American story, as Bill Moyers has urged. Our environmental discourse has thus far been dominated by lawyers, scientists, and economists. Now, we need to hear a lot more from the poets, preachers, philosophers, and psychologists.[3]

While Speth shares with Shellenberger and Nordhaus the sense that an environmental movement focused on technical solutions and policy changes has been too narrowly based, his approach to the question of sustainability is focused more clearly on the social, cultural, and political domain, rather than that of technology. No matter whether technological development enables humans to exist more lightly on the earth, the unpredictability of climate change, the rapid rise in the human population, and the economic development of Asia, Latin America, and Africa will likely require the formulation of new values, ethics, and politics that go beyond the paradigm of modernity. While I share the sensibility of ecomodernists that environmentalists have not been nearly radical enough, I share Speth's conviction that any effective environmental movement requires a new political and ideological discourse formed from resistance to, rather than acceptance of, the patterns of historical meaning-making that underpin the modern rush to embrace an ever more technologically dazzling future.

Clearly, the environmental movement is in flux, and within this flux, new ways of thinking about the relationship of culture, technology, and ecology are emerging. In China, there is also a widespread debate about how to reconcile the demands for social and economic development with the demand for environmental protection. Up to now, China's environmental movement has largely followed that of the global environmental movement, focusing on the three key instruments of technological development, policy change, and environmental legislation.[4] Technological development can help generate energy more efficiently and with a lower impact on the environment. In terms of broad-based social policy, the Chinese government continues to mandate population controls, though the former "one-child policy" was expanded in 2015 to make two children the normal maximum. On the one hand, the one-child policy reduced the number of consumers, but at the same time it enabled China to become a richer country with a greater per capita ecological impact than before. Broad-based policy changes must also be accompanied by legislative frameworks so that the power of the state can be applied in a rational way to enact these policy changes and realize these technological developments for the benefit of the people. But as Pan Yue, China's vice-minister of environmental protection, makes clear, environmental legislation is only practically effective when there is broad public consent as to its validity. Strict environmental laws fail if all they do is give polluters an incentive to move to another jurisdiction, or if prosecutors have little interest in pursuing these cases. To back up technological, policy, and legal reform, Pan Yue argues that it is necessary to create a culture of ecological sustainability, or, in contemporary Chinese terms, "ecological civilization" (shengtai wenming 生態文明).[5]

The Chinese government's deployment of this term has yet to be fully assessed. It is not yet evident what this term implies for the future of China's economic growth and social development. Nonetheless, such a term suggests something more comprehensive than traditional techno-scientific approaches to dealing with environmental problems and has the potential to engage with alternative theories of sustainability that involve at the very least ecological sustainability, equity, and the fair distribution of resources among people. Typically, sustainability discourse also aims to unify these various dimensions into a holistic paradigm. Educator Andreas Edwards explains that sustainability involves the integration of at least the four dimensions of awareness, understanding, concern, and commitment:

1) an awareness of the profound spiritual links between human beings and the natural world; 2) a deep understanding of the biological interconnection of all parts of nature, including human beings; 3) an abiding concern with the potential damage of human impact on the environment; and 4) a strongly held commitment to make ethics an integral part of all environmental activism.[6]

Lucas Johnston, in his discussion of the concept of sustainability, notes that "nearly all definitions of sustainability envision a re-orientation of the 'metaobjectives' of a society, whether it is a new ethic, an alternative anthropology, or a new vision of where humans stand in relation to the rest of the world or cosmos."[7] Sustainability, then, is at the very least a conceptual framework that challenges modernity as a social, political, and cultural organizing principle. It also implies a new worldview, complete with narrative framework and ritual habits to inculcate in people the feelings that provide the social and psychological justification for ecologically responsible decisions. Without such feelings, rituals, and narratives, sustainability remains a technical term that may resonate in the corridors of government but that does not have a widespread social impact. With the right cultural framework, sustainability moves from a technical policy discourse to popular practice. When sustainability is embedded in broader culture, it has the chance to shape the habits of thinking and the patterns of behavior in ways that people barely notice. In short, it comes to define people's way of life, their civic values, and their sense of identity.

The difficulty that China faces is that such an "ecological civilization" at a deep level contradicts the culture of modernity that has shaped China over the last one hundred years and the value of rapid economic development that has shaped it over the last thirty years. Modernity, as a cultural framework, produces a sense of human beings oriented fundamentally by time that progresses in a linear, nonrepeatable, and progressive way. As Wang Hui notes, "This conception of time as evolving, progressive and irreversible not only provided us with a way of reading history and reality, but also incorporated the entire meaning of our existence and struggles into a progression of time, a sequence of ages, and a set of future goals."[8] In this particular sense, therefore, the culture of sustainability stands as a refusal to embrace the paradigm of modernity. Sustainability, at least as conventionally understood, suggests a model of maintenance and stability, not of infinite linear progress. In fact, the extension of contemporary cultural and economic values into the future in an unlimited way is precisely what the culture of sustainability seeks to reject.

In this regard, the paradigm of sustainability also draws for its legitimacy on the new sciences of evolution, ecology, and the environment. Evolutionary science teaches that our thinking selves are the product of 13.7 billion years of cosmic evolution. Although the linear story of evolution is clearly a product of modernity as a pattern of thinking about history, it also relativizes human history by enclosing it within a much larger framework, namely, the deeper history of the universe story. From this larger perspective, human agency within linear time is eclipsed by a deeper sense of cosmic time produced by the drama of the cosmos itself.

The sciences of ecology and environment also challenge the modern sense of historicity by inscribing human life within the broader systems of vitality that make the human species possible, and by construing the value of human action not through an overarching historical narrative about the production of patterns of freedom and individuality, but through the impact of human beings on the worlds that they inhabit and affect in powerful and sometimes destructive ways. The movement for ecological sustainability depends on embedding the holistic picture that has emerged in the new sciences into the operative norms of our culture. This requires confronting and transgressing the conventions of modernity conceived, ultimately, as the production of a linear pattern of historical meaning.

Inasmuch as modernity produces meaning chiefly within the realm of history, and posits the creation of the future, or "innovation," as the chief goal of human livelihood, it also produces the "environment" as the backdrop against which such history takes place. So long as environmentalists advocate the preservation of the environment as simply the backdrop for the production of human meaning, they deepen the logic of modernity in which meaning is produced solely within the realm of human historicity. And so long as ecomodernists urge people to respect, heal, or value nature as an object beyond the hermetically sealed walls of their bodies, they unconsciously reinforce the default dualisms that posit an absolute separation between human beings and their lived environments. What is necessary, therefore, is to rewrite the discourse of ecological sustainability so as no longer to perpetuate the false reification of nature as a thing outside human bodies and no longer to imagine that meaning is the product of human subjectivity within a purely human historical framework.

To create a culture of ecological sustainability depends, then, on a deeper transformation in the way that people feel and perceive their place in the world. In my view, sustainability at its deepest level is an aesthetic transformation, changing the way human beings sense, feel, and cognize their location in space and time. It is consequently an ethical and a political transformation in which human civilizations learn to produce meaning not by fleeing the terrors of an imagined past for the comforting arms of an imagined future that lies perpetually beyond the horizon, but rather in cultivating well-being from the engagement of the human species with the forms of vitality that emerge constantly within and beyond us.

A key term that operates within the Daoist tradition to define Daoist praxis is that of "cultivating the Dao" (*xiudao*). While this may seem a somewhat innocuous term and call to mind all manner of cultivation practices that may be familiar from Buddhist, Hindu, or Confucian traditions, the notion that Dao should be the object of one's cultivation rather than oneself, on the face of it, requires some explanation. A more familiar term within Confucian discourse might be "self-cultivation." Here, the Confucian is trained to develop his or her own "self" so as to promote ever greater harmony between, and integration of, self and world. Confucius famously described this as a lifetime process in which only the willfully persistent and long-lived disciple could manage to achieve something close to sagehood, defined as the integration of self-identity with the will of heaven itself.[9] In this way, the adaptation of self, social ethics, and external circumstances (fate, or the will of heaven) could be defined as the ultimate spiritual task for the Confucian. But the Daoist task, identified as cultivating, enhancing, or developing the Dao, takes on something of a different characteristic. It suggests that the reality that frames the self-understanding of the individual, or we might say the "environment," is something that is capable of being shaped or enhanced in some way through the cultivation activities of the practitioner. That is to say, Daoist spiritual cultivation does not seem to imply the passive acquiescence of the practitioner to his or her circumstances (following the will of heaven), but rather a lively engagement with it within an overall ecology of cosmic power.

The view of sustainability that ensues from this is not of preservation or maintenance but of creative flourishing. This idea thus directly challenges the notion of sustainability as demanding the "maintenance" or "conservation" of the natural environment. Indeed, such a notion depends on the idea that the environment is largely to be understood as a collection of resources that must be carefully managed in such a way as to preserve enough for future generations. The notion of preserving nature as a pristine and immaculate "garden of Eden" free from human activity respects neither the transformative power of nature itself, nor the natural desires and operations of human beings as part of nature.

The notion of cultivation can thus be defined as the deliberate pursuit of a process of transformation in which one thing slowly becomes something else. Within the Daoist tradition, this takes place in the arenas of spiritual practice, martial arts, music and poetry, ritual performance, philosophical reflection, tea-making, alchemy, medicine, and calligraphy. All these arenas, many of which would not ordinarily be captured by the English word "religion," were, and continue to be, regularly practiced by Daoists as part of their cultivation work. It is not the arena in which cultivation happens that defines Daoism: it is the mode in which that cultivation takes place, and its relation to the foundational conception of Dao. For this reason, cultivation must be regarded as involving some kind of transformation and not as the preservation of the status quo. If the goal of the Daoist monk is to engage in the transformation of Dao, then it is inevitable that this should in some basic sense involve the transformation of his or her "environment," whether through music, religious ritual, medicine, martial arts, or other performative acts.

At the same time, however, given that Dao grounds the multiple subjectivities of the natural world, producing an abundance of transformation and vitality through the heavens and earth, the process of cultivation demands that humans also transform as part of this cultivation process. The flourishing that emerges from this is one in which both the self and the world transform together to continue to flourish within the overall ecology of cosmic power. The way this transformation takes place can be understood in four levels, akin to Edwards's four features of sustainability (awareness, understanding, concern, and commitment), as defined previously. These four levels are cultivating the aesthetic of flourishing; cultivating the ethic of flourishing; cultivating the politics of flourishing; and cultivating the spirituality of flourishing.

The Aesthetics of Flourishing

Cultivating the aesthetics of flourishing means learning to cultivate the porosity of the body, so as to feel the transformative power of the multiple subjectivities that constitute the environment in which the body lives. Daoist traditions developed a range of techniques for cultivating the sense of the body in relation to the cosmos, and recent studies suggest that body cultivation disciplines can produce not only a transformed sense of one's own body but, crucially, a transformed sense of one's own body in relation to the world. The first example of this is an autoethnographic study by Denver Nixon, who discusses his experience of modern *qi* cultivation practices. Specifically, he is interested in how his own experience of his body changed as a result of those practices. He begins by noting that, ordinarily, only when people are ill do they develop this kind of "dialog" with their own bodies. He writes:

Kathy Charmaz . . . describes the manner in which those suffering from chronic illness tend to develop a dialectic self, comprised of the physical self and the monitoring self. By going through the ordeal of illness, people develop a heightened sense of awareness of their own bodies, and can thus respond to their body's needs. This monitoring self, once created, usually remains after the illness has subsided. Regarding her ill body, Sara Shaw explained, "I got to know it; I got to understand it . . . I got to respect it . . . [I got to know] how my body was doing, how my body was feeling."[10]

Most people, however, when they are healthy do not have a sense of their own bodies as things that constitute their own identity: they are not truly aware that they are embodied beings until their body stops functioning "normally." Nixon then uses this as a springboard for explaining how the practice of qigong (the discipline of *qi* cultivation) affected his own perceptual sensitivity:

During my research, it seemed that qigong also cultivated sensitivity and awareness, but in a way that did not objectify and thereby bifurcate experience along an inward/outward fracture. That is, the awareness generated through the practice of qigong does not stop at the skin, but rather "knows" the body as whole and part of its environment.[11]

Nixon suggests, therefore, that even basic *qi* movement practices can have the effect of reshaping the mode of awareness of one's body within its lived environment. In his experience, *qi* cultivation led to an increased sensitivity to the emerging context of his lived world and overcame the conventional bifurcation of reality into subject and object. It did so by improving "perceptive depth" and transfiguring the mode of bodily perception and engagement with the lived environment.

In the second example, a recent study of tai chi practitioners in the United Kingdom suggested that there is evidence for what Ulrich Beck calls a "cosmopolitan vision of ecology" in such physical cultivation practices.[12] Beck's notion of a cosmopolitan vision of ecology derives from his idea that a new, green modernity requires a new vision for prosperity, one that is not determined wholly by economic growth, but overall as "well-being."[13] The idea of well-being, from a Daoist perspective, must pay

A tai chi practioner at
Mt. Heming, Sichuan
Province. (Author)

attention to the idea of the insistence of the natural world within the
body, and the notion that the well-being of the porous body is ultimately
dependent upon the well-being of its context. The development of heightened perceptions of the porous body must then require the practitioner
to be concerned not only with his or her or own transfigured body but at
the very least also with the local environments and contexts in which that
body performance takes place.

The authors of the study refer to D. V. S. Kasper's idea of an "ecological
habitus," which refers "to the embodiment of a durable yet changeable
system of ecologically relevant dispositions, practices, perceptions, and
material conditions—perceptible as a lifestyle—that is shaped by and
helps shape socioecological contexts."[14] While it may be easy to dismiss
such practices as being solely focused on the "lifestyle" of the individual,

these studies suggest that the point of such practices is that they engage the individual as a "practitioner" and also engage with the way in which those individuals are shaped by and shape their contexts. From the perspective articulated in this book, this implies the development of a transfigured sense of the body as porous to a world of insistent subjectivity, not simply a social context of relationships, habits, and practices, but also a natural, liquid context of breath, vitality, and power insisting within and pervading the body of the individual.

The Ethics of Flourishing

The cultivation of an aesthetic must necessarily be the foundation for the cultivation of an ethic of flourishing. Given that the body is a body precisely because it lives within a context, any sense of the self as being indwelt by the material world produces a deeper perception of, and sensitivity to, the context in which one's body lives and breathes. This is at one level a social context, but it is also, in the contemporary Chinese world, an ecological context in which people's health is routinely compromised by the polluted environments in which they live.

The sensitivity to the porosity of the body thus leads to the development of ethical sensibilities characterized in Daoist tradition as simplicity, purity, and the gradual lessening of the ego. One way to understand this ethical tradition is in relation to the production of violence in society. At one level, the engagement between the individual and his or her context must involve some change, some consumption, and even death. All processes of life are transactions within an ecology of cosmic power in which one form of life is absorbed, ingested, and transfigured by another. From this point of view, violence is at some level built into the process of transformation. One can live only at the expense of something else. While contemporary consumer capitalism in essence legitimizes the freedom of the individual to construct his or her own life through the endless consumption of natural resources, and the productive labor of others, Daoist ethical codes were resolutely focused on the minimization of violence as a mode of relationality.[15]

From the *Daode jing* onward, Daoists have been horrified by the state exercise of violent power in ways that do not promote the goals of ethical cultivation. The *Daode jing* (chap. 30) states that "when the ruler of the people is assisted by the Dao then the force of weapons is not used in the world."[16] The next chapter states that "weapons are the tool of ill omen" and that the noble man uses them only "when he cannot do otherwise. . . . To regard [weapons] with delight—this is to enjoy the killing of people. Well, by enjoying the killing of people, one is unable to get what one wants in the world."[17] The author of this saying is clearly not a pacifist, neither in the sense that he does not engage in violence, nor in the sense that he absolutely withdraws from the world. Rather, the question is how best to accomplish what is ultimately desirable. The only answer given is negative: delighting in killing will prove ultimately fruitless. In this case, it is not the act itself but the attitude of the actor that is key. The author of this passage, therefore, advocates the transformation of the world through a mode of activity that does not involve delight in weaponry or warfare. But, it does define transformation as a goal and it does recognize that transformation may involve violence. The ethical question is what kind of violence is necessary, and what attitude one should have to violence.

To be alive, therefore, is to have a body that is porous to the world. This necessarily involves the consumption and transformation of the world's resources. Cultivating a sensitivity to this eternal process of consumption thus produces an ethical sensibility in which consumption is not pursued as a goal in and of itself but rather solely as a means toward the ethical transformation of both the human and the greater ecological world. The notion of the porosity of the body thus demands an ethic of responsibility in which the individual allows the other to insist within his or her own body and is mindful of the way his or her own insistence impinges upon the subjectivities of others. This latter point is key, because all too often it seems that contemporary Chinese culture has absorbed the first point—that the natural world produces an profusion of vitality for the human body—without considering the ethical dimensions of relationality that this entails. The result of this can be seen in the increasing consumption of rare and exotic animal and plant species due to the belief that they are beneficial for the human body. Despite international treaties to end the trafficking in pangolins, for instance, news media continue to report the consumption of black market pangolins among wealthy Chinese. The Pangolin Specialist Group estimated in June 2014 that over one million of these creatures had been taken from the wild in the past decade and that populations across Asia were "in precipitous decline."[18] While this tradition is clearly rooted in traditional Chinese cultural beliefs about medicine and well-being, it also draws on the fact that modernity produces a disenchanted social affect in which the natural world is felt as something purely to be consumed and not part of any ethic of relationship.

In relation to this particular concern for endangered species, it is worth noting that the Daoist tradition has consistently rejected blood sacrifices at temples, and that Daoist monks and nuns have long adopted vegetarianism as part of their ethical code. The rapid growth of the middle class across the world has produced an exponential increase in the numbers of animals farmed on an industrial scale for human consumption. It also comes at severe ecological cost as large amounts of energy, water, and chemicals are used solely to grow animals for food. In contrast, traditional Chinese agriculture over a century ago produced levels of food with relatively low amounts of meat and without the use of chemical fertilizers.[19]

A second ethical relation that derives from the aesthetic of the porous body is a renewed sensitivity to the landscape as a body that lives and breathes. In such an understanding, the land itself can become sick, just as the human body can become sick. This is evident in contemporary China in the phenomenon of "cancer villages" where industrial pollution has made the groundwater so toxic that inhabitants have experienced vastly increased rates of cancer.[20] Here, we see the mutual permeability of the body and the landscape: the water and soil are made toxic by the industrial pollution produced by unchecked industrial activity. As a consequence, the ground itself becomes "sick." Secondly, the porosity of the human body to the landscape means that this "sickness" is shared by the humans who live in that area. The mutual porosity of bodies and landscapes thus entails an ethic of relationship between humans and their local contexts: this is not simply a matter of social relations, but also considers the relation between the body and the local landscape. Indeed, human ethics must take place within the context of ecological ethics, because ensuring the health of local biospheres always already entails ensuring the health of the human bodies that mediate human social relations.

Whereas in traditional societies it might have been possible to consider ethical relations solely as regards the human world, the vast scale of human activity now demands an ethic of mutual relationality between the land itself and the humans who inhabit it. This might, in the Western ethical tradition, involve assigning "rights" to animals, ecosystems, or aquifers, as some environmental lawyers argue,[21] but the Chinese context might also benefit from drawing on indigenous values based on the idea of transaction within an ecology of cosmic power. This could simply involve the promotion of the concept of interdependent mutuality, or "stimulus and response" (*ganying*), a basic ethical value, widespread within Daoist and traditional Chinese culture. At its simplest level, this notion suggests that human moral actions, both positive and negative, produce equal reactions upon the actor. If such a value were as widely promoted as Confucian moral values of filial piety, or modern nationalistic values such as patriotism, it would go a long way to mitigating the impact of the rapidly growing Chinese middle class on the large-scale extinction of species.

The Politics of Flourishing

To cultivate an aesthetic and an ethic of flourishing might suggest that this is a process that is to be pursued at an individual level, that the process of "transfiguration" required to enact a culture of flourishing is something that begins and ends at the level of the individual. I would like to argue, however, that although transfiguration begins with the individual, it does not necessarily end there. Individuals can engage in a gradual process of expanding the range of transfiguration through engagement with their local landscapes, whether it is their backyards, their balconies, or their local parks. In so doing they take charge of their own immediate spaces and cultivate a sense of engagement with the subjectivity of nature, overcoming the boredom and apathy that modernity produces in individuals as regards to the natural environment. While such individual transactions are clearly key to cultivating a politics of sustainability, it would be particularly invidious to suggest that responsibility for ethical action is distributed equally across all levels of society. The ecological crisis is as much a crisis of justice, as the economic culture of late-modern capitalism produces increasingly uneven patterns of wealth across the world. As a result, the rich are largely able to insulate themselves from the effects of global environmental devastation, while the poor feel its effects more keenly. This is particularly true in regard to relations between China and the West where the West (and also the new Chinese rich) enjoy consumer goods at relatively cheap prices while the environmental costs are borne by the poor in China and across the developing world in terms of industrial pollution or dangerous levels of air quality.

From this point of view, the cultivation of flourishing also demands a transfiguration of human politics. Politically speaking, I believe this need derives from an inability to pay attention to the voices of local contexts. It is a fault in Chinese politics that gives overwhelming power to the center and an increasing emphasis on the cultivation of nationalism and patriotism. Environmental leaders such as Pan Yue, for instance, conflate the process of creating an "ecological civilization" with the goal of nationalist development:

> The rejuvenation of the Chinese nation is a century-old dream—the unremitting pursuit of Chinese people living all over the world. A key foundation of national revival is cultural revival. The rise in the culture of environmentalism in the world creates a great opportunity for the revival of Chinese culture. The development of a socialist environmental culture with Chinese characteristics is to strive for the revival of Chinese culture and the rejuvenation of the Chinese nation.[22]

While contemporary Chinese leaders might be understandably keen to focus on the "rejuvenation" of the Chinese nation and the pursuit of a "Chinese dream," this cannot be achieved at the expense of rural spaces, marginalized peoples, or through prejudice against ethnic minorities. An example of this was given earlier in terms of the forced migration of the Tibetan herders in the Qinghai-Tibetan plateau. National concerns for the protection of water in China's three major river systems forced the Tibetans to be relocated against their will. The work of Chinese scholars, however, suggests that this move may not have been necessary at all. However, once national values were invoked, there was nothing that could be done by local authorities to resist the overwhelming power of the central government.

Given that China's constitution and the Communist Party's constitution have together created a powerful central government, one in which functionaries work their way up from local to provincial and to state level in search of increasing power and authority, the result is perhaps inevitably a failure to pay attention to the way that national policies produce devastating environmental effects at the local level. One response to this might be that the local level fails properly to implement the directives issued from higher up, and that local politics is prey to the powerful and corrupt interests of local business. At the same time, it may well be that the reverse is true: it is precisely because the local level is impoverished politically, financially, and educationally that such failures are likely. In short, if China is to develop a culture of ecological sustainability, it will inevitably have to give higher priority to local pressures, local government, and local politics. Rather than resisting such protests as the NIMBYism of a local citizenry that fails to appreciate national priorities, perhaps these protests could be viewed as the emergence of a politics focused on the local, where people's experience of and engagement with the natural environment is felt most keenly. The political notion here is that "everywhere is local to someone."[23]

An argument often made by Western scholars about developing an environmental culture in China has to do with the relative lack of democratic politics in China's communist system. Judith Shapiro, for instance, argues in *Mao's War Against Nature* that Mao's disastrous environmental policies were abetted in part by the lack of democratic representation that could have resisted the urgency of his utopian fantasies. At the same time, she argues, democracy could have helped local areas resist the efforts to impose standard models of development across China in ways that were entirely unsuitable to their local contexts.[24] While there have been some successful efforts of local cultures to resist the policies of the central government in China,[25] it is not necessarily the case that democracy in the form of "one person, one vote" is in itself the solution.

One of the key transformations of modernization is the process of urbanization. In what has been called the greatest migration in human history, China's urban population is expected to reach one billion by 2030, its cities accounting for one in eight people on the planet.[26] In such a situation, the vast majority of China's wealth and power will be concentrated in the highly modernized, urban centers. A democratic system based on the concept of one person, one vote will effectively further empower the values, affects, and sensibilities of the urban classes, to the detriment of China's poorer, rural, and agricultural areas. From the perspective of a Daoist notion in which human flourishing resides in the flourishing of the collective subjectivities of the natural world, such a concentration of power is unbalanced. A democratic system would need to be tempered by a democracy of the local space. In such a system, some measure of political power would be distributed evenly across rural and urban areas, giving a voice to rural spaces, wild and relatively uninhabited spaces, and the spaces home to ethnic minorities on the margins of

China's current political system. The aim of such a system would be to achieve a balance of interests between the urban majority and the rural minority on whose life and livelihood the urban centers are ultimately dependent. In so doing, it would help inscribe the politics of urban modernity within the overall functioning of an ecology of cosmic power, ensuring that the decisions made by the urban elite are also in the interests of the rural regions that provide the food and water that make urban life possible.

Moreover, given that the Daoist concept of cultivation is rooted in the capacity of nature to produce growth and change from within itself, it is particularly important for democratic politics not to surrender wholly to the affect of compliance produced by the banal, regular spaces of modern cities. Although the project of massive and rapid urbanization may provide economic benefits to Chinese citizens, it will also increasingly inscribe them within regimes of obedience that primarily serve the interests of the state. This is hardly in China's long-term interests if it is to foster cultural creativity, social development, and scientific progress.

The Spirituality of Flourishing

For some, the achievement of a politics of flourishing should be the goal of China's "green religion," which implies that the overall positive function of religion in the contemporary world is to reshape politics and transform the social order into one that is ecologically sustainable and flourishing. The interpretation of the Daoist tradition offered here, however, suggests that the religious concept of transfiguration should be the final goal of such a transformation. Flourishing, from this point of view, is not about changing society and politics so as to enable future generations simply to continue what the current generation has been doing, but rather transforming both the self and the world to produce an overall continuity of flourishing. While environmentalists might be interested in this from the perspective of transforming ethical and political relationships, this process can also be understood from a deeper, spiritual perspective. At the spiritual level, the transformation of the world and the flourishing of vitality involve the question of death. All transformations within the ecology of cosmic power produce the death of one state and the emergence of another. In fact, the flourishing of vitality in and around the human world demands also the constant death of things, whether consumed as food, used up as natural resources, or destroyed through medicine to promote another kind of life. How, then, should we respond to the production of death all around us, its relation to the ongoing process of the creation of life, and the transformation of death into something that is ultimately productive?

The main contribution of the Daoist tradition to this question has to do with its refusal to imagine death as the end point of life, but rather to theorize life and death together, like yang and yin, as a continuous mode of production in which one thing transforms into another. The spirit world (the realm of "dead" agents) interacts and engages with the material world (the realm of "living" or "predead" agents). Both these worlds constitute each other in an overall process of transformation, or Way. From this perspective, the continuous production of vitality is at the same time the continuous production of death. Managing the relationship between life and death is thus a key function of religion.

To theorize religion from this "Daoist-inspired" viewpoint is to consider religions in terms of the collective symbolic representation of violence, the ritual performance of violence, and the ethical management of violence as the principal mode of relating life and death together in the world. This approach shares with many others the emphasis on religious systems as providing collective symbolic representations of aspects of human culture.[27] This means that religious traditions function as networks of symbol systems that both represent human interactions with reality and also construct those interactions, shaping the ways that human beings experience, and derive meaning from, their experience of the world. These symbolic systems are enacted through social performances in religious rituals, whether collective, public rituals or private behaviors through which the individual engages in cultivation practices. Religious systems, moreover, manage key ethical issues regarding the production of violence in the world, such as which animals may be eaten, how animals may be killed, how to sacrifice animals to gods, in what circumstances outsiders may be killed, and the like.

To those familiar with Catholic Christianity, this framework for theorizing religion should resonate well. The Christian Eucharist can be interpreted as a rich meditation on the violent death of Jesus and the celebration of his resurrection. Symbolically, Christians drink Jesus's blood and eat his body and thereby ingest his resurrection life, and thus they win the assurance of their own resurrection. Contemporary Catholic moral theology, moreover, is focused on questions of life and death, including abortion and sexuality, and maintains a steadfast opposition to the death penalty. Similar interpretations could be adduced for other traditions, including, for instance, the South Asian adoption of ahimsa, or nonharm, as a core value in Hinduism, Buddhism, and Jainism, with each of those traditions distinguishing itself from the others on the basis of how precisely to understand and implement this doctrine.

In this regard, religion as a collective system for the representation and ritual conduct of violence shares much in common with sport, another mass cultural system devoted to the promotion of controlled violence. Perhaps it is not surprising that religious people could develop an affinity with martial arts or other cultural practices centered on the ritual performance of violence. But given that death is the ultimate act of violence, it would seem that a key social function of religion, however, is to provide rites for the disposal of the dead and a symbolic framework through which human beings can interpret the transition from life to death in a way that is productive for the community. Notions of resurrection, immortality, transcendence, afterlives, and reincarnation make the ultimate violence of human death into something transformative and conducive to the ongoing vitality of human communities.

The relevance of this interpretation of religion for the purposes of ecological flourishing is tragically clear. Humans are pursuing the death of the natural world, the extinction of species, and the collapse of the biosphere through the rapidly increasing human population accompanied by an increasing rate of consumption of natural resources. The issue is not simply whether nature should be "saved" or species should be "preserved," but that of managing the quality and quantity of human "violence" so that it produces new life, new possibilities, and creative transformation. How should the human species mourn the death of nature? How could this mourning promote a new collective identity and an ultimately sustainable form of shared belonging in the world? How can consumption be reframed in positive and creative ways rather than as the desire for endless innovation, technology, and consumer goods? How can technology enhance and preserve the ongoing vitality of the world rather than contribute to its gradual death? The fact that human cultures do not grasp these questions at present demonstrates our inability to collectively symbolize the interactions between nature and human beings together in a way that promotes the ongoing viability of the human species. To do so requires the collective social imagination not that we can save nature, but that nature can save us.

To interpret Daoism from the perspective of sustainability and to interpret sustainability from the perspective of Daoism is, in the end, to begin to decolonize Daoism and decolonize nature. It is to recognize the power of Daoist culture to resist and reframe the false dichotomies inherent in modern categories of understanding, and simultaneously to recognize the subjectivity of nature and its capacity to resist human attempts to colonize it, whether through the unending depletion of natural resources or through our attempts to "save" it in national parks. It is, instead, to propose a much richer vision of nature's capacity to infuse human life with meaning and to articulate strategies for human livelihood that are based on nature's capacity to allow the maximal flourishing of human life.

Crucially, however, this new vision is not produced first and foremost by the adoption of a new "worldview" or "way of thinking" about the world centered on sustainability as a "concept." Rather, it is produced by a new (or perhaps rediscovered) aesthetic experience of the local world in the personal body. From this experience can flow more sustainable ethics of performing the body in the world and more sustainable politics of inhabiting the landscapes that give liquid vitality to all. Rather than the impossible and ceaseless quest for innovation, the relentless desire for more consumption, and the projection of hopes into an impossible and unrealizable future, an ecological aesthetics founded upon the sensitivity of the porous body produces ethics, cultures, and politics grounded in the ecology of cosmic power. Through this reintegration of nature and culture, the multiple subjectivities of the natural world that emerge from the unfathomable liquid vitality of the Dao transfigure human lives in an unceasing process of transformation and flourishing.

Notes

Introduction

1. The concept of a normative culture that I draw on here derives from Robert Cummings Neville, *Normative Cultures* (Albany: State University of New York Press), 1995.

2. Gary Gardner, *Invoking the Spirit: Religion and Spirituality in the Quest for a Sustainable World*, Worldwatch Paper 164 (Washington, DC: Worldwatch Institute, 2002), 12.

3. James Miller, "Is Religion Environmentally Friendly? Connecting Religion and Ecology," in *Controversies in Contemporary Religion, Education, Law, Politics, and Spirituality*, ed. Paul Hedges, vol. 2, *Debates in the Public Square and Ethical Issues* (Santa Barbara, CA: Praeger, 2014), 156.

4. The relationship of academic scholarship to the views of believers, commonly known as the insider-outsider debate, is clearly one that is complex and contentious. For a full discussion of the various positions, see Russell T. McCutcheon, ed., *The Insider/Outsider Problem in the Study of Religion: A Reader* (London: Continuum, 1999).

5. Weiming Tu, "Implications of the Rise of 'Confucian' East Asia," *Daedalus* 129, no. 1 (2000): 195–218. See also his essay "Cultural China: The Periphery as the Center," *Daedalus* 134, no. 4 (2005): 145–167.

6. Bruno Latour, *We Have Never Been Modern*, trans. Catherine Porter (Cambridge, MA: Harvard University Press, 1993), 9.

7. Michael LaFargue, "Hermeneutics and Pedagogy: Give Me That Old-Time Historicism," in Gary Delany DeAngelis and Warren G. Frisina, eds., *Teaching the Daode jing* (New York: Oxford University Press), 169.

8. Michael LaFargue, *The Tao of the* Tao Te Ching (Albany: State University of New York Press, 1992), 201.

9. Hans-Georg Moeller, trans., *Daodejing* (La Salle, IL: Open Court, 2007), 79. Of the many translations of the *Daode jing*, Moeller's is framed by a philosophical approach that I have found helpful for my own interpretation.

10. "DZ" refers to the index to Daoist texts in the *Ming Zhengtong Daozang* (Daoist canon of the Ming Zhengtong reign period) in Kristofer M. Schipper, *Concordance du Tao Tsang: Titres des ouvrages* (Paris: Publications de l'Ecole Française d'Extrême-Orient, 1975). An updated encyclopedic overview of all these texts can be found in Kristofer Schipper and Franciscus Verellen, eds., *The Taoist Canon: A Study of Taoist Literature in the Daozang of the Ming Dynasty* (Chicago: University of Chicago Press, 2008).

11. Julius N. Tsai, "Reading the 'Inner Biography of the Perfected Person of Purple Solarity': Religion and Society in an Early Daoist Hagiography," *Journal of the Royal Asiatic Society* 18, no. 2 (2008): 206.

12. See Bron Taylor, *Dark Green Religion: Nature Spirituality and the Planetary Future* (Berkeley: University of California Press, 2010), for an analysis of how modern nature spirituality can challenge (even violently) modern social order.

13. Lai Chi-Tim notes that this rejection of conventional practice was not because of a common ground or interest shared with the ruling authorities. It derived, rather, from the Daoist theological system in which the Dao, arising from nonbeing, has no shape or form. Lai's argument is based on the notion of a religious rivalry, in which Daoists were seeking to demonstrate the superiority of their own religious rituals and theological system. Clearly, however, such an opposition ran counter to prevailing norms and would also upset the social and economic system centered on the popular temples. It is not simply a religious response, as though religion can be separated from other aspects of culture and society. See Chi-Tim Lai, "The Opposition of Celestial-Master Taoism to Popular Cults During the Six Dynasties," *Asia Major* 11, no. 1 (1998): 13.

1. Religion, Modernity, and Ecology

1. Talal Asad, *Formations of the Secular: Christianity, Islam, Modernity* (Stanford, CA: Stanford University Press, 2003), 21–66.

2. Michael B. McElroy, "Perspectives on Environmental Change: A Basis for Action," *Daedalus* 130, no. 4, special issue: *Religion and Ecology: Can the Climate Change* (2001): 31–57.

3. Emile Durkheim, *The Elementary Forms of the Religious Life* (New York: Free Press, 1965).

4. See Robert Bellah, *Religion in Human Evolution: From the Paleolithic to the Axial Age* (Cambridge, MA: Harvard University Press, 2011).

5. Stephen Prothero, *God Is Not One: The Eight Rival Religions that Run the World* (San Francisco: HarperOne, 2011).

6. Indeed, I was one of the coeditors of the volume on Daoism and ecology published in that series.

7. Jennifer Lemche, "The Greening of Chinese Daoism: Modernity, Bureaucracy, and Ecology in Contemporary Chinese Religion" (M.A. thesis, Queen's University, Kingston, Canada, 2010), http://hdl.handle.net/1974/6035.

8. See especially the collection of essays in N. J. Girardot, James Miller, and Xiaogan Liu, eds., *Daoism and Ecology: Ways Within a Cosmic Landscape* (Cambridge, MA: Harvard University Center for the Study of World Religions, 2001).

9. This is discussed in further detail in James Miller, "Daoism and Nature," in *The Oxford Handbook of Religions and Ecology*, ed. Roger Gottlieb, 220–235 (Oxford: Oxford University Press, 2006).

10. James Miller, "Is Green the New Red? The Role of Religion in Creating a Sustainable China," *Nature and Culture* 8, no. 3 (2013): 249–264.

11. Der-Ruey Yang, "New Agents and New Ethos of Daoism in China Today," *Chinese Sociological Review* 45, no. 2 (2012–2013): 49.

12. Bron Taylor, *Dark Green Religion: Nature Spirituality and the Planetary Future* (Berkeley: University of California Press, 2010), 10.

13. Kristofer Schipper, "The 180 Precepts of Lord Lao," in Girardot, Miller, and Liu, *Daoism and Ecology*, 79–93.

14. See Talal Asad, *Genealogies of Religion: Discipline and Reasons of Power in Christianity and Islam* (Baltimore, MD: Johns Hopkins University Press, 1993).

15. Charles Taylor, *A Secular Age* (Cambridge, MA: Harvard University Press: 2007), 37–38.

16. Taylor, *A Secular Age*, 307.

17. Ernest Gellner, *Culture, Identity and Politics* (Cambridge, UK: Cambridge University Press, 1987), 153.

18. Steve Pile, *Real Cities: Modernity, Space, and the Phantasmagorias of City Life* (London: SAGE, 2005), 1; emphasis in the original.

19. Jane Bennett, *The Enchantment of Modern Life: Attachments, Crossings, and Ethics* (Princeton, NJ: Princeton University Press, 2001), 9.

20. See, for instance, Paul Waldau and Kimberly Patton, eds., *A Communion of Subjects: Animals in Religion, Science, and Ethics* (New York: Columbia University Press, 2006).

21. See, for instance, Gavin D'Costa, Paul Knitter, and Daniel Strange, *Only One Way? Three Christian Responses to the Uniqueness of Christ in a Religiously Pluralist World* (London: SCM Press, 2013).

22. See Brian Thomas Swimme and Mary Evelyn Tucker, *Journey of the Universe* (New Haven, CT: Yale University Press: 2013).

23. Bruno Latour, *We Have Never Been Modern*, trans. Catherine Porter (Cambridge, MA: Harvard University Press, 1993), 43.

24. See Bronislaw Szerszynski, *Nature, Technology, and the Sacred* (Oxford: Blackwell: 2005).

25. Stephen Jay Gould, "Nonoverlapping Magisteria," *Natural History* 106 (March 1997): 16–22.

26. Latour, *We Have Never Been Modern*, 11.

27. Paul Bourdieu, for instance, discusses the way that class privilege structures the dominant tastes of societies in *Distinction: A Social Critique of the Judgement of Taste* (New York: Routledge, 1986).

28. Ulrich Beck, *Risk Society: Towards a New Modernity* (London: Sage Publications, 1992), 19.

29. Sino Daily, "Rising Sea Levels Present China with Unimaginable Challenges," February 16, 2007, http://www.sinodaily.com/reports/Rising_Sea_Levels_Present_China_With_Unimaginable_Challenges_999.html.

30. Mayo Clinic, *MRSA Infection*, September 9, 2015, http://www.mayoclinic.org/diseases-conditions/mrsa/basics/causes/con-20024479.

31. Alex Broom, "Infection Control: Why Doctors Over-Prescribe Antibiotics," *The Conversation*, March 26, 2014, http://theconversation.com/infection-control-why-doctors-over-prescribe-antibiotics-24785.

2. The Subjectivity of Nature

1. Robert Ford Campany, *To Live as Long as Heaven and Earth: A Translation and Study of Ge Hong's Traditions of Divine Transcendents* (Berkeley: University of California Press, 2002).

2. "China's Tu Youyou Wins Nobel Prize in Medicine," *China.org.cn*, October 6, 2015, http://www1.china.org.cn/china/2015–10/06/content_36748337.htm.

3. See James Miller, "Authenticity, Sincerity, and Spontaneity: The Mutual Implication of Nature and Religion in China and the West," *Method and Theory in the Study of Religion* 25, no. 3 (2013): 283–307.

4. See James Miller, "Nature," in *The Wiley Blackwell Companion to Chinese Religions*, ed. Randall Nadeau (Chichester, UK: Wiley Blackwell: 2012), 349–368.

5. Francis Bacon, "The New Atlantis," in *The Works of Francis Bacon*, ed. James Spedding et al., 15 vols. (Boston: Houghton Mifflin, 1872–1878), 8:398, quoted in Donald Worster, *Nature's Economy: A History of Ecological Ideas*, 2nd ed. (Cambridge, UK: Cambridge University Press, 1994), 30.

6. See James Miller, "Philosophical and Religious Sources of Modern Chinese Environmental Ideology," *Journal of the Royal Asiatic Society, Shanghai* 74, no. 1 (2010): 4–21.

7. See Reza Aslan, *No God but God: The Origins, Evolution, and Future of Islam* (New York: Random House, 2006), for a liberal, Shia interpretation of Islam.

8. Zhimin Zhang, *Personalities in the Commune*, quoted in *Rand-McNally Illustrated Atlas of China* (New York: Rand-McNally, 1972), frontispiece. Shapiro notes that no other bibliographic information is available; see Judith Shapiro, *Mao's War Against Nature: Politics and the Environment in Revolutionary China* (Cambridge, UK: Cambridge University Press, 2004), 217.

9. *Daode jing*, chap. 25; my translation. The Chinese term here translated as "subjective nature" is *ziran* 自然. This is the modern Chinese term for "nature," but in classical Chinese it denotes "thusness" or "being so-in-and-of-oneself."

10. Brian Thomas Swimme and Mary Evelyn Tucker, *Journey of the Universe* (New Haven, CT: Yale University Press, 2013), 2.

11. One way to read this phrase from within the context of the Daoist alchemical tradition might be that the Daoist practitioner in fact does not care about the natural environment because everything that is necessary for him or her to carry out the cultivation process is already contained within the body. My argument here is that what made this inner alchemy possible is a view of the body as always and already "worlded," hence the later alchemical depictions of the body as a landscape.

12. Livia Kohn, *The Taoist Experience* (Albany: State University of New York Press, 1993), 177.

13. See Edward Slingerland, *Trying Not To Try: Ancient China, Modern Science, and the Power of Spontaneity* (New York: Crown [Random House], 2014), and *Effortless Action: Wu-wei as Conceptual Metaphor and Spiritual Ideal in Early China* (New York: Oxford University Press, 2003).

14. Karen Barad, "Posthumanist Performativity: Towards an Understanding of How Matter Comes to Matter," *Signs: Journal of Women in Culture and Society* 28, no. 3 (2003): 815.

3. Liquid Ecology

1. Louis Althusser, "Ideology and Ideological State Apparatuses (Notes Towards an Investigation)," in *Lenin and Philosophy and Other Essays* (London: Verso, 1970), 11.

2. Guo Pu, *The Book of Burial*, trans. Stephen L. Field, quoted in "In Search of Dragons: The Folk Ecology of Fengshui," in *Daoism and Ecology: Ways Within a Cosmic Landscape*, ed. N. J. Girardot, James Miller, and Liu Xiaogan (Cambridge, MA: Harvard Center for the Study of World Religions, 2001), 190; see also Zhang Juwen, *A Translation of the Ancient Chinese The Book of Burial (Zang Shu) By Guo Pu (276–324)* (Lewiston, NY: Edwin Mellon Press, 2004), 58–74. The translated quote is from Chris Coggins, "When the Land Is Excellent: Village Feng Shui Forests and the Nature of Lineage, Polity, and Vitality in Southern China," in *Religion and Ecological Sustainability in China*, ed. James Miller, Dan Smyer Yü, and Peter van der Veer, 97–126 (New York: Routledge, 2014), 105–106.

3. Coggins, "When the Land Is Excellent," 106.

4. Coggins, "When the Land Is Excellent," 106.

5. Trans. Zhang, *The Book of Burial*, 55, quoted in Coggins, "When the Land Is Excellent," 106.

6. See http://www.nsbd.gov.cn/zx/english/ for the official website for this project. The project, estimated to cost US$62 billion, has been criticized in China and outside for its expense and impracticability. For one example, see Yue Wang,

"Chinese Minister Speaks Out Against South-North Water Diversion Project," *Forbes*, February 20, 2014, http://www.forbes.com/sites/ywang/2014/02/20/chinese-minister-speaks-out-against-south-north-water-diversion-project/.

7. Sarah Allan, trans., *The Way of Water and the Sprouts of Virtue* (Albany: State University of New York Press, 1997).

8. Allan, *The Way of Water*, 76.

9. Chapter 9 of the *Classic of Filial Piety* (*Xiao jing* 孝經) notes: "The son derives his life from his parents, and no greater gift could possibly be transmitted" (父母生之，续莫大焉). See http://ctext.org/xiao-jing for the Chinese text and James Legge's English translation.

10. Vassili Kryukov, "Symbols of Power and Communication in Pre-Confucian China (On the Anthropology of *De*): Preliminary Assumptions," *Bulletin of the School of Oriental and African Studies* 58 (1995): 314–333.

11. Allan, *The Way of Water*.

12. Kryukov, "*Symbols of Power*," 319.

13. Kryukov, "*Symbols of Power*," 315.

14. Allan, *The Way of Water*, 102.

15. Roger T. Ames, "Putting the *Te* Back in Taoism," in *Nature in Asian Traditions of Thought: Essays in Environmental Philosophy*, ed. J. Baird Callicott and Roger Ames (Albany: State University of New York Press, 1989), 113–143.

16. Kryukov, *Symbols of Power*, 330.

17. Yue Pan, *Thoughts on Environmental Issues* (Beijing: China Environmental Culture Promotion Association, 2007).

18. *Wenxuan*, chap. 59, p. 9b, translation adapted from Joseph Needham, *Science and Civilisation in China* (Cambridge, UK: Cambridge University Press, 1956), vol. 2, p. 238.

19. *Shi ji*, chap. 74, p. 3a; trans. Needham, *Science and Civilisation in China*, 2:233.

20. Manfred Porkert, *The Theoretical Foundations of Chinese Medicine* (Cambridge, MA: MIT Press, 1978).

21. *Huainanzi*, chap. 3, pp. 2a–2b; trans. John B. Henderson, *The Development and Decline of Chinese Cosmology* (New York: Columbia University Press, 1984), 25.

22. Karen Barad, "Posthumanist Performativity: Towards an Understanding of How Matter Comes to Matter," *Signs: Journal of Women in Culture and Society* 28, no. 3 (2003), 846.

23. This table is derived from Louis Komjathy, *Daoism: A Guide for the Perplexed* (London: Bloomsbury, 2014), 92.

24. Komjathy, *Daoism*, 92.

25. Porkert, *Theoretical Foundations*.

26. Alfred Forke, *The World-Conception of the Chinese: Their Astronomical, Cosmological, and Physico-Philosophical Speculations* (London: Arthur Probsthain, 1925), 214, quoted in Robin Wang, *Yinyang: The Way of Heaven and Earth in Chinese Thought and Culture* (Cambridge, UK: Cambridge University Press, 2013), 7.

27. James Miller, *Daoism: A Beginner's Guide* (Oxford: Oneworld Publications, 2006), 53.

28. Wang, *Yinyang*, 8.

29. Wang, *Yinyang*, 9–11.

30. Wang, *Yinyang*, 37.

31. Porkert, *Theoretical Foundations*, 179–180.

32. Huangdi neijing *suwen*, 2.4; trans. Paul O. Unschuld, *Medicine in China: A History of Ideas* (Berkeley: University of California Press, 1985), 286.

33. Trans. Unschuld, *Medicine in China*, 283.

34. Huangdi neijing *taisu*, 1.1; trans. Unschuld, *Medicine in China*, 243.

35. *Siji tiaoshen dalun*; trans. Unschuld, *Medicine in China*, 283.

36. See Anna M. Hennessey, "Chinese Images of Body and Landscape: Visualization and Representation in the Religious Experience of Medieval China" (Ph.D. diss., University of California, Santa Barbara, 2011).

37. *Duren jing neiyi*, pref., 8b–9a; trans. Catherine Despeux and Livia Kohn, *Women in Daoism* (Cambridge, MA: Three Pines Press, 2003), 186–187.

38. See Louis Komjathy, *Cultivating Perfection: Mysticism and Self-Transformation in Early Quanzhen Daoism* (Leiden: Brill, 2007).

39. Catherine Despeux, *Immortelles de la Chine Ancienne: Taoïsme et Alchimie Féminine* (Grez-sur-Loing: Pardès, 1990), 195; see also Hennessey, "Chinese Images," 133.

40. Hennessey, "Chinese Images," 133.

41. Hennessey, "Chinese Images," 133–134.

4. The Porosity of the Body

1. James Miller, trans., *The Way of Highest Clarity: Nature, Vision, and Revelation in Medieval China* (Magdalena, NM: Three Pines Press, 2008), 172–173.

2. Miller, *Highest Clarity*, 191.

3. Fabrizio Pregadio, *Great Clarity: Daoism and Alchemy in Early Medieval China* (Stanford, CA: Stanford University Press, 2005), 135.

4. *Baopuzi*, 6:129; trans. Pregadio, *Great Clarity*, 136.

5. Pregadio, *Great Clarity*, 136.

6. Isabelle Robinet, "Shangqing: Highest Clarity," in *Daoism Handbook*, ed. Livia Kohn (Leiden: Brill, 2000), 196–224.

7. *Scripture of the Salvation of Humankind* (*Duren jing*, DZ1), preface, 4a; trans. Isabelle Robinet, *Taoist Meditation* (Albany: State University of New York Press, 1993), 23.

8. Robinet, *Taoist Meditation*, 23.

9. Robinet, *Taoist Meditation*, 27–28.

10. The Neo-Confucian philosopher Zhu Xi wrote: "When a man dies, his material force necessarily disintegrates. However, it does not disintegrate completely at once. Therefore, in religious sacrifices we have the principle of spiritual influence and response. Whether the material force . . . of ancestors of many generations ago is still there or not cannot be known. Nevertheless, since those who perform the sacrificial rites are their descendants, the material force

between them is after all the same. Hence there is the principle by which they can penetrate and respond." Wing-tsit Chan, trans., *A Source Book in Chinese Philosophy* (Princeton, NJ: Princeton University Press, 1963), 645.

11. Miller, *Highest Clarity*.

12. Miller, *Highest Clarity*, 37.

13. Miller, *Highest Clarity*, 44.

14. Louis Komjathy, *Daoism: A Guide for the Perplexed* (London: Bloomsbury, 2014), chap. 7.

15. Komjathy, *Daoism*, 178–179.

16. Benjamin Penny, "Immortality and Transcendence," in Kohn, *Daoism Handbook*, 109–133.

17. See James Miller, "Nature," in *The Wiley-Blackwell Companion to Chinese Religion*, ed. Randall L. Nadeau, 349–368 (Oxford: Wiley-Blackwell, 2012), for more detail.

18. See Miller, *Highest Clarity*; Julius N. Tsai, "Reading the 'Inner Biography of the Perfected Person of Purple Solarity': Religion and Society in an Early Daoist Hagiography," *Journal of the Royal Asiatic Society* 18, no. 2 (2008): 193–220.

19. Miller, *Highest Clarity*, 111.

20. Miller, *Highest Clarity*, 122.

21. Miller, *Highest Clarity*, 123.

22. Gil Raz, "The Way of the Yellow and the Red: Re-Examining the Sexual Initiation Rite of Celestial Master Daoism," *Nan Nü* 10 (2008): 87.

23. Raz, "Yellow and Red," 90.

24. Kristofer Schipper, *The Taoist Body*, trans. Karen C. Duval (Berkeley: University of California Press, 1993), 148–149.

25. Catherine Despeux and Livia Kohn, *Women in Daoism* (Cambridge, MA: Three Pines Press, 2003), 106.

26. Raz, "Yellow and Red," 96.

27. DZ639.13a8, trans. Steven R. Bokenkamp, *Early Daoist Scriptures* (Berkeley: University of California Press, 1993), 330–331, quoted in Raz, "The Yellow and the Red," 119.

28. See Judith Butler, *Gender Trouble: Feminism and the Subversion of Identity* (New York: Routledge, 1990). See also Timothy Morton, "Guest Column: Queer Ecology," *PMLA* 125, no. 2 (2010): 273–282.

5. The Locative Imagination

1. For a philosophical treatment of this position, see Roger T. Ames, "The Local and the Focal in Realizing a Daoist World," in *Daoism and Ecology: Ways Within a Cosmic Landscape*, ed. N. J. Girardot, Liu Xiaogan, and James Miller, 125–147 (Cambridge, MA: Harvard University Center for the Study of World Religions, 2001).

2. Robert F. Campany, "Ingesting the Marvelous," in Girardot, Miller, and Liu, *Daoism and Ecology*, 125–147.

3. Willis Jenkins, *The Future of Ethics* (Washington, DC: Georgetown University Press, 2013), 75.

4. Jenkins, *Ethics*, 79.

5. Dana Phillips, "Ecocriticism, Literary Theory, and the Truth of Ecology," *Ecocriticism* 3, no. 3 (1999): 577–602

6. Phillips, "Ecocriticism," 580.

7. Donald Worster, "Nature and the Disorder of History," *Environmental History Review* 18, no. 2 (1994), 7–8, cited in Phillips, "Ecocriticism," 580.

8. Joel B. Hagen, *An Entangled Bank: The Origins of Ecosystem Ecology* (New Brunswick, NJ: Rutgers University Press: 1992), 194.

9. Worster, "Nature and the Disorder of History," 7.

10. Jenkins, *Ethics*, 93.

11. Iris Marion Young, *Responsibility for Justice* (New York: Oxford University Press, 2011), 105, quoted in Jenkins, *Ethics*, 113.

12. *Esoteric Biography of Perfected Purple Yang (Ziyang zhenren neizhuan*; DZ103); trans. James Miller, *The Way of Highest Clarity: Nature, Vision, and Revelation in Medieval China* (Magdalena, NM: Three Pines Press, 2008), 151.

13. *Daode jing*, chap. 11: "Thirty spokes are united in one hub. It is in its [space of] emptiness, where the usefulness of the cart is. Clay is heated and a pot is made. It is in its [space of] emptiness, where the usefulness of the pot is. Doors and windows are chiseled out. It is in its [spaces of] emptiness, where the usefulness of a room is"; trans. Hans-Georg Moeller, *Daodejing* (LaSalle, IL: Open Court, 2007), 27.

14. Edward H. Schafer, *Pacing the Void: T'ang Approaches to the Stars* (Warren, CT: Floating World Edition, 2005), 235.

15. Livia Kohn, trans., *The Taoist Experience* (Albany: State University of New York Press, 1993), 256.

16. Schafer, *Pacing the Void*, 241.

17. *Wei furen neizhuan*, in *Sandong zhu'nang*, 8.22b; trans. Schafer, *Pacing the Void*, 233.

18. Schafer, *Pacing the Void*, 233.

19. Wang Ming, *Baopuzi neipian xiaoshi* (Beijing: Zhonghua shuju, 1985), 74; trans. Jianmin Gai, "From Mountainforest Daoism to Urban Daoism: Preliminary Discussion on Environmental Contexts and Characteristics of Contemporary Urban Daoism (unpublished manuscript), 6. Completion of the cinnabar means the completion of an alchemical recipe to produce an elixir of immortality.

20. *Daode jing*, chap. 80, advocates a small state with a small government: "Although your neighboring states are within eyesight, And the sounds of their dogs and cocks are within earshot, Your people will grow old and die without having anything to do with them"; trans. Roger T. Ames and David L. Hall, *Daoism: A Philosophical Translation* (New York: Ballantine Books), 2003.

21. Campany, "Ingesting the Marvelous," 128. The five sacred mountains are, by location: East, Mt. Tai 泰, Shandong Province; West, Mt. Hua 華, Shanxi Province; South, Mt. Heng 衡, Hunan Province; North, Mt. Heng 恒, Shanxi Province; Center, Mt. Song 嵩, Henan Province.

22. Trans. Campany, "Ingesting the Marvelous," 128.

23. Campany, "Ingesting the Marvelous," 128.

24. Campany, "Ingesting the Marvelous," note 9.

25. *Baopuzi neipian,* 19:336, quoted in Campany, "Ingesting the Marvelous," 134.

26. Trans. Miller, *Highest Clarity,* 139.

27. Julius N. Tsai, "Reading the 'Inner Biography of the Perfected Person of Purple Solarity': Religion and Society in an Early Daoist Hagiography," *Journal of the Royal Asiatic Society* 18, no. 2 (2008): 193–220.

28. In North America, this parallels the experience of nature writers such as Thoreau and Muir. In particular, Muir's writing about his own experience walking in forests became the inspiration for the conservation movement.

29. John Lagerwey, *Wu-shang pi-yao: Somme taoïste du VI siècle* (Paris: Publications de l'École Française d'Extrême-Orient, 1987), 172–193.

30. See Russell Kirkland, *Taoism: The Enduring Tradition* (New York: Routledge, 2004).

31. Miller, *Highest Clarity,* 148.

32. Trans. Miller, *Highest Clarity,* 158.

33. Kuang-ming Wu, *On Chinese Body Thinking: A Cultural Hermeneutic* (Leiden: Brill, 1997), 237.

34. Wu, *On Chinese Body Thinking,* 236.

6. The Political Ecology of the Daoist Body

1. Tim Ingold, *The Perception of the Environment: Essays on Livelihood, Dwelling, and Skill* (London: Routledge, 2000), 157.

2. Ingold, *The Perception of the Environment,* 171.

3. Ingold, *The Perception of the Environment,* 169.

4. Maurice Merleau-Ponty, "Husserl et la Notion de Nature (Notes Prises au Cours de Maurice Merleau-Ponty)," *Revue de Metaphysique et de Morale* 70 (1965): 261, quoted in Hwa-Jol Jung, "Merleau-Ponty's Transversal Geophilosophy," in *Merleau-Ponty and Environmental Philosophy: Dwelling on the Landscapes of Thought,* ed. Sue Cataldi and William Hamrick (Albany: State University of New York Press, 2007), 241.

5. Francisco J. Varela, Evan Thompson, and Eleanor Rorsch, *The Embodied Mind: Cognitive Science and Human Experience* (Cambridge: MIT Press, 1997).

6. Giovanna Colombetti and Evan Thompson, "The Feeling Body:" Towards an Enactive Approach to Emotion," in *Developmental Perspectives on Embodiment and Consciousness,* ed. Willis F. Overton et al., 45–68 (New York: Lawrence Erlbaum Associates, 2007), 46.

7. Colombetti and Thompson, "The Feeling Body," 56.

8. Mark Rowlands, *The Body in Mind: Understanding Cognitive Processes* (Cambridge, UK: Cambridge University Press, 1999), 31.

9. Hilary Puttnam, "The Meaning of 'Meaning,'" in *Language, Mind, and Knowledge: Minnesota Studies in the Philosophy of Science,* ed. Keith Gunderson, 175–193 (Minneapolis: University of Minnesota Press, 1975).

10. Rowlands, *The Body in Mind,* 30.

11. James J. Gibson, *The Ecological Approach to Visual Perception* (Boston: Houghton Mifflin, 1979).

12. Rowlands, *The Body in Mind*, 116.

13. David C. Rubin, *Memory in Oral Traditions: The Cognitive Psychology of Epic, Ballads, and Counting-out Rhymes* (New York: Oxford University Press, 1995).

14. Rowlands, *The Body in Mind*, 141.

15. David Abram, "Merleau-Ponty and the Voice of the Earth," *Environmental Ethics* 10, no. 2 (May 1, 1988): 119.

16. Richard Shusterman, "Body Consciousness and Performance: Somaesthetics East and West," *The Journal of Aesthetics and Art Criticism* 67, no. 2 (2009): 139.

17. Sundar Sarukkai, "Inside/Outside: Merleau-Ponty/Yoga," *Philosophy East and West* 52, no. 4 (2002): 462.

18. Sarukkai, "Inside/Outside: Merleau-Ponty/Yoga," 466.

19. Jane Bennett, *Vibrant Matter: A Political Ecology of Things* (Durham, NC: Duke University Press, 2010), 102.

20. Livia Kohn, *Cosmos and Community: The Ethical Dimension of Daoism* (Cambridge, MA: Three Pines Press, 2004).

21. Kohn, *Cosmos and Community*, 2.

22. In *Mencius* 6A, for instance, the philosopher famously chastises King Hui of Liang for concentrating on "profit" rather than "benevolence."

23. DZ786, 4a–12b; trans. Kohn, *Cosmos and Community*, 136.

24. Kristofer Schipper, "The 180 Precepts of Lord Lao," in *Daoism and Ecology: Ways Within a Cosmic Landscape*, ed. N. J. Girardot, Liu Xiaogan, and James Miller, 79–83 (Cambridge, MA: Harvard University Center for the Study of World Religions, 2001).

25. Schipper, "180 Precepts," 82.

26. Trans. Kohn, *Cosmos and Community*, 144.

27. See Pulitzer Center, "Congo's Bloody Coltan," n.d., http://pulitzercenter.org/video/congos-bloody-coltan, accessed October 12, 2016.

28. This idea may resonate well in the Western context with James Lovelock's Gaia hypothesis, in which the earth is recognized as a single, living organism.

29. Leonardo da Vinci and Irma A. Richter, *Selections from the Notebooks of Leonardo da Vinci* (London: Oxford University Press, 1977 [1952]), 45–46, quoted in Rod Giblett, "The Tao of Water," *Landscapes: The Journal of the International Centre for Landscape and Language* 3, no. 2, article 4 (2009): 4, http://ro.ecu.edu.au/landscapes/vol3/iss2/4.

30. Henry D. Thoreau, *The Journal of Henry D. Thoreau*, vols. 1–14, ed. B. Torrey and F. Allen (New York: Dover: 1962), 9:394, quoted in Giblett, "The Tao of Water," 6.

31. Giblett, "The Tao of Water," 8.

32. World Wildlife Fund China, Wetland Conservation and Restoration, n.d., http://en.wwfchina.org/en/what_we_do/freshwater/wetland_conservation/.

33. He Zuoxiu, "Man Need Not Revere Nature," *Friends of Nature* 2 (2005): 20.

34. Liang Congjie, "Is It True that Man Need Not Revere Nature?," *Friends of Nature* 2 (2005): 14.

35. James Miller, "Is Green the New Red? The Role of Religion in Creating a Sustainable China," *Nature and Culture* 8, no. 3 (2013): 249–264.

36. James Miller, "Authenticity, Sincerity, and Spontaneity: The Mutual Implication of Nature and Religion in China and the West," *Method and Theory in the Study of Religion* 25, no. 3 (January 1, 2013): 290. See also Richard Delgado, "Trust Theory of Environmental Protection, and Some Dark Thoughts on the Possibility of Law Reform," *Issues in Legal Scholarship* 3.1 (2003): article 4 (1–15), doi:10.2202/1539-8323.1042.

37. Miller, "Authenticity," 290.

38. Robert P. Weller, *Discovering Nature: Globalization and Environmental Culture in China and Taiwan* (Cambridge, UK: Cambridge University Press, 2006).

39. Weller, *Discovering Nature*, 76.

40. Weller, *Discovering Nature*, 77.

41. Jinyu Qi, "'Ecological Migration' and Cultural Adaptation: A Case Study of the Sanjiangyuan Nature Reserve, Qinghai Province," in *Religion and Ecological Sustainability in China*, ed. James Miller, Dan Smyer Yu, and Peter van der Veer, 181–193 (New York: Routledge, 2014).

42. Qi, "Ecological Migration," 187.

43. Qi, "Ecological Migration," 189–190.

7. From Modernity to Sustainability

1. N. J. Girardot, *The Victorian Translation of China: James Legge's Oriental Pilgrimage* (Berkeley: University of California Press, 2002).

2. Louis Komjathy, *The Daoist Tradition: An Introduction* (London: Bloomsbury, 2013), 6.

3. Komjathy, *The Daoist Tradition*, 5.

4. Komjathy, *The Daoist Tradition*, 6.

5. Michel Strickmann, "On the Alchemy of T'ao Hung-Ching," in *Facets of Taoism*, ed. Holmes Welch and Anna Seidel, 123–192 (New Haven, CT: Yale University Press, 1981).

6. Prasenjit Duara, "Knowledge and Power in the Discourse of Modernity: The Campaigns Against Popular Religion in Early Twentieth-Century China," *Journal of Asian Studies* 50, no. 1 (1991): 67–83.

7. See James Miller, "Religion, Nature, and Modernization in China," in *Technology, Trust, and Religion: Roles of Religions in Controversies on Ecology and the Modification of Life*, ed. Willem B. Drees, 107–122 (Leiden: Leiden University Press, 2009).

8. See *The Economist*, "China's Chicago," July 26, 2007, http://www.economist.com/node/9557763, on the emergence of Chongqing as a megacity.

9. Particularly relevant here is the development of Asian studies at Columbia University, under the leadership of Theodore de Bary, who was instrumental in producing source books in Chinese civilization published by Columbia University Press. More recent examples of the attempt to distinguish the core motifs of Chinese and Western philosophy can be found in the comparative projects un-

dertaken by David L. Hall and Roger T. Ames, *Thinking Through Confucius* (Albany: State University of New York Press, 1987); *Anticipating China: Thinking Through the Narratives of Chinese and Western Culture*, (Albany: State University of New York Press, 1995); and *Thinking from the Han: Self, Truth, and Transcendence in Chinese and Western Culture* (Albany: State University of New York Press, 1997).

10. See *The Economist*, "A Message from Confucius," October 22, 2009, http://www.economist.com/node/14678507, on the role of Confucius Institutes in China's "soft power" initiative.

11. See Martin Jacques, *When China Rules the World* (London: Penguin, 2012).

12. Prasenjit Duara, *The Crisis of Global Modernity: Asian Traditions and a Sustainable Future* (Cambridge, UK: Cambridge University Press, 2014).

13. Duara, *The Crisis of Global Modernity*, 2; emphasis in the original.

14. Vincent Goossaert and David A. Palmer, *The Religious Question in Modern China* (Chicago: University of Chicago Press, 2011).

15. J. Z. Smith, *Imagining Religion* (Chicago: University of Chicago Press, 1982), xi.

16. Ninian Smart, *Dimensions of the Sacred: An Anatomy of the World's Beliefs* (Berkeley, University of California Press, 1996), 10–11.

17. Simon C. Estok, "Shakespeare and Ecocriticism: An Analysis of 'Home' and 'Power' in King Lear," *Journal of the Australasian Universities Language and Literature Association* 103 (May 2005): 15–41, doi:10.1179/000127905805260537.

18. Dana Phillips, "Ecocriticism, Literary Theory, and the Truth of Ecology," *Ecocriticism* 3, no. 3 (1999): 577–602.

8. From Sustainability to Flourishing

1. Michael Shellenberger and Ted Nordhaus, *The Death of Environmentalism: Global Warming Politics in a Post-Environmental World*, 2004, http://www.thebreak through.org/images/Death_of_Environmentalism.pdf.

2. For the full text, visit www.ecomodernism.org.

3. James Gustave Speth, "Environmental Failure: A Case for a New Green Politics," *environment360*, October 20, 2008, http://e360.yale.edu/content/feature .msp?id=2075.

4. For a fuller discussion of the globalization of the environmental movement in China and Taiwan, see Robert P. Weller, *Discovering Nature: Globalization and Environmental Culture in China and Taiwan* (Cambridge, UK: Cambridge University Press, 2006).

5. Yue Pan, "Looking Forward to an Ecological Civilization," *China Today* 57, no. 11 (2008): 29–30.

6. Andres Edwards, *The Sustainability Revolution: Portrait of a Paradigm Shift* (Gabriola Island, BC: New Society Publishers, 2005), 14–15.

7. Lucas F. Johnston, *Religion and Sustainability: Social Movements and the Politics of the Environment* (New York: Routledge, 2014), 29.

8. Hui Wang, *The End of the Revolution: China and the Limits of Modernity* (New York: Verso, 2009), 70.

9. Confucius says, in *Analects* 2.4: "At fifteen, I set my mind on learning. At thirty, I stood firm. At forty, I had no doubts. At fifty, I knew the will of Heaven. At sixty, my ear was obedient. At seventy, I could follow what my heart desired, without overstepping the mark" (my translation).

10. Kathy Charmaz, *Good Days, Bad Days: The Self in Chronic Illness and Time* (New Brunswick, NJ: Rutgers University Press, 1991): 70–71, quoted in Denver Vale Nixon, "The Environmental Resonance of Daoist Moving Meditations," *Worldviews* 10, no. 3 (2006): 389–390.

11. Nixon, "Environmental Resonance," 390.

12. David Brown, George Jennings, and Andrew Sparkes, "Taijiquan the 'Taiji World' Way: Towards a Cosmopolitan Vision of Ecology," *Societies* 4, no. 3 (September 2014): 380–398.

13. Ulrich Beck, "Climate for Change, or How To Create a Green Modernity?" *Theory, Culture, Society* 27 (2010): 254–266.

14. D. V. S. Kasper, "Ecological Habitus: Toward a Better Understanding of Socioecological Relations," *Organization and Environment* 22, no. 3 (2009): 318.

15. See Livia Kohn, *Cosmos and Community: The Ethical Dimension of Daoism* (Cambridge, MA: Three Pines Press, 2004), for a complete discussion of Daoist ethical codes.

16. Trans. Hans-Georg Moeller, *Daodejing* (LaSalle, IL: Open Court, 2007), 75.

17. Trans. Moeller, *Daodejing*, 77.

18. See IUCN SSC Specialist Pangolin Group, *Scaling Up Pangolin Conservation*, July 2014, http://www.pangolinsg.org/files/2012/07/Scaling_up_pangolin _conservation_280714_v4.pdf.

19. Franklin Hiram King, *Farmers of Forty Centuries; Or, Permanent Agriculture in China, Korea, and Japan* (n.p., 1911), http://www.gutenberg.org/ebooks/5350.

20. See RT.com, "China Admits Pollution Brought About 'Cancer Villages,'" February 23, 2013, http://www.rt.com/news/china-water-pollution-cancer-346/.

21. See Earth Law Center, "California Waterways," http://www.earthlawcenter .org/california-waterways.

22. Yue Pan, *Thoughts on Environmental Issues* (Beijing: China Environmental Culture Promotion Association, 2007), 1.

23. Thanks to Jason Kelly for coining this phrase.

24. Judith Shapiro, *Mao's War Against Nature: Politics and the Environment in Revolutionary China* (Cambridge, UK: Cambridge University Press, 2004).

25. James Miller, "Monitory Democracy and Ecological Civilization in the People's Republic of China," in *Civil Society in the Age of Monitory Democracy*, ed. Lars Trägårdh, Nina Witoszek, and Bron Taylor, 137–148 (Oxford: Berghahn Books, 2013).

26. Tom Miller, *China's Urban Billion: The Story Behind the Biggest Migration in Human History* (London: Zed Books, 2012), 1.

27. The classic example of this approach can be seen in Clifford Geertz, "Religion as a Cultural System," in *Anthropological Approaches to the Study of Religion*, ASA Monograph 3, ed. Michael Banton, 1–46 (London: Tavistock Publications, 1966).

Bibliography

Abram, David. "Merleau-Ponty and the Voice of the Earth." *Environmental Ethics* 10, no. 2 (May 1, 1988): 101–120.

Allan, Sarah. *The Way of Water and the Sprouts of Virtue.* Albany: State University of New York Press, 1997.

Althusser, Louis. "Ideology and Ideological State Apparatuses (Notes Towards an Investigation)." In *Lenin and Philosophy and Other Essays,* trans. Ben Brewster, 127–186. New York: Monthly Review Press, 1971.

Ames, Roger T. "Putting the *Te* Back in Taoism." In *Nature in Asian Traditions of Thought: Essays in Environmental Philosophy,* ed. J. Baird Callicott and Roger Ames, 113–143. Albany: State University of New York Press, 1989.

——. "The Local and the Focal in Realizing a Daoist World." In *Daoism and Ecology: Ways Within a Cosmic Landscape,* ed. N. J. Girardot, James Miller, and Liu Xiaogan, 265–282. Cambridge, MA: Harvard University Center for the Study of World Religions, 2001.

Ames, Roger T., and David L. Hall. *Daoism: A Philosophical Translation.* New York: Ballantine Books, 2003.

Asad, Talal. *Genealogies of Religion: Discipline and Reasons of Power in Christianity and Islam.* Baltimore, MD: Johns Hopkins University Press, 1993.

——. *Formations of the Secular: Christianity, Islam, Modernity.* Stanford, CA: Stanford University Press, 2003.

Aslan, Reza. *No God but God: The Origins, Evolution, and Future of Islam.* New York: Random House, 2006.

Barad, Karen. "Posthumanist Performativity: Towards an Understanding of How Matter Comes to Matter." *Signs: Journal of Women in Culture and Society* 28, no. 3 (2003): 802–831.

Beck, Ulrich. *Risk Society: Towards a New Modernity.* London: Sage Publications, 1992.

——. "Climate for Change, or How To Create a Green Modernity?" *Theory, Culture, Society* 27 (2010): 254–266.

Bellah, Robert. *Religion in Human Evolution: From the Paleolithic to the Axial Age.* Cambridge, MA: Harvard University Press, 2011.

Bennett, Jane. *The Enchantment of Modern Life: Attachments, Crossings, and Ethics.* Princeton, NJ: Princeton University Press, 2001.

——. *Vibrant Matter: A Political Ecology of Things.* Durham, NC: Duke University Press, 2010.

Bokenkamp, Steven R., with a contribution by Peter S. Nickerson. *Early Daoist Scriptures.* Berkeley: University of California Press, 1993.

Bourdieu, Paul. *Distinction: A Social Critique of the Judgement of Taste.* New York: Routledge, 1986.

Broom, Alex. "Infection Control: Why Doctors Over-prescribe Antibiotics." *The Conversation.* March 26, 2014. http://theconversation.com/infection-control-why -doctors-over-prescribe-antibiotics-24785.

Brown, David, George Jennings, and Andrew Sparkes. "Taijiquan the 'Taiji World' Way: Towards a Cosmopolitan Vision of Ecology." *Societies* 4, no. 3 (September 2014): 380–398.

Butler, Judith. *Gender Trouble: Feminism and the Subversion of Identity.* New York: Routledge, 1990).

Campany, Robert Ford. "Ingesting the Marvelous." In *Daoism and Ecology: Ways Within a Cosmic Landscape,* ed. N. J. Girardot, James Miller, and Liu Xiaogan, 125–147. Cambridge, MA: Harvard Center for the Study of World Religions, 2001.

——. *To Live as Long as Heaven and Earth: A Translation and Study of Ge Hong's Traditions of Divine Transcendents.* Berkeley: University of California, 2002.

Charmaz, Kathy. *Good Days, Bad Days: The Self in Chronic Illness and Time.* New Brunswick, NJ: Rutgers University Press, 1991.

Chan, Wing-tsit. *A Source Book in Chinese Philosophy.* Princeton, NJ: Princeton University Press, 1963.

"China's Tu Youyou Wins Nobel Prize in Medicine." *China.org.cn.* October 6, 2015. http://www1.china.org.cn/china/2015–10/06/content_36748337.htm.

Coggins, Chris. "When the Land Is Excellent: Village Feng Shui Forests and the Nature of Lineage, Polity, and Vitality in Southern China." In *Religion and Ecological Sustainability in China,* ed. James Miller, Dan Smyer Yü, and Peter van der Veer, 97–126. New York: Routledge, 2014.

Colombetti, Giovanna, and Evan Thompson. "The Feeling Body: Towards an Enactive Approach to Emotion." In *Developmental Perspectives on Embodiment and Consciousness,* ed. Willis F. Overton et al., 45–68. New York: Lawrence Erlbaum Associates, 2007.

Da Vinci, Leonardo, and Irma A. Richter. *Selections from the Notebooks of Leonardo Da Vinci.* 1952. Reprint, London: Oxford University Press, 1977.

D'Costa, Gavin, Paul Knitter, and Daniel Strange. *Only One Way? Three Christian Responses to the Uniqueness of Christ in a Religiously Pluralist World.* London: SCM Press, 2013.

Delgado, Richard. "Trust Theory of Environmental Protection, and Some Dark Thoughts on the Possibility of Law Reform." *Issues in Legal Scholarship* 3.1 (2003): article 4 (1–15). doi:10.2202/1539-8323.1042.

Despeux, Catherine. *Immortelles de la Chine Ancienne: Taoïsme et Alchimie Féminine.* Grez sur Loing: Pardès, 1990.

——. *Women in Daoism.* Cambridge, MA: Three Pines Press, 2003.

Duara, Prasenjit. "Knowledge and Power in the Discourse of Modernity: The Campaigns Against Popular Religion in Early Twentieth-Century China." *The Journal of Asian Studies* 50, no. 1 (1991): 67–83.

——. *The Crisis of Global Modernity: Asian Traditions and a Sustainable Future.* Cambridge, UK: Cambridge University Press, 2014.

Durkheim, Emile. *The Elementary Forms of the Religious Life.* New York: Free Press, 1965.

Earth Law Center. "California Waterways." N.d. Accessed October 12, 2016. http://www.earthlawcenter.org/california-waterways.

Economist, The. "A Message from Confucius." October 22, 2009. http://www.economist.com/node/14678507.

——. "China's Chicago." July 26, 2007. http://www.economist.com/node/9557763.

Edwards, Andres. *The Sustainability Revolution: Portrait of a Paradigm Shift.* Gabriola Island, BC: New Society Publishers, 2005.

Estok, Simon C. "Shakespeare and Ecocriticism: An Analysis of 'Home' and 'Power' in King Lear." *Journal of the Australasian Universities Language and Literature Association* 103 (May 2005): 15–41. doi:10.1179/000127905805260537.

Field, Stephen L. "In Search of Dragons: The Folk Ecology of Fengshui." In *Daoism and Ecology: Ways Within a Cosmic Landscape,* ed. N. J. Girardot, James Miller, and Liu Xiaogan, 185–200. Cambridge, MA: Harvard Center for the Study of World Religions, 2001.

Forke, Alfred. *The World-Conception of the Chinese: Their Astronomical, Cosmological, and Physico-Philosophical Speculations.* London: Arthur Probsthain, 1925.

Foucault, Michel. *The Order of Things: An Archaeology of the Human Sciences.* New York: Vintage, 1984.

Gai, Jianmin. "From Mountainforest Daoism to Urban Daoism: Preliminary Discussion on Environmental Contexts and Characteristics of Contemporary Urban Daoism." Unpublished manuscript.

Gardner, Gary. *Invoking the Spirit: Religion and Spirituality in the Quest for a Sustainable World.* Worldwatch Paper 164. Washington, DC: Worldwatch Institute, 2002.

Geertz, Clifford. "Religion as a Cultural System." In *Anthropological Approaches to the Study of Religion,* ASA Monograph 3, ed. Michael Banton, 1–46. London: Tavistock Publications, 1966.

Gellner, Ernest. *Culture, Identity, and Politics*. Cambridge, UK: Cambridge University Press, 1987.

Giblett, Rod. "The Tao of Water." *Landscapes: The Journal of the International Centre for Landscape and Language* 3, no. 2, article 4 (2009): 1–11. http://ro.ecu.edu.au /landscapes/vol3/iss2/4.

Gibson, James J. *The Ecological Approach to Visual Perception*. Boston: Houghton Mifflin, 1979.

Girardot, N. J. *The Victorian Translation of China: James Legge's Oriental Pilgrimage*. Berkeley: University of California Press, 2002.

Girardot, N. J., James Miller, and Xiaogan Liu, eds. *Daoism and Ecology: Ways Within a Cosmic Landscape*. Cambridge, MA: Center for the Study of World Religions, Harvard University, 2001.

Goossaert, Vincent, and David A. Palmer. *The Religious Question in Modern China*. Chicago: University of Chicago Press, 2011.

Gould, Stephen Jay. "Nonoverlapping Magisteria." *Natural History* 106 (March 1997): 16–22.

Hagen, Joel B. *An Entangled Bank: The Origins of Ecosystem Ecology*. New Brunswick, NJ: Rutgers University Press, 1992.

Hall, David L., and Roger T. Ames. *Thinking Through Confucius*. Albany: State University of New York Press, 1987.

——. *Anticipating China: Thinking Through the Narratives of Chinese and Western Culture*. Albany: State University of New York Press, 1995.

——. *Thinking from the Han: Self, Truth, and Transcendence in Chinese and Western Culture*. Albany: State University of New York Press, 1997.

Hedges, Paul. *Controversies in Contemporary Religion: Education, Law, Politics, Society, and Spirituality*. 3 vols. Santa Barbara, CA: Praeger, 2014.

Henderson, John B. *The Development and Decline of Chinese Cosmology*. New York: Columbia University Press, 1984.

Hennessey, Anna M. "Chinese Images of Body and Landscape: Visualization and Representation in the Religious Experience of Medieval China." Ph.D. diss., University of California, Santa Barbara, 2011.

Ingold, Tim. *The Perception of the Environment: Essays on Livelihood, Dwelling, and Skill*. London: Routledge, 2000.

IUCN SSC Specialist Pangolin Group. *Scaling Up Pangolin Conservation*. July 2014. http://www.pangolinsg.org/files/2012/07/Scaling_up_pangolin_conserva tion_280714_v4.pdf.

Jacques, Martin. *When China Rules the World*. London: Penguin, 2012.

Jenkins, Willis. *The Future of Ethics*. Washington, DC: Georgetown University Press, 2013.

Jung, Hwa-Jol. "Merleau-Ponty's Transversal Geophilosophy and Sinic Aesthetics of Nature." In *Merleau-Ponty and Environmental Philosophy: Dwelling on the Landscapes of Thought*, ed. Sue Cataldi and William Hamrick, 235–258 (Albany: State University of New York Press, 2007).

Kasper, D. V. S. "Ecological Habitus: Toward a Better Understanding of Socioecological Relations." *Organization and Environment* 22, no. 3 (2009): 318.

King, Franklin Hiram. *Farmers of Forty Centuries; Or, Permanent Agriculture in China, Korea, and Japan.* N.p., 1911. http://www.gutenberg.org/ebooks/5350.

Kirkland, Russell. *Taoism: The Enduring Tradition.* New York: Routledge, 2004.

Kohn, Livia. *The Taoist Experience.* Albany: State University of New York Press, 1993.

——. *Cosmos and Community: The Ethical Dimension of Daoism.* Cambridge, MA: Three Pines Press, 2004.

Komjathy, Louis. *Cultivating Perfection: Mysticism and Self-Transformation in Early Quanzhen Daoism.* Leiden: Brill 2007.

——. *The Daoist Tradition: An Introduction.* London: Bloomsbury, 2013.

——. *Daoism: A Guide for the Perplexed.* London: Bloomsbury, 2014.

Kryukov, Vassili. "Symbols of Power and Communication in Pre-Confucian China (On the Anthropology of *De*): Preliminary Assumptions." *Bulletin of the School of Oriental and African Studies* 58 (1995): 314–333.

LaFargue, Michael. *The Tao of the Tao Te Ching.* Albany: State University of New York Press, 2001.

——. "Hermeneutics and Pedagogy: Give Me That Old-Time Historicism." In *Teaching the Daode jing,* ed. Gary Delany DeAngelis and Warren G. Frisina, 167–192. New York: Oxford University Press, 2008.

Lagerwey, John. *Wu-shang pi-yao: Somme taoïste du VI siècle.* Paris: Publications de l'Ecole Française d'Extrême-Orient, 1987.

Lai, Chi-Tim. "The Opposition of Celestial-Master Taoism to Popular Cults During the Six Dynasties." *Asia Major* 11, no. 1 (1998): 1–20.

Latour, Bruno. *We Have Never Been Modern.* Trans. Catherine Porter. Cambridge, MA: Harvard University Press, 1993.

Lemche, Jennifer. "The Greening of Chinese Daoism: Modernity, Bureaucracy, and Ecology in Contemporary Chinese Religion." M.A. thesis, Queen's University, Kingston, Canada, 2010. http://hdl.handle.net/1974/6035.

Mayo Clinic. *MRSA Infection.* September 9, 2015. http://www.mayoclinic.org/diseases-conditions/mrsa/basics/causes/con-20024479.

McCutcheon, Russell T., ed. *The Insider/Outsider Problem in the Study of Religion: A Reader.* London: Continuum, 1999.

McElroy, Michael B. "Perspectives on Environmental Change: A Basis for Action." *Daedalus,* 130, no. 4, special issue: *Religion and Ecology: Can the Climate Change?* (2001): 31–57.

Merleau-Ponty, Maurice. *Le Visible et L'Invisible.* Paris: Gallimard, 1964.

——. "Husserl et la Notion de Nature (Notes Prises au Cours de Maurice Merleau-Ponty)." *Revue de Metaphysique et de Morale* 70 (1965): 257–269.

Miller, James. "Daoism and Nature." In *The Oxford Handbook of Religions and Ecology,* ed. Roger Gottlieb, 220–235. Oxford: Oxford University Press, 2006.

——. *Daoism: A Beginner's Guide.* Oxford: Oneworld Publications, 2006.

——. *The Way of Highest Clarity: Nature, Vision, and Revelation in Medieval China.* Magdalena, NM: Three Pines Press, 2008.

——. "Religion, Nature, and Modernization in China." In *Technology, Trust, and Religion: Roles of Religions in Controversies on Ecology and the Modification of Life,* ed. Willem B. Drees, 107–122. Leiden: Leiden University Press, 2009.

——. "Philosophical and Religious Sources of Modern Chinese Environmental Ideology." *Journal of the Royal Asiatic Society, Shanghai* 74, no. 1 (2010): 4–21.

——. "Nature." In *The Wiley-Blackwell Companion to Chinese Religion*, ed. Randall L. Nadeau, 349–368. Oxford: Wiley-Blackwell, 2012.

——. "Authenticity, Sincerity, and Spontaneity: The Mutual Implication of Nature and Religion in China and the West." *Method and Theory in the Study of Religion* 25, no. 3 (January 1, 2013): 283–307.

——. "Is Green the New Red? The Role of Religion in Creating a Sustainable China." *Nature and Culture* 8, no. 3 (2013): 249–264.

——. "Monitory Democracy and Ecological Civilization in the People's Republic of China." In *Civil Society in the Age of Monitory Democracy*, ed. Lars Trägårdh, Nina Witoszek, and Bron Taylor, 137–148. Oxford: Berghahn Books, 2013.

——. "Is Religion Environmentally Friendly? Connecting Religion and Ecology." In *Controversies in Contemporary Religion, Education, Law, Politics, and Spirituality*, ed. Paul Hedges, vol. 2, *Debates in the Public Square and Ethical Issues*, 153–176. Santa Barbara, CA: Praeger, 2014.

Miller, Tom. *China's Urban Billion: The Story Behind the Biggest Migration in Human History*. London: Zed Books, 2012.

Moeller, Hans-Georg. *Daodejing*. LaSalle, IL: Open Court, 2007.

Morton, Timothy. "Guest Column: Queer Ecology." *PMLA* 125, no. 2 (2010): 273–282.

Needham, Joseph. *Science and Civilisation in China*. Vol. 2. Cambridge, UK: Cambridge University Press, 1956.

Neville, Robert Cummings. *Normative Cultures*. Albany: State University of New York Press, 1995.

Nixon, Denver Vale. "The Environmental Resonance of Daoist Moving Meditations." *Worldviews* 10, no. 3 (2006): 380–403.

Pan, Yue. *Thoughts on Environmental Issues*. Beijing: China Environmental Culture Promotion Association, 2007.

——. "Looking Forward to an Ecological Civilization." *China Today* 57, no. 11 (2008): 29–30.

Penny, Benjamin Penny. "Immortality and Transcendence." In *Daoism Handbook*, ed. Livia Kohn, 109–133. Leiden: Brill, 2000.

Phillips, Dana. "Ecocriticism, Literary Theory, and the Truth of Ecology." *Ecocriticism* 3, no. 3 (1999): 577–602.

Pile, Steve. *Real Cities: Modernity, Space, and the Phantasmagorias of City Life*. London: SAGE, 2005.

Porkert, Manfred. *The Theoretical Foundations of Chinese Medicine*. Cambridge, MA: MIT Press, 1978.

Pregadio, Fabrizio. *Great Clarity: Daoism and Alchemy in Early Medieval China*. Stanford, CA: Stanford University Press, 2005.

Prothero, Stephen. *God Is Not One: The Eight Rival Religions that Run the World*. San Francisco: HarperOne, 2011.

Pulitzer Center. "Congo's Bloody Coltan." N.d. Accessed October 12, 2016. http://pulitzercenter.org/video/congos-bloody-coltan.

Puttnam, Hilary. "The Meaning of 'Meaning.'" In *Language, Mind, and Knowledge: Minnesota Studies in the Philosophy of Science*, ed. Keith Gunderson, 175–193. Minneapolis: University of Minnesota Press, 1975.

Qi Jinyu. "'Ecological Migration' and Cultural Adaptation: A Case Study of the Sanjiangyuan Nature Reserve, Qinghai Province." In *Religion and Ecological Sustainability in China*, ed. James Miller, Dan Smyer Yu, and Peter van der Veer, 181–193. New York: Routledge, 2014.

Rand-McNally Illustrated Atlas of China. New York: Rand-McNally, 1972.

Raz, Gil. "The Way of the Yellow and the Red: Re-Examining the Sexual Initiation Rite of Celestial Master Daoism." *Nan Nü* 10 (2008): 86–120.

Robinet, Isabelle. *Taoist Meditation*. Trans. Norman Girardot and Julian Pas. Albany: State University of New York Press, 1993.

——. "'Shangqing: Highest Clarity." In *Daoism Handbook*, ed. Livia Kohn, 196–224. Leiden: Brill, 2000.

Rowlands, Mark. *The Body in Mind: Understanding Cognitive Processes*. Cambridge, UK: Cambridge University Press, 1999.

RT.com. "China Admits Pollution Brought About 'Cancer Villages.'" February 23, 2013. http://www.rt.com/news/china-water-pollution-cancer-346/.

Rubin, David C. *Memory in Oral Traditions: The Cognitive Psychology of Epic, Ballads, and Counting-out Rhymes*. New York: Oxford University Press, 1995.

Said, Edward W. "Orientalism Reconsidered." In *Literature, Politics, and Theory*, ed. Francis Baker et al., 210–229. New York: Methuen, 1986.

Sarrukai, Sundar. "Inside/Outside: Merleau-Ponty/Yoga." *Philosophy East and West* 52, no. 4 (2002): 459–478.

Schafer, Edward H. *Pacing the Void: T'ang Approaches to the Stars*. Warren, CT: Floating World Edition, 2005.

Schipper, Kristofer. *The Taoist Body*. Trans. Karen C. Duval. Berkeley: University of California Press, 1993.

——. "The 180 Precepts of Lord Lao." In *Daoism and Ecology: Ways Within a Cosmic Landscape*, ed. N. J. Girardot, James Miller, and Liu Xiaogan, 79–93. Cambridge, MA: Harvard University Center for the Study of World Religions, 2001.

Shapiro, Judith. *Mao's War Against Nature: Politics and the Environment in Revolutionary China*. Cambridge, UK: Cambridge University Press, 2004.

Shellenberger, Michael, and Ted Nordhaus. *The Death of Environmentalism: Global Warming Politics in a Post-Environmental World*. 2004. http://www.thebreak through.org/images/Death_of_Environmentalism.pdf.

Shusterman, Richard. "Body Consciousness and Performance: Somaesthetics East and West." *The Journal of Aesthetics and Art Criticism* 67, no. 2 (2009): 133–145.

Sino Daily, "Rising Sea Levels Present China with Unimaginable Challenges." February 16, 2007. http://www.sinodaily.com/reports/Rising_Sea_Levels _Present_China_With_Unimaginable_Challenges_999.html.

Slingerland, Edward. *Effortless Action: Wu-wei as Conceptual Metaphor and Spiritual Ideal in Early China*. New York: Oxford University Press, 2003.

———. *Trying Not To Try: Ancient China, Modern Science, and the Power of Sponta-neity.* New York: Crown (Random House), 2014.

Smart, Ninian. *Dimensions of the Sacred: An Anatomy of the World's Beliefs.* Berkeley: University of California Press, 1996.

Smith, Jonathan Z. *Imagining Religion: From Babylon to Jonestown.* Chicago: University of Chicago Press, 1982.

Speth, James Gustave. "Environmental Failure: A Case for a New Green Politics." *environment360.* October 20, 2008. http://e360.yale.edu/content/feature.msp?id=2075.

Strickmann, Michel. "On the Alchemy of T'ao Hung-Ching." In *Facets of Taoism*, ed. Holmes Welch and Anna Seidel, 123–192. New Haven, CT: Yale University Press, 1981.

Swimme, Brian Thomas, and Mary Evelyn Tucker. *Journey of the Universe.* New Haven, CT: Yale University Press, 2013.

Szerszynski, Bronislaw. *Nature, Technology, and the Sacred.* Oxford: Blackwell, 2005.

Taylor, Bron. *Dark Green Religion: Nature Spirituality and the Planetary Future.* Berkeley: University of California Press, 2010.

Taylor, Charles. *A Secular Age.* Cambridge, MA: Harvard University Press, 2007.

Thoreau, Henry D. *The Journal of Henry D. Thoreau.* Vols. 1–14. Ed. B. Torrey and F. Allen. New York: Dover, 1962.

Trägårdh, Lars, Nina Witoszek, and Bron Taylor, eds. *Civil Society in the Age of Monitory Democracy.* Oxford: Berghahn Books, 2013.

Tsai, Julius N. "Reading the 'Inner Biography of the Perfected Person of Purple Solarity': Religion and Society in an Early Daoist Hagiography." *Journal of the Royal Asiatic Society* 18, no. 2 (2008): 193–220.

Tu, Weiming. "Implications of the Rise of 'Confucian' East Asia." *Daedalus* 129, no. 1 (2000): 195–218.

———. "Cultural China: The Periphery as the Center." *Daedalus* 134, no. 4 (2005): 145–167.

Unschuld, Paul O. *Medicine in China: A History of Ideas.* Berkeley: University of California Press, 1985.

Varela, Francisco J., Evan Thompson, and Eleanor Rorsch. *The Embodied Mind: Cognitive Science and Human Experience.* Cambridge: MIT Press, 1997.

Waldau, Paul, and Kimberly Patton, eds. *A Communion of Subjects: Animals in Religion, Science, and Ethics.* New York: Columbia University Press, 2006.

Wang, Hui. *The End of the Revolution: China and the Limits of Modernity.* New York: Verso, 2009.

Wang Ming. *Baopuzi neipian xiaoshi.* Beijing: Zhonghua shuju, 1985.

Wang, Robin. *Yinyang: The Way of Heaven and Earth in Chinese Thought and Culture.* Cambridge, UK: Cambridge University Press, 2013.

Wang, Yue. "Chinese Minister Speaks Out Against South-North Water Diver-sion Project." *Forbes.* February 20, 2014. http://www.forbes.com/sites/ywang/2014/02/20/chinese-minister-speaks-out-against-south-north-water-diver-sion-project/.

Weller, Robert P. *Discovering Nature: Globalization and Environmental Culture in China and Taiwan*. Cambridge, UK: Cambridge University Press, 2006.

World Wildlife Fund China. "Wetland Conservation and Restoration." N.d. Accessed October 12, 2016. http://en.wwfchina.org/en/what_we_do/freshwater/wetland_conservation/.

Worster, Donald. "Nature and the Disorder of History." *Environmental History Review* 18, no. 2 (1994): 1–15.

——. *Nature's Economy: A History of Ecological Ideas*. 2nd ed. Cambridge, UK: Cambridge University Press, 1994.

Wu, Kuang-ming. *On Chinese Body Thinking: A Cultural Hermeneutic*. Leiden: Brill, 1997.

Yang, Der-Ruey. "New Agents and New Ethos of Daoism in China Today." *Chinese Sociological Review* 45, no. 2 (2012–2013): 48–64.

Young, Iris Marion. *Responsibility for Justice*. New York: Oxford University Press, 2011.

Zhang, Juwen. *A Translation of the Ancient Chinese* The Book of Burial (Zang Shu) *By Guo Pu (276–324)*. Lewiston, NY: The Edwin Mellon Press, 2004.

Index

CPSIA information can be obtained
at www.ICGtesting.com
Printed in the USA
LVHW030031110320
649645LV00001B/1